Fundraising with
The Raiser's Edge®

Additional Praise for *Fundraising with The Raiser's Edge*

"Bill Connors has written the Raiser's Edge book we've all been waiting for . . . to help all of us as fundraisers use this powerful software more effectively. It's the book that tells you how to do the things you really want to do in The Raiser's Edge, and more importantly, why to do it the way he recommends. Bill's background as a fundraiser means he's grounded the book in what is practical and useful for fundraisers on the front lines of raising funds in challenging times."
    Theresa Nelson, Founder and Principal, Theresa Nelson & Associates

"Bill Connors' book is a long overdue contribution to the fundraising world. If you are a novice Raiser's Edge user, this is a mandatory starting point. If you are a seasoned development professional, you will discover indispensable information to help you focus on raising money. Bill has written a uniquely practical and logical guide to The Raiser's Edge system."
    Marilyn Cahill, Director of Membership, California Academy of Sciences

"This is a really useful book. Bill Connors was a successful fundraiser before he became a fundraising software guru and you can see that from the way he writes this book. His enthusiasm for fundraising, and for The Raiser's Edge's role in supporting fundraisers, shines through on every page."
    John Kelly, President, Brakeley—International Fundraising Consultancy

"*Fundraising with The Raiser's Edge: A Non-Technical Guide* is a must-read for current users or anyone considering The Raiser's Edge. It is filled with tips and tricks and gives plenty of real-world examples from nonprofits that have used The Raiser's Edge to work more efficiently and improve their fundraising results."
    Dawn Bailey, Senior Consultant, Blackbaud, Inc.

"The next best thing to having a Raiser's Edge consultant and expert in your office? This book! Welcome to what I call the Fundraiser's Official Bible! I've had the pleasure of working with Bill as he helped us—now you can benefit from his wisdom and guidance as well. This will help you raise money—and help you contain costs. A CEO and Development Director's best friend."
    Patricia Wilson, Executive Director, Greater Bay Area Make-A-Wish Foundation

"Connors comprehensively reveals how fundraisers can better understand and deploy the many capabilities of the Raiser's Edge software. As a Blackbaud RE user at my institution for nearly a decade, I truly didn't know how much I didn't know until I reviewed Connors' book. With *Fundraising with the Raiser's Edge* serving as a useful guide, I and countless other "non-technical" fundraisers will be equipped to better understand and utilize the robust capability of Blackbaud's fundraising software. Connors has produced a great book which should be of significant value to the advancement profession."
    Dick Johnson, Executive Vice President, U.S. Naval Academy Foundation

Fundraising with The Raiser's Edge®

A Non-Technical Guide

BILL CONNORS, CFRE

WILEY
John Wiley & Sons, Inc.

Published by John Wiley & Sons, Inc., Hoboken, New Jersey.
Published simultaneously in Canada.

Screenshots from The Raiser's Edge software are used by permission of Blackbaud, Inc. All rights reserved. The Raiser's Edge and other Blackbaud product and service names are trademarks of Blackbaud, Inc., in the U.S.A. and other countries, and are used with permission.

This book is based upon The Raiser's Edge version 7.91.

For general information on our other products and services or for technical support, please contact our Customer Care Department within the United States at (800) 762-2974, outside the United States at (317) 572-3993 or fax (317) 572-4002.

Wiley also publishes its books in a variety of electronic formats. Some content that appears in print may not be available in electronic books. For more information about Wiley products, visit our web site at www.wiley.com.

Library of Congress Cataloging-in-Publication Data:

Connors, Bill.
  Fundraising with the raiser's edge : a non-technical guide / Bill Connors.
    p. cm.
  Includes bibliographical references and index.
  ISBN 978-0-470-56056-3 (pbk.)
  1. Fund raising.   2. Nonprofit organizations–Finance.   I. Title.
  HG177.C66 2010
  658.15′224–dc22

                                                          2009038772

Printed in the United States of America

10 9 8 7 6 5 4 3 2

Contents

Acknowledgments

As with most worthwhile things in life, this book is by no means just my own creation. It is only possible because of the support, education, and experiences shared by many good people in my life over many years. Although I alone am responsible for any mistakes and shortcomings in this book, I wish to give public thanks, as all good fundraisers must, to those who made this book possible. My apologies to the people whose names should be listed here but are not.

I have been fortunate to work with many outstanding co-workers and colleagues over the years who have taught me much about fundraising, The Raiser's Edge, and so much more. They include Mark Anello, Lou Attanasi, John Auwaerter, Dawn Bailey, Jim Ballou, Tracy Barry, Sally Beckett-Jeffery, Loraine Brown, Kevin Brunson, Suzanne Bryer, Jim Bush, Joy Clay, Cathleen Collins, Bill Conner (yes, I worked for someone with almost exactly the same name), Rich Conte, Michael Culler, Maurin Dajani, Reggie Daniel, Derek Drockelman, Frank Evans, Carolyn Ferrell, Mark Fetner, Anne Finch, Paul Finch, Leslie Franchs, Richard Geiger, Peter Gross, Kyle Haines, Keith Heller, Lawrence Henze, Debra Holcomb, Amy Jajuga, Kathryn Johnson, Adria Kamau, Lisa Lane Kasperzak, Martin Kaufman, John Kelly, Kevin Knight, Kevin Kreamer, Marty Lee, David Loring, Stu Manewith, Liz Marenakos, Amy Matthews, Jason Metcalfe, Cindy McElhinney, Trit Mulligan, Nicci Noble, Beth Parsons, Heather Paul, Leslie Payne, Karen Powell, Deepa Ranjith, Esther Ratterree, Andy Sabine, Cindy Scarbrough, Glenda Scott, Kimberley Sherwood, Renee Simi, Wayne Smith, Suzann Squire, Scott Staub, Jeff Stowe, John Stubbs, Shaun Sullivan, Steve Swain, Gina Tan, Jon Temple, Mark Terrero, Jeff Terry, Marc Van Baar, Tom Walker, Dorie Wallace, Robert Weiner, Brad West, Brandon Woods, David Zeidman, and Jerry Zink. Although the names are too numerous to mention and many of them aren't known to me, I have also learned much from the many members of the Blackbaud professional services; customer support, particularly electronic support; product design and development; and documentation teams.

I have also learned much from and with hundreds of clients from consulting since 1998—thank you for what you shared and what you enabled me to experience and learn. Of particular note I wish to mention Beth Basham, Lindy Ebbs, Paul Greenblatt, Linda Hulten, JC Minton, and Janice May Pinkowski. I especially have to thank the staff of the Greater Bay Area Make-A-Wish Foundation including Lynne Durie, Rachael Brent, and executive director Patricia Wilson—an amazing fundraiser and visionary leader for supporting the importance of the fundraising database.

The drafts of this book have been reviewed by colleagues who have contributed many hours of their own time to make this book better: Dawn Bailey, Rachael Brent, Kristin Caid, Rachel Hutchisson, Lisa Lane Kasperzak, Shawn O'Hara, and Gail Yates.

Their work has been an invaluable contribution and I can't express my appreciation enough. I would also like to thank others who reviewed and commented on specific chapters: Beth Basham, Kevin Brunson, Marilyn Cahill, John Kelly, Nicole Leventhal, Theresa Nelson, and Trini Ramos.

Since this is my first book, I am indebted to the team at Wiley & Sons who guided me gently and patiently through the process: Susan McDermott, who instantly embraced the idea for this book and became an internal champion; and Judy Howarth and Michael Lisk, wise and patient editors.

Although this book is a production independent of Blackbaud, Blackbaud's leaders believed in the value of this project for its customers and have supported it every step of the way. Particular thanks to Rachel Hutchisson, who spearheaded Blackbaud's involvement and was an editor extraordinaire; Marc Chardon, President; Charlie Cumbaa, Senior Vice President; Dawn Bailey, Professional Services; and the many other "Blackbaudians" who helped.

As every fundraiser knows, it is about relationships. And no more important relationships exist than those in our personal lives. To be energetic, present, and positive fundraisers requires good people in our lives at home. The same is true with writing a book.

There are two people who deserve very special mention, the two people most responsible for this book. Shawn O'Hara has been a friend, "big sister," colleague, mentor, and inspiration. No one has provided me more professional guidance and encouragement since I was a high school participant in Junior Achievement when she worked there. And Gail Yates—friend, former boss, mentor, encourager—someone who put my interests above her own early in my career and truly made possible my entrée into the world of The Raiser's Edge, supporting it every step of the way.

My thanks and love to Andy, Kris and her family, Brian, and my partner Jeff—thank you, Jeff, for your patience, support, love, and laughter—lots and lots of laughter!

And finally, to the two people to whom this book is dedicated, my mother and father Isabelle and Tom Connors. No son could have more support, encouragement, and love than they have given.

To all these special people and many more not mentioned, two words that no fundraiser can say too often: thank you.

About the Author

Bill Connors, CFRE, is an independent consultant and trainer on The Raiser's Edge.

In high school Bill was in Junior Achievement, an international organization that teaches students about business, economics, and personal finance. After participating in the after-school program and summer conferences, he began working for the national headquarters in the summers during college and graduate school. That led to a full-time job after graduate school as the assistant director of the international student conference.

Bill knew the real work of Junior Achievement happened in the 165 field offices of the organization throughout the country. He left the headquarters and moved to Phoenix, Arizona, where he became director of development for the central Arizona office in 1991.

At the time, Junior Achievement had an old DOS database that was more for accounting purposes than a true fundraising database. A team in the Phoenix office embarked on a project to develop a better tool, which got subsumed into a national project. The national organization bought 200 copies of The Raiser's Edge for Windows in 1995, one for each field office.

Bill left the Phoenix office after five years of successful fundraising, program management in the rural areas of Arizona, and doing some IT work for the office. He returned to the national office overseeing the rollout of The Raiser's Edge to the field offices. He and his colleague developed and delivered a training curriculum, wrote documentation, developed custom reports, and worked with Blackbaud on Junior Achievement's needs.

After his experience at Junior Achievement, Bill moved to San Francisco in 1998 and joined Blackbaud to help start the consulting program for the company. Previously Blackbaud had customer support over the telephone from Charleston, South Carolina, and on-site trainers. However, there was no one to help organizations with on-site implementation, customization, and use of the software to accomplish each organization's specific objectives. Bill spent the next seven years doing that in addition to helping build the Blackbaud consulting practice.

During a one-year break from his employment at Blackbaud, Bill was a senior consultant for fundraising technology in the United Kingdom and Europe for Brakeley Ltd., a fundraising consulting firm in London.

During his time at Blackbaud, Bill consulted with hundreds of organizations of all types and sizes in their use of The Raiser's Edge throughout the United States and Canada. He also taught classes, moderated user groups, and spoke at conferences. As principal consultant he was the chief liaison for the consulting department with the product development department. In the process he contributed to the development and design of the software.

After 10 years of national and international travel for Junior Achievement, Blackbaud, and Brakeley, Bill left Blackbaud in 2005. Later that year he became an independent consultant and trainer on The Raiser's Edge. To this day he works exclusively on The Raiser's Edge with clients, helping them convert to, set up, clean up, learn, and use The Raiser's Edge.

Bill is an honors graduate of Yale University with a master's degree from Brigham Young University. He is actively involved in the Association of Fundraising Professionals and has served on the board of directors of the Golden Gate Chapter. He continues to speak at Blackbaud and fundraising conferences.

Bill lives in San Francisco. He can be reached at bill@billconnors.com and www.billconnors.com.

Introduction

The Raiser's Edge is a large, sophisticated database. There is no question about that. But the premise of this book is quite simple: if you are smart and capable enough to be a fundraiser in the twenty-first century, you are smart and capable enough to learn what every fundraiser should know about The Raiser's Edge.

Perhaps it is a fair expectation to assume that, if you are like most fundraisers, you have never opened a software book. You have never gone into a bookstore, walked to the computer section, and pulled off the shelves one of the dozens of books about Microsoft Word, Excel, or Windows. Well, that is okay, because this is not one of those books.

This book is written by a fundraiser for fundraisers who work in development and advancement offices that use The Raiser's Edge. This book is not written for the database administrators, gift processors, "power users" who generate the mailings and reports, or support staff. I do hope these Raiser's Edge users will also read the book and learn more about the fundraiser's perspective on The Raiser's Edge. I hope it will improve their abilities to understand and work with fundraisers. However, this book is written for fundraisers, using fundraising terminology and fundraising concepts, with a focus on accomplishing fundraising objectives.

This is a non-technical guide to make your life easier. It will help you, as a fundraiser, do three things:

1. Understand the capabilities, terminology, and concepts of The Raiser's Edge so you can work with your database staff to meet your fundraising objectives with the greatest results and the least confusion and stress.
2. Learn a few of the areas of The Raiser's Edge that you—yes, you—can and should use yourself without having to become a database expert.
3. Manage the database staff to ensure this critical tool for your department's success is set up, maintained, and used as it should be.

The screenshots that appear in this book should not imply that this is a typical software manual. The screenshots are intended to help you visualize the fields and functions discussed so the concepts are more concrete. For those fundraisers who do love computers, do not worry. The concepts in this book will be just as applicable, meaningful, and informative to you.

I use the word "fundraiser" in the loosest of terms. Your organization might be a "nonprofit" or "school." Your department might be the "development" or "advancement" or even "resource generation" office. And your title might be Vice President of Advancement, Director of Development, Annual Fund Manager, Major Gifts Officer,

Special Events Director, Membership Manager—maybe even Executive Director! I use "fundraiser" and "fundraising" in the broadest sense and, for variety, use some of the other common terms in our profession. The intent is to cover everyone who does fundraising in any form.

Today's Fundraising Technology

Sometimes in the fundraising profession we sell ourselves short, not quite believing that we are and should be professionals engaged in a profession. "Fundraiser" does not mean "bake sale" for us. We are engaged in a serious, sophisticated profession that is a combination of art and science. To do that job well, we need serious, sophisticated tools. Although perhaps not as hip and sexy as the constant discussion about what the Internet offers, the fundraising database is the technological workhorse that keeps development departments going day in and day out.

How would you feel if you walked into your bank, it was the teller's first day on the job, and she had yet to receive training? Would you entrust her to take your deposit, properly process it, and get it into your account using the bank's software? What if you walked up to the check-in desk at the airport and discovered it was the agent's first day on the job, and he had yet to receive training? Do you think you'll have the right seat on the plane or your luggage will arrive as scheduled?

The software that we use in today's development offices is just as sophisticated as these niche database products. The bank's database software tracks you, your accounts, deposits, and withdrawals and creates your monthly statements. The airline's database software tracks you, your ticket purchases, and your seat assignments. These activities are similar to the tasks we use for our fundraising databases to track gifts and events. In the for-profit world the programs are called customer relationship management (CRM) systems.

Fundraisers should not hire someone off the street, regardless of background, and expect that person to sit down to The Raiser's Edge and start using it. The Raiser's Edge is not Microsoft Word where all you really have to know is how to start the program, type, and save the document. The Raiser's Edge is not Microsoft Internet Explorer where all you really have to do is start the program, enter a web site address, and click on little blue text with underlines. The Raiser's Edge is a sophisticated database that helps us manage the myriad details that are necessary to run a successful development office. You do not have to have a degree in Information Technology (IT) to be successful with The Raiser's Edge. However, you and your staff need to know some things awfully hard to learn by just sitting down and trying to figure them out on your own. This book addresses the critical elements you as a fundraiser should know about The Raiser's Edge.

Overview of Chapters

The organization of this book is not directed by the screens and "pages" of The Raiser's Edge itself. The software is organized as it is for a reason. This book is going to walk you through The Raiser's Edge in the order that will resonate best with a fundraiser.

Any well-run fundraising department starts each new fiscal year with a fundraising plan. Chapter 1 explains how the process of fundraising is structured and organized in the software. How does your office raise money? What solicitation methods do you employ over a year and toward what ends? We don't want "the tail to wag the dog." The Raiser's Edge should reflect how you fundraise, not vice versa. With that in mind, the first chapter is about understanding the concepts and terminology behind setting up The Raiser's Edge to track and measure your fundraising performance.

All fundraising involves people and organizations. The second chapter addresses how The Raiser's Edge stores biographical and contact information. The primary objective of this chapter is to help you confidently open the record of a person or organization in The Raiser's Edge, know where to go to find what you want, understand what you are looking at, and access a few tools to help you use that data. We do not get bogged down in the details of proper data entry because most fundraisers are not doing the data entry themselves.

As a fundraiser, you should be recording your interactions with your prospects and donors. If you are capable of using e-mail, I promise you are capable of entering notes and interactions in The Raiser's Edge. The second chapter also helps you learn how to do that.

Although gifts are the outcome of fundraising efforts (at least that's what we hope for), we talk about gifts in Chapter 3 before getting into the fundraising processes. It is important to understand how gifts work in The Raiser's Edge to understand how to perform and track your fundraising efforts in the system. The purpose of this chapter is not to teach anyone how to be a gift processor. Its focus is to teach you how to look at the gifts in The Raiser's Edge and understand their complexity and nuances. This enables you to properly understand a donor's history, work with the database staff to get mailings out correctly, and request reports—and get them!—that really reflect what you want to see. Because fundraisers are ultimately responsible for the proper controls over the money, we also take a high-level walk through the typical gift-processing steps. This includes discussion about how The Raiser's Edge relates to accounting and assists you in preventing fraud.

In Chapter 4 we address mass communications with constituents. Every development office does many mailings. In fact, "communications" is often part of the department head's responsibility. Direct mail appeals, event invitations, newsletters, magazines, annual reports—these mailings should come from The Raiser's Edge. To reduce the headaches and mistakes I often see, we talk about the concepts you should understand as a fundraiser when providing direction and review of other's work to ensure the mailings are being generated correctly. The content here also applies to other mass appeals like telemarketing (phonathons) and e-mail campaigns.

Chapter 5 discusses two specialized uses of The Raiser's Edge that raise money for organizations: events and membership programs. Because the system is used by so many organizations for these purposes, the chapter explains how these activities are integrated into the larger system. The chapter also discusses the functions and concepts unique to events and membership.

Chapter 6 addresses major gifts and grants fundraising from individuals and institutions. We discuss tools that can be used to help you ask for and get the big gifts, however you define "major" and "big" for your organization. We walk through the process in the life cycle of a major gifts prospect and show how The Raiser's

Edge can be used each step of the way. We also look at some management tools for overseeing this process.

In Chapter 7 we address getting data out of The Raiser's Edge in useful ways. I believe that The Raiser's Edge, like all databases, is simply a tool and not the end in itself. We fundraise to support the programs that meet our organization's mission, not to raise money in and of itself. Likewise we use the fundraising database to support our fundraising, not just to manage data. Getting meaningful, actionable information out of The Raiser's Edge is important. The output capabilities of The Raiser's Edge are one of the facets that set it apart from its competitors and why many clients have told me over the years they have converted to The Raiser's Edge. Yet, sadly, there are so many reports and other output tools in The Raiser's Edge that, in my experience, most users get overwhelmed and don't put them to use. In Chapter 7 I break down the Reports and Dashboards features with a practical focus on results. I suggest specific reports and dashboards you and your organization should consider running and a suggested schedule for running them. Key concepts are discussed so that when you ask for a report you get the information you are expecting and can be assured the results are correct.

In Chapter 8 we discuss the fundraiser's role in managing the database administrator. Someone in the development office, not IT, has to be responsible for The Raiser's Edge. It just does not take care of itself any more than any other technology does. Although that day-to-day responsibility usually does not lie with a fundraiser, usually a fundraiser is that person's manager. Is your database set up and maintained the way it should be so your organization and its data are safe? Chapter 8 discusses recommendations in a non-technical way about what someone in your office should be doing to get The Raiser's Edge in tip-top shape.

At the end of the book are three appendixes that should be of practical use for you and your organization. If you are implementing The Raiser's Edge or considering such an undertaking, there is an appendix that walks you through what the process should look like. There is a checklist that your database administrator should be following daily, weekly, and monthly to keep your database healthy and happy. And there is an example of my recommended approach to creating policy and procedure documentation for The Raiser's Edge, a process discussed in Chapter 8.

The Database Administrator

The roles and responsibilities of the database administrator are discussed in great detail in Chapter 8, but the position is referred to many times in the earlier chapters. In summary, the database administrator is the person responsible for the database, for its setup, use, and maintenance. This person is usually the most knowledgeable about The Raiser's Edge and for things not known, is responsible for finding the answers. Large organizations might have a person in a full-time job with this responsibility, while smaller organizations often combine this role with responsibilities for data entry and reporting. In some organizations this person is a fundraiser. Whatever the job title, someone in your organization should have final responsibility for the database. That is the person referred to in this book as your database administrator.

Some Additional Thoughts

One thing before we go much further: please note that the name of the software is The Raiser's Edge. It is "Raiser's" and not "Razor's"—a play on the word fundraiser, of course. If you really want to do things right, such as impress potential job candidates and future employers that you really know what you are talking about, it is The Raiser's Edge—yes, "The" is an official part of the name, only dropped when the name is used as a modifier, such as,

"Are you a Raiser's Edge user?"

"Yes! I'm a fundraiser so of course our office uses The Raiser's Edge, and I'm a Raiser's Edge user."

(For you English Lit majors, I have read *The Razor's Edge* by W. Somerset Maugham and watched the DVD of the movie starring Bill Murray. Although money is somewhere among the themes of this work, I think The Raiser's Edge was chosen for the clever play on the word "fundraiser" and has nothing to do with Maugham's book.)

Saying and writing The Raiser's Edge all the time is a mouthful, so the standard nickname is "RE." I have heard other nicknames and acronyms as well, but "RE" is the most common and closest to an "official" shortened form.

Some mistakenly refer to The Raiser's Edge as "Blackbaud," but that's not correct. Blackbaud is the name of the company that makes The Raiser's Edge. Just as Microsoft makes Word, Excel, Outlook, Windows, and other products, Blackbaud makes software exclusively for the nonprofit and education market, including The Raiser's Edge as its flagship product; The Financial Edge, a nonprofit accounting software package; The Education Edge, admissions and registrar office software for independent schools; nonprofit Internet marketing and community building programs, most of which interface with The Raiser's Edge; and prospect research products and services sold under the Target Analytics name.

The name "Blackbaud" shows the company's origin in education in the early 1980s, combining the words "blackboard" and "baud," the old technology term for the speed of a modem (anyone remember those?). With this start, The Raiser's Edge is now used by the majority of independent schools in the United States. But these days it is also used by hospital foundations, museums, universities and colleges, social service agencies, religious organizations, and foundations that both raise and give away money. More than 13,000 organizations across the world use The Raiser's Edge, making it by far the most widely used fundraising package.

Some other details of note:

- The Raiser's Edge is sold in modules so that organizations only have to pay for functionality they need, such as the Alumni module for schools and the Membership module for museums, zoos, and aquariums. Some modules have broad applicability, such as Tribute for honor and memorial giving; Events for special events; Prospect for major gifts prospect research and tracking; and EFT for monthly donor programs. These optional modules are touched on throughout this book in the contexts in which they naturally occur. If functionality is discussed which you cannot find in your copy of The Raiser's Edge, it is likely your organization has not purchased that module. Check with your database administrator for confirmation.

- The Raiser's Edge is sold throughout the world. Five major English editions exist, one each for the United States, Canada, the United Kingdom, Australia, and New Zealand. Most of the concepts in this book are at such a level that the aspects of fundraising unique to these and other areas of the world should not have an impact. But having done fundraising database consulting in three of these five countries and others as well, there will be occasional references to international differences. For my international readers who sense a preponderance of Americanisms in the book, I apologize. I assure you I respect and appreciate the contributions you are making to our profession (a case in point: I still believe most fundraisers in the United States have much to learn about the value of implementing monthly giving programs; see my Blackbaud whitepaper on this point).

- The current version of The Raiser's Edge, having been out since 2000, is The Raiser's Edge version 7. As of this writing, the most current update is 7.91, getting very close to version 8. Version 8 has been in development for years and will be a whole new program of The Raiser's Edge. It has been written from the ground up with new technology and new design just as version 7 was after The Raiser's Edge for DOS versions 5 and earlier and The Raiser's Edge for Windows version 6. Although the future release of version 8 is briefly discussed in the last chapter, my point here is to assure readers who have heard of version 8 that I, too, am aware of it and of two other thoughts:

  1. Its release and your organization's conversion to it are far enough in the future to justify the investment of time and energy in this book to learn more about the current version, to implement those learnings, and to benefit from them.

  2. The Raiser's Edge version 8 is still The Raiser's Edge and still designed by Blackbaud. As noted in this introduction, this book is much more conceptual than about button-clicking. The concepts in this book will largely carry over to future versions of The Raiser's Edge and will most assuredly assist in the implementation and use of version 8 of The Raiser's Edge. Having provided some guidance to the designers of version 8 and having had some hands-on and other exposure to it, I feel confident this is true.

- There are many examples throughout the book based on my consulting experience with organizations of all types. However, two organizations are frequently named to provide examples of how everything discussed came together in a "real" environment. Some mention is made of Junior Achievement, my first implementation of The Raiser's Edge and my first experience as a user of it. More mention is made of the Greater Bay Area Make-A-Wish Foundation in San Francisco, California. I recently completed several years there as contract database administrator for The Raiser's Edge in addition to my other consulting work. This gave me a long-term opportunity to "practice what I preach," the results of which I share with you in this book with their permission.

Summary

Blackbaud has assisted in the production of this book and provided permission for the screenshots, for which I express my gratitude. But as a former Blackbaud customer and employee and as a current Raiser's Edge consultant and occasional Blackbaud competitor, my objective is to share with you what I honestly think of The Raiser's Edge as I have always tried to do. You deserve honesty and directness as you invest your organization's money into this software and your time into reading this book.

The Raiser's Edge is not without its challenges. It is by no means perfect. My list of recommendations for things to add, change, and remove is endless. The passion with which I feel this is almost endless as well (as many of my colleagues at Blackbaud, especially in product development and support, will tell you). But no software package is perfect. I believe The Raiser's Edge strikes a good balance of affordability, ease of use, and needed functionality.

In summary, I think that The Raiser's Edge is a terrific piece of software. On a daily basis I am reminded of the level of sophistication this product allows us fundraisers to achieve. What we do as fundraisers is not easy and anyone who says otherwise has clearly never been a fundraiser. This software strives to find the impossible balance between the high degree of functionality needed by the larger and more sophisticated organizations and the accessibility and usability needed by smaller and more basics-oriented organizations. That perfect balance is unachievable, but from my observations The Raiser's Edge does it better than any other product.

Furthermore, our needs change over time as we become more sophisticated users, our organizations grow, and our fundraising strategies get more creative and advanced. The Raiser's Edge is well poised to support you as that becomes true for you and your organization. This book is not about helping you use all or even most of The Raiser's Edge (a comment I hear often from prospective clients). This book is about helping you understand the parts of The Raiser's Edge you and your organization should be using now so you can focus on raising money to support your mission rather than fussing with data.

So with that, let us get started learning more about fundraising with The Raiser's Edge.

Additional Resources and Follow-up to the Book on the Web

Given the technology subject matter of this book and the book's purpose to be a resource for fundraisers and their organizations, more information and resources can be found on Bill Connors' web site at www.billconnors.com/book at no charge. Included are:

- Bill's answers to frequently asked questions from readers of the book.
- More examples and documentation for the concepts discussed in the book.
- Other resources for The Raiser's Edge Bill has developed from his consulting and training practice, for both fundraisers and database administrators.

CHAPTER 1

Organizing Fundraising

The Raiser's Edge has been designed as both a "front office" and "back office" system. What do we mean by that? Think of the back office as tasks such as gift entry and acknowledgement, interfacing with accounting, and running after-the-fact reports of money received. The front office is you, the frontline fundraiser out raising money. The Raiser's Edge was designed to be used by and for you and not just as an administrative system.

Therefore gift coding in The Raiser's Edge is not just about gift data entry fields. Gift coding should represent how you and your organization fundraise. It has two purposes:

1. To help you organize and manage your fundraising.
2. To help you track and report on your progress toward your fundraising objectives.

The codes used with gifts apply to functionality throughout The Raiser's Edge, not just the gifts you receive. For example, these codes also affect the setup of your fundraising staff, fundraising volunteers, prospects, and donors in the system.

This chapter is about how to reflect in The Raiser's Edge the ways your organization raises money. The primary structure to do this uses the following three types of "records" (I explain a "record" shortly):

1. Campaigns
2. Funds
3. Appeals

Matching your fundraising structure with these records seems easier than it usually is in practice. Blackbaud provides definitions for each of these records in The Raiser's Edge, but often I see two situations that I would like to help you avoid:

1. Confusion on the organization's part—among the fundraisers and the database staff alike—about what their campaign, fund, and appeal structure should be.
2. Rigid adherence to the user guide definitions that do not make sense for the particular organization. This adherence results in the need to do development, senior management, and board reports in Excel and Word documents, defeating the investment the organization has made in The Raiser's Edge.

There are three objectives for this chapter:

1. *Help you understand campaigns, funds, and appeals.* These are concepts you encounter repeatedly in looking at data and asking for reports. Fundraisers need to understand the terms and roles these records play in data entry and output.
2. *For organizations already using The Raiser's Edge, help fundraisers evaluate whether your campaign, fund, and appeal structure is set up and being used to best effect for your fundraising needs.* Many organizations struggle with reporting and question whether this structure is set up right. This chapter helps you decide whether the way your database is set up best meets your fundraising needs.
3. *For organizations implementing The Raiser's Edge, help fundraisers decide what the campaign, fund, and appeal structure should be.* These are key concepts and fields in the database and much forethought needs to go into deciding how to use them. Setting up campaigns, funds, and appeals correctly helps determine your success and happiness with The Raiser's Edge.

If you follow fundraising best practice, you enter each fiscal year with a fundraising plan. Let us talk about how to apply that plan to The Raiser's Edge so you can use the software to perform and track your fundraising through the year.

Getting Started with The Raiser's Edge

When you log into The Raiser's Edge, you are not going to see a screen that says "Organizing Your Fundraising" or anything similar. The Raiser's Edge is laid out based on the different "parts" you need over the course of using the database. Think of starting to use The Raiser's Edge like walking into a kitchen. The pots and pans are in the cabinets below the counter, the spices are in the cupboards above, some of the ingredients are in the refrigerator while others are in the pantry. The utensils you need to whip it all together are in the drawers. You have to take out the tools and food from the various locations in the order you need them to make each meal. They are not neatly lined up for you in just the right order.

The Raiser's Edge is like that kitchen. When you log in, you are presented on the main screen, called the "shell," with the various tools and parts that make up the system as shown in Figure 1.1. When you use The Raiser's Edge, you need to select the particular functions and resources available to accomplish a task. These functions are not grouped together or labeled with the particular task at hand because the same tools can be used many different ways for a number of different purposes.

Blackbaud is changing this in the next generation of The Raiser's Edge, but understand this rationale when approaching the system. There *is* a lot there. But just as a kitchen with only a spoon and knife will not allow you to make much of a meal, if The Raiser's Edge only had a few options you would not be able to do much fundraising with it. With the blender, food processor, and double ovens, you can do so much more.

When you log in, you see a list of options down the left side of the screen as shown in Figure 1.1. These options are called "pages." The Raiser's Edge was designed to look similar to a web site. A web site has a home page and many other pages; so does The Raiser's Edge. There is the Home page, Records page, Reports page, and so forth.

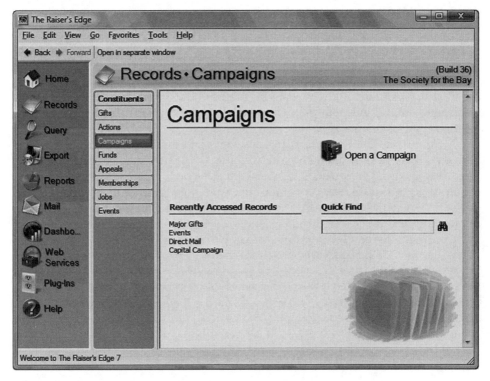

FIGURE 1.1 The Raiser's Edge "Shell"

What pages you see depends on your security rights. As we discuss in Chapter 8, most fundraisers do not see all the pages that are available. Some of the pages are for tasks that only the database administrator needs to do.

Your database administrator should have assigned you a login name and password. Contact your database administrator if you have any challenges logging in. Your database administrator can also assist you if you are not able to access or use the functions discussed in this book.

Please protect your login name and password carefully. Create a password impossible to guess. Try to avoid writing it down (your database administrator can always reset your password if you forget it). Your login name and password provides access to sensitive name, address, telephone, wealth, relationship, gift, and other information that needs to be protected carefully. It also identifies you to The Raiser's Edge, giving you ownership of the items you create and the settings you prefer to use.

Accessing Campaign, Fund, and Appeal Records

To see the setup of your fundraising, click on **Records** in the upper left corner of The Raiser's Edge. There are three types of records on the Records page shown in Figure 1.1 that are relevant to organizing fundraising in The Raiser's Edge:

1. Campaigns
2. Funds
3. Appeals

You need to know where these records are located so you can see the list of them and to track their individual performance. For example, to most powerfully measure the performance of an appeal, you want to use the Appeal Summary available within the appeal record (discussed in Chapter 7).

Our intent here is not for you to do data entry. In a well set-up system typically only the database administrator for The Raiser's Edge has access to add and edit campaigns, funds, and appeals. Occasionally only the annual fund manager will have add and edit rights to just appeals.

A "record" in The Raiser's Edge is an entity that is big enough and important enough to have its own file in the database. It is not just an item in a list but instead has many fields of information related to it. "Record" means "database record." Your prospects, donors, and other individuals and organizations have records in the database because they have name fields, address fields, notes, gifts, and much more information associated with them.

Campaigns, funds, and appeals—the way we organize fundraising in The Raiser's Edge—are records because they are more than just names, as shown in the fund record in Figure 1.2. They are more than just options in a list of choices when doing gift entry. They have dates, goals, notes, ways to categorize them, possibly solicitors raising money for them, and relationships to each other (e.g., the direct mail appeal raises money for the unrestricted fund). Funds have the ability to be set up to relate to your accounting software. Appeals let you track how many constituents were

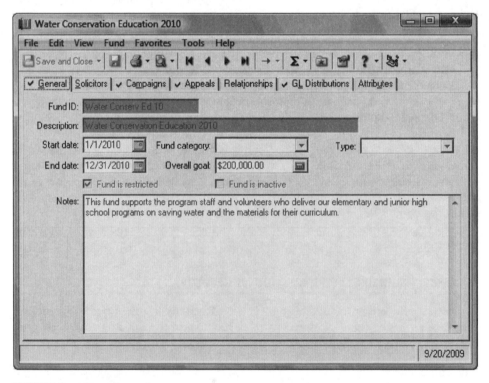

FIGURE 1.2   A Fund Record

solicited, how much the appeal cost, and what steps are necessary to accomplish the appeal.

To open a campaign, fund, or appeal record, type the name of the record in the **Quick Find** field on the relevant Records page. If you do not know the name of the record you are seeking, click the **Open a** ... option on the screen. When the Open screen appears, if it does not automatically show you all of the campaign, fund, or appeal records in your system then click on the **Find Now** button and it will. Then simply double-click on the campaign, fund, or appeal you would like to see to open it.

Defining Campaign, Fund, and Appeal

The data entry for campaigns, funds, and appeals is easy for your staff as shown in the sample fund record in Figure 1.2. Where organizations struggle, and what is most important for you as a fundraiser to understand, is what the campaigns, funds, and appeals should be.

Why This Is Important

The standard fundraising plan usually addresses four primary points:

1. How much needs to be raised for each program or purpose, including unrestricted money.
2. How that money is going to be raised.
3. From whom it is going to be raised.
4. Who is going to raise it.

Therefore fundraisers want and need to measure four things about the money they raise:

1. What the money is for.
2. How the money is raised.
3. Who gave the money.
4. How much each fundraiser raised.

The best way to measure these by using The Raiser's Edge is to *assign a different field for each of these metrics*. Although one might inform the other—it is likely you have different fundraising methods for your corporate donors than your other donors—fundamentally "*Who* gave?" and "*How* were they asked and *why* they gave?" are two different questions.

As a modern database, The Raiser's Edge takes the approach of putting the answers to each of these questions in their own fields. You should do this also, as you define your campaigns, funds, and appeals.

There are many functions and rules about campaigns, funds, and appeals, but let us focus on the common challenges and solutions to help you determine if your campaigns, funds, and appeals are set up well. It is the work of *determining* what they should be that is the most important and hardest challenge. Once you have the structure designed or fixed, they are easy to enter or modify in The Raiser's Edge.

User Guide Definitions

The user guide for The Raiser's Edge defines these records as follows:

- *Campaign:* "A campaign is your overall objective to raise money. For example, a museum can have a New Building Campaign with the objective to raise money for a new location. Of campaigns, funds, and appeals, campaigns are the broadest type of record. Campaigns act as an umbrella over funds and appeals."
- *Fund:* "A fund identifies where to track gifts and pledges for financial purposes."
- *Appeal:* "An appeal is a solicitation that brings in your gifts. Solicitations can include auctions, direct mailings, and phonathons."[1]

The classic Blackbaud training example is to pretend for a moment that we are the Red Cross. We are doing a direct mail piece asking our supporters to send in a gift and allowing them to designate the disaster they would like their relief gift directed to. So:

- We have a "Disaster Relief Campaign."
- There would be one fund for each of the following donor designation options:
  - Relief Fund for those in Location X affected by Fires.
  - Relief Fund for those in Location Y affected by Floods.
  - Relief Fund for those in Location Z affected by Hurricanes.
- The appeal would be the Disaster Relief Direct Mailing of June 201X.

There is nothing wrong with these user guide definitions. However, in the real world it can be difficult figuring out how to overlay an organization's specific development plan into this structure.

Another Perspective

Let me give you my perspective on defining campaigns, funds, and appeals. Although this perspective is not as short as those provided in the Blackbaud documentation, I hope they help you understand the intent of them in the software and how they should work for you.

It helps to understand that The Raiser's Edge uses standard fundraising terms with "campaign," "fund," and "appeal." It can be confusing using these words of broad meaning for a specific purpose in the software. For example, some organizations do "direct mail *campaigns*" that should be set up as *appeals* in The Raiser's Edge. In my work with Catholic dioceses, the "Bishop's Annual *Appeal*" is best set up in The Raiser's Edge as a *campaign*.

The user guide definitions often work, and mine will be very similar, but here is the fundamental concept: *campaigns, funds, and appeals are merely categories for organizing your fundraising.* Do not be too concerned about matching the literal meaning of the words used to name these categories in the software. Focus on their *function* instead.

The primary purpose of these records is twofold:

1. *Reporting* by these categories, such as getting statistics such as total dollars raised, number of donors and gifts, average gift size, and so forth. The Campaign Performance Analysis Report is shown as an example in Figure 1.3.
2. Quickly and easily *filtering* all gift output by any combination of these three categories. They show up as filters on all gift output so you can see just the gifts and giving totals you want. For example, see Figure 1.4, the filters for the Constituent Giving History Report.

Let us explore these two purposes a little more. Understanding what campaigns, funds, and appeals *do* in The Raiser's Edge is critical to understanding what they should *be*.

As the primary way to categorize and track your fundraising, there are numerous campaign, fund, and appeal reporting tools. We discuss these more in Chapter 7, but they include:

- *Summaries*, affectionately known as the "thermometer screens," because they use the classic fundraising performance measurement to graphically represent your progress toward a goal. They also provide a number of useful breakouts of gifts received by calendar year, fiscal year, gift type, and so forth.
- *Performance Analysis Reports* that show total dollars raised, number of donors and gifts, average gift size, goal, and progress against goal. For appeals they also include cost per gift and response percentages. Figure 1.3 is an example of a Campaign Performance Analysis Report.
- *Statistical Reports* show these statistics and others for one time period you define; two time periods with variances (e.g., how are we doing so far this year to date as compared to last year to date?); and three to five time periods shown side-by-side.
- *On-screen "dashboards"* that give you graphs and data in tables that allow for drill-through capability for greater detail.

You can easily use these tools for one campaign, fund, or appeal; for all of this year's fundraising broken out by campaign, fund, and appeal; or for multiple years fundraising by campaign, fund, and appeal.

Furthermore, when doing all gift-related output such as lists, reports, and exports, you can filter by campaign, fund, and appeal. For example:

- When doing invitations for an event, if the events are reflected in appeals you can easily filter for and find all those who have given to the event before.
- When calculating total giving, we usually want separate lists for capital campaign giving and annual campaign giving. The report we run from The Raiser's Edge to get lists for the annual report provides an easy filter for campaign to create these lists. A tab similar to the Filters tab shown in Figure 1.4 shows up in almost all reports.

The Society for the Bay Campaign Performance Analysis
Fiscal Year to Date

Campaign	Number of Donors	Average/Donor	Number of Gifts	Average/Gift	Total Given	Goal	Over (Under)	% Goal
Capital Campaign	78	$17,120.83	214	$ 6,240.30	$1,335,425.00	$2,000,000.00	($664,575.00)	66.77%
Direct Mail	115	$ 252.23	201	$ 144.31	$ 29,007.00	$ 50,000.00	($ 20,993.00)	58.01%
Events	39	$ 5,901.99	102	$ 2,256.64	$ 230,177.00	$ 150,000.00	$ 80,177.50	153.45%
Internet	55	$ 190.14	94	$ 111.25	$ 10,457.50	$ 15,000.00	($ 4,542.50)	69.72%
Major Gifts	86	$ 9,313.90	231	$ 3,467.51	$ 800,995.00	$ 750,000.00	$ 50,995.00	106.80%
Membership	41	$ 609.20	83	$ 300.93	$ 24,977.00	$ 50,000.00	($ 25,023.00)	49.95%
Planned Giving	9	$32,316.67	10	$29,085.00	$ 290,850.00	$ 350,000.00	($ 59,150.00)	83.10%
GRAND TOTALS	**423**	**$ 6,434.73**	**935**	**$2,911.11**	**$2,721,889.00**	**$3,365,000.00**	**($643,111.00)**	**80.89%**
Actual Counts	**170**	**$16,011.11**	**916**	**$2,971.49**				
A Total of 7 Campaign(s) Listed								

FIGURE 1.3   The Campaign Performance Analysis Report

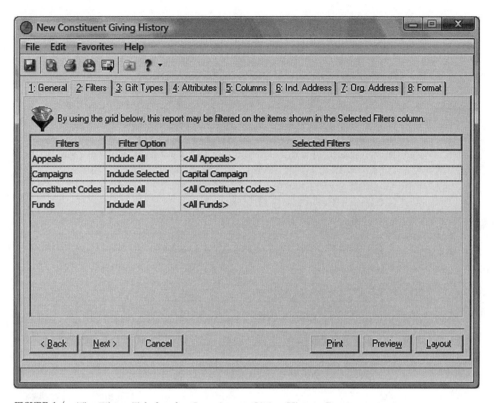

FIGURE 1.4   The Filters Tab for the Constituent Giving History Report

- When you get close to the end of the year, you might want to run the LYBUNT report—those who have given Last Year But Unfortunately Not This year. Filters for campaign, fund, and appeal make it easy to say, "show me everyone who gave a major gift last year but has not this year" so event, direct mail, and other small gifts do not confuse the matter.
- When working with direct mail consultants, they often want to know the prospects' last and largest gifts for RFM (Recency, Frequency, and Monetary value) segmentation. They probably do not want event or unsolicited tribute gifts counted in the "last" and "largest" calculations. In this case filtering by appeals makes it easier for your staff to include only those gifts of interest.

Your campaigns, funds, and appeals should be the categories you want to use to report and filter giving.

The purpose of this discussion is to encourage use of the functionality of The Raiser's Edge in the way that is meaningful to your organization. If the user guide definitions work for your organization, use them. What you should not be doing is setting up The Raiser's Edge to match those definitions and then struggling to report on the money raised in the categories that management and the board actually want to see. Do not feel you have to be forced into a structure that is artificial and unnatural for you because the database seems to require it—it does not.

Based on this context, here are my definitions and descriptions of campaigns, funds, and appeals. Campaign is usually the level that organizations struggle with the most in their Raiser's Edge setup. Let us leave campaigns for last so there is more context when we discuss them.

Funds

The intention and primary use of Funds in The Raiser's Edge is to record what the money is for, the program or purpose the money is to be spent on. We do not raise money to raise money; we raise money so the organization can spend it to accomplish the organization's objectives. For example:

- A hospital foundation might have funds for Patient Services, Cardiology, Pediatrics, and Oncology.
- A school might have funds for Scholarships, Library Books, and Athletics.
- A zoo might have funds for the African Exhibit, the Bear Exhibit, and Educational Programs.

Every organization has a fund for Unrestricted, whether by that name, "Annual Fund" or some other variation, to indicate the money was given to be spent however the organization best sees fit.

Fund is a required field for every gift in your system and is the pivotal category.

Fund is also the category in The Raiser's Edge that is supposed to correspond to your accounting software, whether The Financial Edge from Blackbaud or another accounting software package. If you are doing your initial setup of funds in The Raiser's Edge for a forthcoming implementation, or you are evaluating the accuracy of your funds because of problems with them, read the accompanying note on "How Funds in The Raiser's Edge Relate to Accounting."

Note: How Funds in The Raiser's Edge Relate to Accounting

Fund is the field in The Raiser's Edge that should correspond to the coding in your accounting software. Donors give to support the mission of the organization: we hope, as nonprofit managers, the money is given without restrictions, but often donors will restrict their gifts. We also deliberately ask for money for specific purposes knowing that donors are more likely to give to mission than overhead.

The expectation is that your accounting software will have accounts (or, in The Financial Edge, "projects") to track what the money is for. The accounting department has several reasons to need to know gift restrictions, among them:

- It is one of accounting's roles at a nonprofit organization to ensure that the organization is a proper steward of donations. They help make sure money gets spent for the purpose it was given. Although accounting might track how money is raised and by whom it is given, that is detail for internal analysis and decision making. Honoring donor intent is the more important fiduciary responsibility of the organization that accounting helps to ensure is accomplished.

- Another of accounting's roles is to manage the expenditure of the organization's money. Accounting needs to know how much money each program has received, so they can approve and deny expense requests by program staff.
- The accounting department also has audit, accounting, and legal responsibilities in their recording and reporting of money. For example, donor intent helps drive their classification of money as unrestricted, temporarily restricted, and permanently restricted.

Fund is intended to be the categorization level in The Raiser's Edge that corresponds to the accounting software's chart of accounts. If you use The Financial Edge and wish to integrate your two Blackbaud products, it is critical that you, your accounting staff, and if necessary, your senior management, work together to determine what your funds in The Raiser's Edge and accounts and projects in The Financial Edge should be.

If you do not use The Financial Edge or your organization has no desire to integrate it with The Raiser's Edge (not a recommended approach), you have more flexibility about how you structure your funds. However, it is best practice that The Raiser's Edge and your accounting software be reconciled each month. Although this can be a difficult task initially, it is an achievable and recommended one (we talk more about this in Chapter 3). The Greater Bay Area Make-A-Wish Foundation has been reconciling The Raiser's Edge and the accounting system Peachtree to the penny every month on more than $6 million of annual income. Other organizations do this as well.

To be able to reconcile with accounting, your copy of The Raiser's Edge should have a field that corresponds with the structure of your accounting software. It is highly unlikely you want to balance a month based on total revenue and if the month does not balance, ask your staff to compare every batch or every single gift between the systems. Fund in The Raiser's Edge is usually the level at which you reconcile the two systems.

However, none of this means your funds have to be defined as what the money is for or its program purpose. Some organizations simply do not need to give up all functionality in The Raiser's Edge for funds to track the fact that almost all gifts are unrestricted or for a single program purpose. What is perhaps more useful instead, and what may be so ingrained in the organization that it is reflected in the accounting chart of accounts as well, is how the money is *raised*. Fund can be defined that way instead.

At Junior Achievement, the vast majority of money was raised as unrestricted. There was no value in defining fund records as "the purpose of the gift" because one fund would contain almost all the money raised. This would make this functionality almost useless for any meaningful reporting or filtering. The way we wanted to track money was by how it was raised, not what it was for. The campaign, fund, and appeal structure was a hierarchy, like an organizational chart, of how money was raised. The broad groupings were the campaigns and the most detailed levels were the appeals. For example:

- There was a "Board Fundraising" campaign with funds for each of the ways the board was involved in fundraising.
- There was a "Special Events" campaign with each of the events as a fund, such as "Bowl-a-thon" (BAT). The appeals for each fund were the ways money was raised by each event, such as "BAT Event Sponsorships," "BAT Bowler Sponsorships," and "BAT Registration Fees."
- The "Personal Giving" campaign only had one fund but there were several appeals for the efforts used to raise money from people, such as direct mail.

Another common exception to the standard definition is that many organizations will assign each large special event to a fund even if the other funds refer to program purposes. The gala, bowl-a-thon, golf tournament, and other such events each have corresponding fund records. I am usually not an advocate of this approach because it is not a consistent definition of fund—some funds are defined as the purpose of the money while others are defined as the way it is raised. Events are not held to raise money for events, events are held to raise money either for unrestricted or restricted purposes. Ideally the fund for event money would stay true to that intent, and the event would be reflected in the appeal and by linking the gift to the event (for those with the RE:Event optional module). But many organizations do create funds for events, and those events are represented in the accounting system the same way.

Tip: Funds for the VSE Report for Educational Institutions

If your organization participates in the Voluntary Support of Education (VSE) survey from the Council for Aid to Education, there are further considerations you should understand before setting up your funds in The Raiser's Edge. Funds should play a pivotal role in defining the categories to complete this survey. To learn more, reference the Blackbaud documentation and Knowledgebase on this topic. Also consult the Council for Advancement and Support of Education (CASE) *CASE Reporting Standards & Management Guidelines*, 4th edition.

Because the VSE survey plays an important role in fundraising reporting for educational institutions, tips such as this one will appear throughout the book where particularly important. Similar tips do not appear for other sectors in the nonprofit field because no other sectors have the reporting standardization that has developed in the educational sector.

Appeals

Appeals are probably the easiest fundraising record type to understand in The Raiser's Edge. They are the most consistently defined across organizations. Although The Raiser's Edge does not require the **Appeal** field for every gift, most organizations modify their copy of the software and make it a required field.

Quite simply, appeal is used to indicate *how the money was raised, what prompted the donor to make the gift*. This is intentionally highly specific. It is appropriate that your copy of The Raiser's Edge have hundreds or thousands of appeals from years of fundraising. Typical examples include:

- July 201X Direct Mailing
- Winter 201X Newsletter (if it includes a gift reply envelope)
- Fall 201X Alumni Telemarketing
- Gala 201X Invitation

Assigning specific dates to most appeals is best and most common practice. With this field we are tracking the specific ask that resulted in the gifts and measuring the performance of those specific asks, not general types of asks.

Other common appeals that are correct but have no date specificity include:

- *Unsolicited.* This appeal is needed if the gift **Appeal** field is made a required field. It simply indicates that your organization has no idea what prompted the donor to give but should be used sparingly.
- *Personal Ask.* You might call this "Face-to-Face Ask" or something else, but this is used for major gift asks that happen on a one-off basis.
- *Grant Application.* Use this for other one-off asks that are by application or proposal rather than a direct ask.
- *Tribute.* Some organizations want to break tributes out by "Memorial" and "In Honor Of" if they get a number of these gifts. "Tribute" covers gifts you did not directly ask for but were the recipient of either because of family member requests or simply from the donor's own motivation.

Packages

Appeals have further functionality not yet mentioned: Packages. A "package" in The Raiser's Edge is a subset of an appeal. While, at your discretion, campaigns, funds, and appeals can be used in any combination, each package always belongs to one specific appeal. Packages are typically used in three ways:

1. As the name implies, package can be used to indicate different packaging of the appeal. This lets you test, as direct mail professionals like to do, which of the formats of the appeal are most successful. For example, a direct mail appeal might be divided between versions offering a premium and those not providing that option to test which has the best net results. Another example of different versions of an appeal would be telemarketing, in which different scripts are tested for effectiveness. Each script would be assigned a different package code when recording gifts from the calls.
2. Another use of package is for segmentation. There are two common examples of this.
   a. For direct mail programs that do RFM segmentation (Recency, Frequency, and Monetary value), the codes assigned to the prospects can be recorded as packages. Blackbaud has a software program that will handle this directly with The Raiser's Edge. Most organizations, however, have their direct mail consultant or mail house do this coding outside The Raiser's Edge and afterward import the segmentation codes back into the system.

b. At the end of the year, many organizations do an end-of-year or holiday ask. Typically, this is segmented so that board members and major donors do not get the same letter as smaller donors. Given that it is really the same appeal—the "End-of-Year 201X Direct Mail appeal"—the segments assigned are usually recorded as packages. All copies of The Raiser's Edge have the ability to do this using the Mail page we will talk about in Chapter 4.

3. A third typical use of packages in The Raiser's Edge is to record the source lists when doing acquisition mailings. The names of the mailing recipients are not in The Raiser's Edge when doing acquisitions unless you use this type of mailing to renew long-lapsed donors. When your newly acquired donors give, their gifts can be entered, based on codes from the reply device, with the source list so you can measure the performance of each list purchased or traded.

Packages do not have to be used on every appeal. If you decide to use them on an appeal, however, all packages within that appeal need to follow one of these definitions. For example, one acquisition appeal cannot have packages for both packaging format and source list. However, an acquisition appeal could use packages for source list while another appeal in your system uses packages for packaging format.

Both appeals and packages are typically entered in two places in The Raiser's Edge after they are set up in Records:

1. They are entered on the Appeals tab of constituent records to indicate the constituent was sent the appeal and package, regardless of the constituent's response. This should be done for every solicitation your organization sends and can be done globally. This is called an "assigned appeal."

2. They are entered on the gifts that are received in response to the appeals so you can measure their success. This is called a "gift appeal."

Campaigns

Campaigns are the hardest fundraising record type to define. They are also the most difficult for which to find the proper role at most organizations. Applying the "overall objective" definition is harder than it sounds.

Deciding what to define as a campaign is not hard when there is a capital or endowment campaign in progress. The capital and endowment campaigns become campaigns in The Raiser's Edge with clearly defined goals and date ranges. For example, we can have the "Campaign for the 21st Century" to build a new building, we need $2.5 million to do that, we kicked off the campaign on July 1, 2009, and plan to complete it by August 31, 2012.

The challenge is how to use the campaign record in The Raiser's Edge for fundraising not related to a classic capital or endowment campaign. For efforts to raise money for the organization's annual needs, what should the campaigns be?

The key is that your *campaigns should be the topmost, broadest grouping and categorization of your fundraising efforts* that you want to use for

- Reporting
- Filtering giving output

When you ask for reports for your development department, how do you want to see fundraising broken out? What reports do you give to your organization's senior management? To the development committee of the board? To the board of directors or trustees?

What you do not want to do is to force your Raiser's Edge campaigns to match some user guide definition and then make your staff jump through hoops to create reports for these audiences in Word or Excel. Even if you want a specific presentation formatted in Word or Excel rather than using a standard report from The Raiser's Edge, your staff should be able to run campaign reports and just take the numbers off them for your Word or Excel versions. If your staff tells you they have to run a lot of queries, reports, or exports to give you your regular reports, something is probably amiss.

Here are some common examples of what organizations do for their campaigns:

- *Do not use campaigns.* Some organizations are small and straightforward enough that the funds and the appeals track what is primarily needed and adding another layer of categorization is not needed. These organizations choose not to use the campaign records at all, which is fine because **Campaign** is not a required field on a gift.
- *Use one campaign per year.* Another option is to create one campaign for each fiscal year, perhaps simply named "Annual Campaign 201X." There is nothing wrong with this approach as long as in doing so you are not then asking your staff to group your funds or appeals into other categories to give you the reports you really want.
- *Use campaigns to group appeals.* Some organizations use campaigns to group appeals together. Senior management and the board do not want to see how each and every appeal is doing but they do want to see how money is being raised. The campaigns might be ways to categorize the appeals for this purpose. For example, here are the campaigns used by a boys school in Northern California:
  - Direct Mail
  - Major Gifts
  - Planned Gifts
  - Corporate and Foundation Grants
  - Special Events

  "Membership" could be added to this list for organizations that have membership programs.
- *Use campaigns to group funds.* Other organizations are more focused on what reason the money is being raised, but senior management and the board do not want to see a report of every fund in the system. This would be applicable in large organizations that have a relatively large number of active funds, such as hospital foundations and schools. The campaigns could then be ways to group funds. For example, a hospital foundation might have the following campaigns:
  - Pediatrics
  - Cardiology
  - Oncology

  The funds would be more specific uses of money within each of these campaigns, such as Cardiac Research, Healthy Heart Community Education, and Cardiology Patient Services and Follow-up as funds for a Cardiology campaign.

- *Use campaigns for divisions or departments.* Large organizations that have multiple divisions or departments might find it best to use those units as the campaigns. At the Greater Bay Area Make-A-Wish Foundation we set up our campaigns as the departments of the organization. Our primary campaigns are Development, Corporate, Events, and Programs because these represent the teams of staff that fundraise, for whom budget numbers have been assigned, and whose performance toward goals we want to track.

     At four universities where I have implemented The Raiser's Edge the campaigns have been the schools in the university, such as the:
- Business School Campaign
- Law School Campaign
- College of Arts and Sciences Campaign

There is no right or wrong way to set up your campaigns as long as they reflect the most helpful ways to report on your giving at the broadest level and filter your giving in reports and other output.

Tip: The Raiser's Edge Enterprise

If your organization has The Raiser's Edge Enterprise edition of The Raiser's Edge, you have much more sophisticated setup and reporting functionality available to use than discussed here for campaigns and funds. Consult with your database administrator for more information.

Other Considerations

There are a few other points to keep in mind for fundraisers when analyzing and setting up your campaigns, funds, and appeals.

Interrelationships

Campaigns, funds, and appeals are not a strict hierarchy like an organizational chart. This is not often clear to fundraisers and lends to their confusion about how their campaigns, funds, and appeals should be set up. The structure is *not* a hierarchy with campaigns at the top, select funds in each campaign, and certain appeals for each fund. Campaigns, funds, and appeal can be entered on a gift in any combination.

     Using our Red Cross example, one appeal was raising money for three different funds. That is fine. You can decide that all the money from one appeal goes to the same fund—it is how you structure and present the appeal to your prospects.

     Sometimes, such as a typical capital campaign, a campaign will include its own set of funds (funding areas within the campaign) and will include its own appeals (solicitation efforts to raise money just for that campaign). But campaigns can also be used as a way to group just appeals together, thereby making a hierarchy that does not include funds. Any campaign or appeal could "feed" any fund. Or, campaigns could be a way to group funds together and one appeal could "feed" multiple campaigns and funds. It is up to you as to how the three levels interrelate.

Avoid the "Fruit Bowl"

One of the strongest recommendations I can make is to avoid what I call the "fruit bowl." The fruit bowl occurs when *one* field in The Raiser's Edge is used to track and report on categories like the following combinations:

- Board
- Major Gifts
- Direct Mail
- Tribute
- Bequests
- Special Events
- Corporate
- Foundation

I call this a fruit bowl because the options are not "apples to apples"; this is a combination of apples, oranges, bananas, cherries, and more fruit. That is, these options are based on:

- Who gave the money (board, corporate, foundation).
- The size of the gift (what I usually hear is "put all gifts of $1,000 or more in Major Gifts").
- How the money was raised (direct mail, tribute, events).
- The giving vehicle (bequests).

How do you then code a $2,000 gift given by a board member in a special event in honor of his recently deceased mother? Is that Board, Major, Tribute, or Event? Of course, everyone responds with an answer, but it is based on a hierarchy of importance and consideration. These sentences always seem to begin with "Well...," followed by case-by-case analysis. Is it more important that a board member gave it to track it as board giving? Is it more important to give the event credit because it was raised at the event?

The fruit bowl approach is also discouraged as the format to request for a report. The problems with this kind of reporting, which is extremely common, are:

- *It makes data entry difficult.* Who makes the decision and when every time a gift might fall into more than one category?
- *It makes all but the topmost category meaningless.* You might feel you have good reporting, but the categories are meaningless because they are incomplete.

The better way to do this with modern technology like The Raiser's Edge is to give each aspect a different field. Each aspect gets its own "bucket"—field—with similar type data that answers the same question. Each bucket only has one kind of "fruit" so you can do "apples to apples" comparisons.

Campaigns, funds, and appeals should each be defined so they are "exhaustive and exclusive" for gift entry:

- *Exhaustive.* Every gift has a campaign, fund, and appeal that are appropriate for it.
- *Exclusive.* There is only one campaign, fund, and appeal that apply to each gift.

In summary, make sure your campaigns in particular do not reflect this mistake. Define campaign, fund, appeal, and constituent code (discussed in Chapter 2) each for one purpose, to measure one thing. And when requesting reports, only ask each report to report on one thing at a time.

Note: Fixing the Fruit Bowl with Accounting

One of the most common reasons for this "fruit bowl" type of structure in The Raiser's Edge is that it is often found in the financial reports for the organization for fundraising revenue. Fundraisers have had such poor track records of being detail-oriented and trustworthy with numbers, the accountants have long been called on by organizational leadership to do most of the reporting. This includes fundraising reporting, such as how the money was raised and who gave it. However, accounting systems typically were not set up to avoid this fruit bowl problem either. They still are not today because accounting software is not designed to track fundraising metrics. The fruit bowl approach is just tradition and inertia, and now is the time to change.

Fund is the level in The Raiser's Edge that should integrate with accounting. Fund is usually defined as what the money is for and how it should be spent, and that is fine. If that is not what makes sense for your organization, that is okay as well, but define fund for one thing. Your accounting system should be set up to track that one thing, too. We have The Raiser's Edge, better technology, better tools, better understanding. We no longer need our colleagues in accounting to report to us, management, or the board about the fundraising metrics.

If you work with your accounting colleagues in a professional and cordial way (often much harder to do for both parties than it should be), they will typically welcome the opportunity to simplify what they track. They will work with you when they occasionally need fundraising data organized differently than they usually track it, such as giving by donor type (e.g., individual, corporate, foundation). My colleagues from the accounting profession have repeatedly assured me that there are no legal or financial requirements otherwise.

This will, also, likely require the involvement of your organization's senior management and the board to help them understand this proposed change in reporting: accounting will provide *financial* reports, which typically indicate the purpose of funds raised, and development will provide the *fundraising* reports, including reports on who has given and how that money has been raised. "Fundraising reports" is plural. There should be two separate reports that answer these questions. Both grand totals will match, but "the *who*" and "the *how*" questions should each have their own reports. The trust in the fundraising reports will be significantly higher if the development and accounting leadership can tell the organization management and board that they are reconciling the departments' systems each month.

Year Designations

Appeals should be specific in most cases, tied to the month and year of the activity. But a common question is, "Should there be date designations in the campaigns and funds?" Should we just have the "Annual Campaign" and "Unrestricted Fund" or should it be the "201X Annual Campaign" and "Unrestricted Fund 201X"? The answer to that depends on two important considerations:

1. *Do you wish to keep a goal in The Raiser's Edge for each fiscal year for the campaign and fund?* If so, you need one for each year because campaigns and funds can only have one goal; they do not allow multiple goals defined for different time periods. For example, if you want to run a report that lists the Annual Campaign for the last five years, each year showing its goal and the performance against goal, you need a campaign for each year. If you just want performance in terms of dollars raised, number of donors, average gift size, and the like, with no reference to goal, you do not need one per year. You only need one per year to keep each year's goal and to measure performance specifically against the goal.

2. *Do you raise and receive money for particular fiscal years outside those years?* When I was a fundraiser for Junior Achievement, a program that offers in-school programs about business and economics, our fiscal year was July through June to match the school year. In April, May, and June it was difficult to raise money for the fiscal year we were concluding because the school year was ending or over. But that did not mean that I just sat around playing Solitaire until July 1 arrived. I kept raising money, but I raised it *for* the next fiscal year's programs.

   When measuring fiscal year fundraising activity and performance, whether for the organization as a whole or for me as a fundraiser, it was not the date of the gift that mattered but the fiscal year designation. This is handled in The Raiser's Edge by putting the fiscal designation in the campaign, fund, or both. At Junior Achievement we filtered to fiscal year not by gift date but by campaign when running reports. If you raise or receive money for a fiscal year before or after that fiscal year (such as event gifts and pledge payments that need to continue to be linked to the previous fiscal year), you should consider this approach. If your internal reporting guidelines are clear that it is absolutely by date received, this consideration is not necessary for you.

Campaigns are easy to add to The Raiser's Edge and the need to do this each year should typically not be a deterrent to this approach. Funds are somewhat harder to add because there are usually more of them and the setup is more complicated if they are linked to the accounting system.

A common approach is to put the fiscal designation in the campaigns and not use a fiscal designation in the funds. By using the campaign and fund together, you know the fiscal year of a gift without having to have the fiscal designation on the fund, too.

This approach does not resolve wanting to store a goal for each year for each fund, however. Funds are only slightly more difficult to set up than campaigns, and the accounting information can be copied from one fund to another. Do not worry too much about the difficulty of creating new funds each year if that is your preferred approach to keep goal history.

Summary

Campaigns, funds, and appeals are core concepts that show up everywhere in The Raiser's Edge. They impact:

- Gift coding
- Assigning staff and volunteer fundraisers to their roles
- Assigning fundraisers to their prospects
- Linking fundraisers' activities to prospects and donors
- Recording solicitations prospects have received
- Giving statistics by each of these levels
- Filtering all other giving by donor, group of donors, and time frames by these levels

They have a dramatic impact on how your database is set up and what you get out of it.

A development strategic plan for a fiscal year discusses the funding needs, from whom you are going to raise that money, how you are going to raise it, and who is going to raise it.

Funds in The Raiser's Edge are where you set up the funding needs and amounts.

Appeals in The Raiser's Edge are where you set up how you are going to raise the money.

Campaigns give you a broader way to classify these areas when you do not want all of your reporting at such detailed levels.

From whom you are going to raise the money are your people and organizations, prospects and donors, called "constituents" in The Raiser's Edge. Constituents are categorized by "Constituency Code." Who is going to raise the money are your "solicitors." These are both tracked by using the Constituent record type and are the subject of our next chapter.

Finish reading this book to get the full context of how campaigns, funds, and appeals work for you. Then evaluate whether your campaigns, funds, and appeals are meeting your needs. If not, take out your fundraising plan; decide and list in writing outside The Raiser's Edge what your campaigns, funds, and appeals will be; coordinate with your accounting colleagues, senior management, and the board;

and work with your database administrator to get them entered and set up in The Raiser's Edge. The Raiser's Edge will be ready to help you raise, track, and report money the way that works best for you.

■ ■ ■

Now let us turn our attention to the prospects and donors.

Note

1. Blackbaud, *Campaigns, Funds & Appeals Data Entry Guide*, version 061908, p. 5.

CHAPTER 2

Prospects, Donors, and Other Constituents

In the fundraising process, there are a variety of people and organizations we work with to raise money:

- Prospects, whether defined as "those who have never given" or "anyone, including previous donors, we are asking for a gift"
- Donors
- Alumni and their parents
- Members
- Volunteers, such as trustees, board members, and event, program, and office volunteers
- Event attendees and sponsors
- Staff
- Community and government organizations we work with and who support our organizations' work
- Political and media contacts

These people and organizations should be stored in The Raiser's Edge as "Constituents." Constituents are primarily the people and organizations with whom we have or wish to have direct relationships. There is a great deal of information we store about our constituents so each one is given its own record in The Raiser's Edge, just like campaigns, funds, and appeals. Constituents are also accessed from the Records and Home pages. The people and organizations we do not have a direct relationship with but whom we want to track, such as spouses, partners, and places of employment, are stored *within* each constituent record rather than having their own constituent records.

For most users of The Raiser's Edge, the constituent record is the heart of the database and the part they access most frequently, especially if they are fundraisers. Although the system offers a great deal of functionality around constituents, in this

Note: Features of The Raiser's Edge

Many of the functions in The Raiser's Edge mentioned in this book are based on options that can be turned on or off for each copy or each user. If your copy of The Raiser's Edge does not have the options or perform as noted in this book, see your database administrator to enable that functionality. If your database administrator is unfamiliar with the option, have him or her contact Blackbaud customer support.

chapter we are going to focus on the following key areas:

- Who should be recorded in your database and which should be constituents.
- Key concepts about constituent biographical, demographic, and activity information so you can understand what you see and discuss it knowledgeably with your database staff.
- The primary tools for fundraisers for meaningfully accessing constituent information.

Who Should Be Recorded in The Raiser's Edge

For fundraisers, The Raiser's Edge should be *the* contact management tool. Who should be recorded in The Raiser's Edge? Everyone.

Every donor should have a record in The Raiser's Edge. The system is built for both major gifts and direct marketing donors (direct mail, telemarketing, and online).

Should prospects be in The Raiser's Edge? Yes! The Raiser's Edge is intended to be used to manage all your prospects as well as those who already give. There is no need to keep prospects in a Microsoft Excel spreadsheet until they give, waiting to transfer them into The Raiser's Edge. Today's database technology is sufficiently advanced to easily handle the additional names your prospects will add.

The only exception to adding prospects is for traded and purchased lists. Typically, you do not have permission to enter these names and addresses into your database until the prospect makes a donation.

When board members and others give you names and addresses to solicit, such as people to invite to events, it is generally best to add these to The Raiser's Edge right away for two reasons:

1. The names may overlap with ones already in the system. Adding the new names to The Raiser's Edge will help you avoid sending duplicate mailings.
2. The Raiser's Edge allows you to record, in each constituent record, the mailings the person or organization receives. Putting names of those you are reaching out to into The Raiser's Edge allows you to use the excellent mailing tools available in the system to generate the mailings and mark the records accordingly.

There are exceptions to this rule about volunteer-provided lists, but adding the lists is a common practice.

All boards and committees should be included in The Raiser's Edge. Other development volunteers should be included as well. Many organizations use The Raiser's Edge to manage all of their volunteers, including program volunteers.

All staff should be included in the system and, ideally, be converted into donors as well. Regardless, using The Raiser's Edge to its full extent requires having the names of the people who interact with your donors entered into the system. That way, you can assign roles and activities and record each interaction.

If you are an educational institution, all alumni should be in The Raiser's Edge. Most schools and colleges that use The Raiser's Edge do this, relying on it as the system of record for alumni. All address, family, and employment updates are recorded for the institution in The Raiser's Edge. All communications to alumni are done by using the mailing capabilities of The Raiser's Edge. Educational institutions also typically include parents and may also include current students and grandparents.

Your fundraising department should work hard to eliminate every spreadsheet and other database that contains constituent information. Instead, all of this data should be recorded in The Raiser's Edge. This includes information from business cards, Rolodexes, and personal Microsoft Outlook contact folders. Unless the contact information is strictly for your personal use, all vendors and other contacts should be entered into The Raiser's Edge. Do not worry, these records can be coded so they are excluded from mailings and other communications they should not receive.

One area where this recommendation is often ignored is in event management. Make no mistake. All event sponsorship and auction item prospects and invitees should be recorded in The Raiser's Edge. Ideally, all event attendees should be in The Raiser's Edge, as well. In Chapter 5 we talk more about this topic.

In many organizations, it is entirely appropriate to use The Raiser's Edge as the *organization's* database, not just the development database. Although this requires greater coordination and resources, it also provides significant benefit, leveraging the system's versatile contact management functionality in a broader way. At Junior Achievement and the Greater Bay Area Make-A-Wish Foundation, we included program management in The Raiser's Edge: the volunteers, teachers, children, families, medical personnel, and others. We record their activities and details of their involvement. The benefits of using The Raiser's Edge as the organization-wide database include:

- Potential cost savings by having one database to buy and support.
- Cross-functional knowledge of the database so staff can work with and back up each other.
- Less duplication in mailings.
- Less effort maintaining data when one constituent serves several roles (e.g., donor and program volunteer).
- A more holistic understanding of your constituencies by being able to see, in one place, all the roles each constituent plays, sometimes referred to as a "360-degree view."

The Raiser's Edge is not intended to be the single database solution for all organizations, but for many, it is an appropriate and successful fit.

Who Should Be a Constituent

Although everyone should be in The Raiser's Edge, not all people and organizations get full constituent records in the database. A "constituent" is a person or organization in The Raiser's Edge who is important enough to have its own record with the screens and fields for data entry. Constituents:

- Make gifts
- Are members
- Attend or sponsor events
- Are prospects to make gifts, be members, and attend and sponsor events
- Have notes and reminders about interactions past and future
- Receive mailings
- Show up on reports

Most people and organizations you deal with *will be* constituents. Notable exceptions include:

- *Spouses and partners*. Each member of married and partnered couples does not need their own record in the database. One of the people can be designated as the main person, with the other person sharing the same constituent record.
- *Places of employment*. As fundraisers, we often want to record where someone works if we are able to secure that information. However, that company or organization does not need to have its own record in the database unless you plan to approach it directly for other reasons.

There are many other examples we discuss later. However, who does and does not merit a constituent record in your database is an important concept for fundraisers to understand when looking up records in the database and when working with data entry staff. You, as a manager or fundraiser working with your database staff, need to provide direction about the importance and roles of people and organizations so they can be entered correctly for successful output.

Definition: Output

Throughout this book, we refer to "output," meaning the numerous ways The Raiser's Edge can produce results from the data you and your staff enter. Output from The Raiser's Edge can include: mailings, reports, lists, on-screen presentations of data, and exports. Because this list is so long, "output" is a more succinct way to refer to those results.

An example: One of your donors works for Bank of America and provides a business address. When that address is entered, a data entry question arises: Should Bank of America be added as its own constituent record? If this company is entered solely for mailing purposes for that one donor, there is no need for it to have its own record. But if your organization has a number of supporters working at Bank of America, you might want the bank to be added as a constituent. Then each employee can be linked to the Bank of America record, and the bank could be approached separately for a corporate gift based on its employees' support of your organization. In the process of soliciting that corporate gift, you can also identify which employees might best assist you in the process.

Names on Checks

Many fundraising database users in the United States say, "The IRS requires that the name on the check be entered as the hard credit constituent in our database." My research and experience have shown this is not the case. The IRS requires acknowledgement letters clearly indicate the name of the true donor. However, the IRS does not dictate how we set up our database and who the constituents are. Correct this belief among your data entry staff to avoid duplicates and difficulty retrieving data.

The most common example I see of this are multiple records for the same corporation resulting from different names that are used on checks from them over the years. This can result in the database housing different records for:

- The corporate office
- Subsidiary offices
- The foundation
- A matching gift processing company out of Princeton, New Jersey

In some situations, these are legitimately different donors and future prospects that need to be distinguished. But often they are not—the money is essentially from the single corporation that should be thanked, recognized, contacted, and re-solicited as that one single entity. The Raiser's Edge is a fundraising database, not solely a check-processing system, so work with your staff toward that end. We discuss this more in the section on soft credits in Chapter 3.

Tip: "Names on Checks" for Your Database Administrator

An approach I have used quite successfully to create the constituent records I want while reflecting the actual name on the check in the acknowledgement letter is to:

- Create a gift attribute named "Name on Check" with a Text data type.
- Enter this attribute on any gift where the name on the check is sufficiently different from the donor's name to warrant calling this out in the letter.
- Include this attribute in the fields to export for the acknowledgment letters.
- Modify the acknowledgement letter to include this field and use the Microsoft Word **If . . . Then . . . Else . . .** function to display the name on the check in the letter only if the attribute is not blank.

If your organization is an educational organization and you participate in the VSE reporting noted in Chapter 1, you will need to make further considerations before implementing this approach to make certain your gifts are categorized properly to determine giving by donor type.

Individual or Organization?

Your data entry staff may need your assistance about whether records should be added as an individual or an organization constituent. The Raiser's Edge has two types of records for constituents, an Individual record type and an Organization record type. Although this might seem self-evident, there are situations where you need to provide guidance.

Most situations will be clear. For example, Robert Hernandez is a board member and should be entered as an individual constituent. The Coca-Cola Company is a corporate donor and should be an organization. However, consider these situations:

- People who own their own businesses
- People with their own foundations
- Contacts and employees of organizations
- Families
- Anonymous donors
- Giving circles

The best approach to answer the question "Should this be an individual or organization?" is to first answer these questions:

- Who is the prospect?
- Who is the donor?
- Who are we actually soliciting?
- Who will be recognized in the annual report?

Also, think about whether having the person change at the organization will affect whether you stay connected with the organization. Or could the person's organization affiliation change and we would still focus on the person? Treat this as a fundraising issue, not a data entry issue, and the answer will be clearer.

Related Organizations

A very common question is, "What should be done with organizations that are closely related? Should there be one record for each or one umbrella record?" Examples include:

- Banks and their branches
- Insurance companies and their independent agents (e.g., State Farm)
- Headquarters and their subsidiaries (e.g., The Dayton Hudson Corporation and the local Target store)
- Companies and their matching gift processors

By now you should have anticipated a consistent theme in addressing these complexities:

- Who is the prospect?
- How will giving be recognized?

■ Are independent decisions made?
■ Will separate mailings be sent?
■ What future contact will be made and with whom?

These situations are not easy to handle and usually require thought and discussion. Your gift entry leadership should participate in the discussion, but this is also a fundraising question that a fundraiser needs to help resolve.

You can use the Name on Check strategy discussed earlier to address many of these situations and to limit each person or organization to one constituent record. Sometimes, it is easiest to manually modify the acknowledgement letter before sending it rather than complicate your database forever so that one letter comes out correctly now. Making those kinds of decisions often requires a fundraiser's leadership and direction.

Constituent Tabs

When you open a constituent record in The Raiser's Edge, think of it as pulling out a hanging folder from a file cabinet. For some of the prospects and donors, that file is going to be so full of information that the staff will have organized it into manila folders within the hanging file. Those manila folders would have names on them identifying the information inside.

That metaphor is applied to the design of The Raiser's Edge. When you open a constituent, there is so much information that can be stored in the record that it is organized into "tabs" just like the tabs on manila file folders as shown in Figure 2.1. When you click on a tab in The Raiser's Edge, you can see the information related to that topic. There is so much information we can track in today's fundraising environment that it is impossible to display it on one screen. In this section, we show you how to find a record, and we walk through each of the tabs in a record. We discuss:

■ The important concepts you should know about each tab for understanding the data you see and providing direction to data entry and output staff.
■ Tools specifically designed for the fundraiser to use and make sense of that data.

With two exceptions, we do not teach you how to do data entry. Data entry concepts are only discussed where it is important for you, as a fundraiser, to provide direction or understand the database to extract the information you want later.

One benefit of this design for a constituent record is that you do not need to go to other places in the software to find information about the person or organization. All of the constituent's data are going to be in this record. There might be a few links in this record to other records, but if your database has been used correctly there is no information anywhere else in The Raiser's Edge about this constituent. It is here alone and easily accessible.

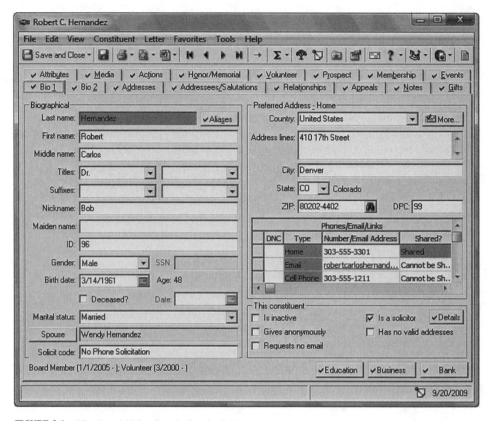

FIGURE 2.1   The Bio 1 Tab of an Individual Constituent

Tip: Raiser's Edge Tabs

- A tab with a red checkmark means there is data on that screen. If a tab has no checkmark, the tab is currently empty.
- If there are tabs you do not need to see and you wish to reduce the amount of information on the screen, talk to your database administrator who can remove tabs from your view.

Searching for Records

To find a constituent in the database, click on either the Home or Records page, though it is best practice to get in the habit of using the Home page.

In the **Quick Find** box you can type:

- A person's first name, space, and the person's last name (e.g., Robert Hernandez).

- A person's last name, comma, space, and the first name (e.g., Hernandez, Robert).
- The initial part of the name of an organization (e.g., "Nestle" to find Nestle USA, Inc.; Nestle UK Ltd; or Nestle Australia Ltd.).

Tip: Searching from the Home Page

The Home page can be customized for the tools you most frequently need. If the **Quick Find** box is not on your Home page already, you can easily add it by clicking the **Customize Home Page** button at the top of the screen and adding a checkmark to **Show quick find.**

If searching **Quick Find** does not find anything or if it finds multiple matches, the Open screen will appear. Here are a few tips to most effectively use this tool:

- Do not worry about using proper casing. The search screen is not case sensitive.
- Do not type the whole name in the search fields. The search fields are "begins with" searches. The Raiser's Edge will find any record that begins with what you type. You do not have to type in the full name for a match. This is especially helpful if you are not sure of the exact name or its spelling.
  - Typing "ander" in the **Last/Org name** search field will find both Anderson and Andersen last names.
  - Typing "british" in the **Last/Org name** search field will find any organization whose name begins with British, such as British Airways, British Museum, British Heart Foundation, and British Schools and Universities Foundation.
- If you know how the name starts but are not sure how it ends, the "begins with" tip above helps. However, if you are not sure how the name begins but know a part of the name, begin the search with an asterisk (*). For example, searching on "*foundation" will find any organization that contains the word "foundation."
- For the most thorough search possible, all of the checkboxes at the bottom of the search screen should have checkmarks in them except **Exact match only.** You only need to add the checkmarks once; The Raiser's Edge will remember the checkmarks for future searches.

When The Raiser's Edge displays the list of records that meet your search criteria, simply double-click the constituent record you want to open.

Search thoroughly before adding a new record or asking someone to add a new record for you. Duplicates are the bane of databases. Check various spellings, and even do a search using address fields to be absolutely certain the constituent is not in the database already. If your searching reveals duplicates, let your database administrator know so those records can be merged.

■ ■ ■

When you open a record, you can click on any tab in any order. We will review the tabs in the order in which they appear in the record as there is a logical progression to their order.

Bio 1 Tab

The Bio 1 tab contains the primary name, biographical, and contact information for an individual as shown in Figure 2.1.

People who are not married or partnered have their own records and the name data entry is straightforward. Determining which person should go in the name fields on the Bio 1 tab requires some thought in the cases of married and partnered couples.

SPOUSES AND PARTNERS   There are two ways to set up spouses and partners in The Raiser's Edge:

1. They share one constituent record.
2. They each have their own constituent record, and the records are linked to each other.

As a fundraiser, it is important for you to think about how you are going to use the system and request information from it. What you decide will help you determine which way to have the data entered. It is usually easier to handle couples as one constituent, but there are times when that setup does not provide sufficient flexibility. If you do not understand the rationale for this important point, you will be confused when you open records and get data back from The Raiser's Edge. Additionally, you will have a difficult time participating in conversations with your database staff when asking for information from the system.

For most organizations using The Raiser's Edge, married and partnered couples share one record. Blackbaud designed The Raiser's Edge to be used this way most of the time. You only need one record per couple if:

- You treat the couple as a couple and there is no distinction between them as people. For example, you get one joint check from them when they give to your direct mail solicitations.
- One of them has a primary relationship with you—board member or volunteer, for example—and the second person is simply the spouse or partner without a separate relationship with you.

Spouses and partners each need to have a separate relationship with you before a constituent record is created for both of them. A common example would be that one of them is a board member and the other is a volunteer. Another example is when both are alumni of your school or college.

When a spouse or partner does not have a constituent record of its own, there is limited information you can record about them. So the rule of thumb is: *If there are fields that need to be filled out for the second person that are only available if the second person has its own record, the second person needs to be added as a constituent.* Examples of those fields include:

- Constituent codes
- Gifts
- Volunteer
- Event participation
- Attributes

We talk about these fields in this chapter.

The determination of whether spouses and partners should be constituents is typically done on a case-by-case basis within a database. All of the spouses and partners you track do not need to be treated the same way. When creating mailings, The Raiser's Edge provides an option to send only one copy of a mailing to a couple even if each spouse or partner has its own record.

If you determine that a shared record is the best approach, you should understand that The Raiser's Edge has no gender expectations about the main person in the couple who is put on the Bio 1 tab. So:

- Put the most important person in the Bio 1 name fields if one of the two has a more direct relationship with you. If the woman is the board member and her husband has no direct relationship with you, she should be recorded in the Bio 1 fields.
- If neither member of the couple has a more direct relationship with you, your organization should develop a policy for how the situation is to be handled. For example, a couple gives a joint check to your direct mail efforts. Options you should consider include:
  - The "traditional" way of the man first. This is, by far, the most common approach.
  - The first name on the check or the signer of the check.
  - If you are an organization for girls or women, it is fine to have a policy that always puts the woman first.
- The Raiser's Edge can handle same-gender couples just fine.

If you determine that each spouse or partner needs to be a constituent, each will have a full Bio 1 screen with name fields to complete. One of them will need to be designated the "Head of Household." This function is used when doing mailings from The Raiser's Edge. If selected, it allows you to send only one copy of a mailing to the couple even though they each have their own record.

Spouses and partners are expected to have the same address and same combined name field, as discussed below. The constituent marked the head of household determines:

- Which of the records will get the indication that the mailing was sent to them.
- The ID put on the reply portion of the mailing, such as a direct mail piece, and therefore into which record resulting gifts will be entered.

When spouses and partners are linked using the spouse functionality, one of them and only one of them will be automatically marked as the head of household. You should indicate which of the two is the most important so that your staff can change this default setting if necessary.

Partners   You should help establish a policy for your organization that reflects when "Spouse" functionality should be used for nonmarried couples. This includes both same- and opposite-gender couples. Design a policy that reflects the philosophy of your organization: when are two people considered a "couple" such that this functionality should be used rather than recording the second person on the Relationships tab?

The Raiser's Edge spouse functionality is important because it defines the constituent, prospect, and donor perspective. For example, most information in the constituent record, such as giving history, is assumed to be *their* combined giving if a spouse or partner is present. The versions of the names we use for mailings and reporting is based on the main constituent and spouse fields.

It is possible to change the name of the spouse functionality throughout The Raiser's Edge. It is often changed to "Partner." Other options to indicate the same thing are typically too long to fit well. Talk to your database administrator.

OTHER BIO 1 CONCEPTS OF NOTE   The discussion on spouses and partners is the most important take-away from the left side of the Bio 1 tab. Most of the fields there are self-explanatory, though there is a large amount of important detail that your data entry staff should pay attention to when filling out these fields.

Other fields on the Bio 1 tab you should understand as a fundraiser:

- **Solicit codes** are the "do not contact" codes such as Do Not Solicit, Do Not Mail, No Newsletter, and so forth.
  Understand:
  - These are codes for what *not* to do.
  - These are not limited to solicitations; they apply to almost all contact methods.
    These codes play a critical role in keeping your mailings and other communications from going to the wrong people, so you should understand the codes your organization is using. These are discussed extensively in Chapter 4 in the context of creating mailings.
- The **Preferred Address** on the right side of the screen is where the constituent prefers to get his or her mail. This defaults to a home address but can be any address, such as a business. If it is a business address, the name of the business can be seen by clicking on the **Business** button in the lower right of the screen.
- Most users of The Raiser's Edge will place all phone and fax numbers and e-mail and web addresses in the **Phones/Emails/Links** area. Confirm your organization's procedure. The intended way to use this area is to only include the phone and contact information for the preferred address. You might need to click on the **Business** button to see business contact information.
  - For e-mail addresses, you can click on the address to start an Outlook e-mail to the constituent. When you send the e-mail, The Raiser's Edge will store a copy of it on the Actions tab of the constituent.
  - You can click on web addresses to go to the web site.
- The section of the lower-right screen labeled **This constituent** contains a number of important functions. You should talk to your database administrator to make sure that you understand and agree with the ways your organization is using those options.

Finally, there are three buttons on the screen that are important to fundraisers that warrant explanation.

1. The **Spouse** button on the left side of the screen: this shows the spouse or partner information.
2. The **Education** button in the lower right side of the screen: if you are an educational institution, this shows the *Primary* education record affiliated with your school. "Primary" is of note because the alumnus might have multiple degrees from your institution and the other degrees are accessed on the Relationships tab. If your organization is not an educational institution, this button is much less important.
3. The **Business** button is the person's primary place of employment, whether it is a business or another type of organization (e.g., hospital, school). The address here can be used for mailing purposes whether or not it is the preferred address.

Org 1 Tab

The Raiser's Edge was designed to support your efforts to raise money from organizations such as corporations and foundations. It is just as powerful a tool in this context as it is raising money from individuals. In fact, most of the constituent record functionality is exactly the same for both record types.

The Org 1 tab is for organizations what the Bio 1 tab is for individuals, but it is more straightforward because the concept of spouses and partners does not apply. The Org 1 tab is shown in Figure 2.2.

- The **Org Name** field should be the official version of the organization's name. This is the name by which the organization wants to be recognized in annual reports, newsletters, donor walls, and the like. Alternative names such as nicknames, acronyms, acronyms that are spelled out, former names, merged company names, misspellings, and other versions by which you might search for the organization go under the **Aliases** button. Help the database staff determine what needs to be the official organization name.

Tip: Alphabetizing Organizations Properly

Organizations whose names begin with "The," such as The Coca-Cola Company, and foundations whose names contain a person's name, such as the Bill & Melinda Gates Foundation, should not be listed alphabetically in reports by the literal first word in the name. Remind your data entry staff to put a backslash (\) instead of a space before the words by which these organizations should be alphabetized. The backslash will only appear in the **Org Name** field; all other instances of the name will display a space instead of the backslash. So:

The\Coca-Cola Company sorts this organization in the Cs
Bill & Melinda\Gates Foundation sorts this organization in the Gs

When searching for these organizations, search by the word after the backslash and not the first word: "Coca" and "Gates," respectively.

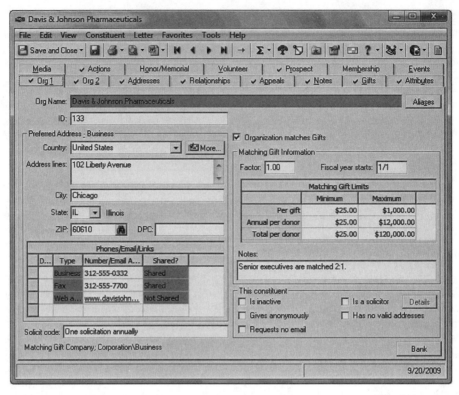

FIGURE 2.2　The Org 1 Tab of an Organization Constituent

- Organizations have a Preferred Address and contact information, too, but these fields play a different role.
  - If you do not have a contact person's name for the organization, this address is the one that will be used for the mail you send to the organization.
  - If you have a contact person at the organization who receives the mail, the process is different. The contact is added on the Relationships tab. The organization's preferred address is assigned to the contact initially but can be changed later if necessary. You would change a contact's address if the contact had a mail drop or room number or worked at a different location than the main organization address.

    Mail sent to the organization in this situation does not go to the preferred address but, instead, to the contact's address. Although organizations' preferred addresses are important, it is more important that you understand contacts for organizations, which will be discussed in the section below on Relationships.
- The most important item in **Organization matches Gifts** is the checkbox next to the section name. This is a tool that can help you *raise* money, not just track it, if your staff takes the time to fill it out. If your staff sets this up properly, they can be notified anytime an individual donor who works for a matching gift company makes a gift.
- **Solicit code** and **This constituent** are just as important for organizations and work the same way as they do for individuals.

Tip: Starting Tab

If you would like a record to always open to a tab other than Bio 1 or Org 1, talk to your database administrator. For example, membership staff might wish records to open to the Membership tab while major gifts officers might wish records to open to the Prospect (major gifts) tab.

Bio 2 and Org 2 Tabs

The second tabs for individuals and organizations, Bio 2 and Org 2, respectively, are very much the same. These are the "miscellaneous" tabs, used for those fields there were not enough of to justify their own tab.

The demographic and credit card fields are not used by most organizations. Although these fields work fine, most organizations have decided this is more detail than they need to track. Feel free to ignore these fields, use them, or even consider working with your database administrator to rename them and use them for different purposes. At Junior Achievement, we renamed the **Religion** field to "T-Shirt Size" given the number of events we did where we handed out T-shirts.

CONSTITUENT CODE KEY CONCEPTS The important fields on this screen are the **Constituent Codes**. The broad-sounding name for this field has led many to think that this is the miscellaneous code area for The Raiser's Edge: if there is something I want to track that I cannot find another field for, here is where I put it.

The intent of this field, however, is to provide the tracking and reporting code we raised in the last chapter regarding donor type. This field is supposed to answer the questions, "Where does our money come from? Who gives to us?" The classic fundraising categories include:

- Individuals
- Foundations
- Corporations

Sometimes "Bequest" and "Government" are included in the classic list as well. Think of the typical annual report that contains a pie chart showing what types of donors support the organization, accounting as shown in Figure 2.3 from the annual report of Lewis & Clark, a college and graduate school in Portland, Oregon.

Because this is such a core classifying and reporting field, a long conversation could ensue about this field. This field is intended to be as important as campaigns, funds, and appeals, and is also a pivotal field for:

- Filtering when running mailings, reports, and exports (e.g., only include board members).
- Reporting so you can see dollars given, number of donors, and so forth by these categories.

Fundraising leadership needs to determine if this intended purpose provides value for reporting. Does fundraising leadership, the organization's accounting senior management, or the board want to see giving by donor type? Is Finance relying on

Sources of Gift Income, 2007–2008
$11,587,912

Estates	$5,388,241	46.5%
Foundations/OICF	$1,875,878	16.2%
Trustees	$1,686,669	14.5%
Alumni	$1,234,726	10.7%
Parents	$477,793	4.1%
Friends	$451,248	3.9%
Corporations/organizations	$395,601	3.4%
Faculty/staff	$77,756	0.7%

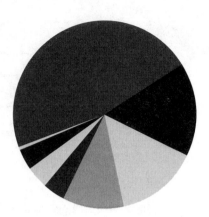

FIGURE 2.3   Sources of Gift Income from Lewis & Clark *Report on Giving 2007–2008*

development and The Raiser's Edge to provide that data for any reporting? If so, reserve this field exclusively for defining donor type, and put other codes elsewhere such as the Attributes tab. If not, it is appropriate to use the functionality available here for other purposes.

If this field is used to define donor type, keep the following best practices in mind:

- Every constituent should have at least one code.
- Usually, the classic categories of Individual, Foundation, and Corporation are too broad to be meaningful within a single database. They are typically broken out further.
- The codes for *individual* constituents typically define the *primary, big picture relationship to your organization*. Keep in mind the categories that are meaningful for your reporting by donor type. Good examples include:
  - *Board Member*. Because giving by board members should be disproportionately larger than gifts from other sources, it is important to note the relationship even though it may currently apply to less than 20 constituents.
  - *Former Board Bember*. This is a common constituent code as it defines the constituent's current role and important history.
  - *Staff and Former Staff*. Typical codes for the same reasons, establishing the relationship with the constituent.
  - Other codes generally depend entirely on the nature of your organization and your use of The Raiser's Edge.
    - Schools will have Alum, Current Parent, Past Parent, perhaps Current Grandparent and Past Grandparent, and Faculty.
    - Hospitals will have Patient and Physician.
    - At the Greater Bay Area Make-A-Wish Foundation, we have Wish Child, Wish Family, and Volunteer.
  - *Friends*. It is not uncommon for the majority of individuals to fall into a "miscellaneous" category. This group is usually called "Individuals" to use the traditional fundraising terminology or "Friends" to avoid confusion with the record type of Individual.

- The codes for *organization* constituents typically define the *type of organization*. Good examples include:
  - *Business or Corporation*. Although "Corporate" is the traditional fundraising term, it is not technically correct for small businesses, so many opt for "Business" instead.
  - *Foundation*. This single value often suffices while those users with significant foundation fundraising work will often break this out into different foundation types (e.g., private, corporate, community).
  - *Government*. Used for federal, state, provincial, and local governments and government agencies.
  - *Community Organization*. Other nonprofits in your community from which you receive money such as Rotary Clubs.
  - *Schools*. This is often a constituent code for organizations that work with schools and are using The Raiser's Edge to track their interactions and include them in mailings.
- When individuals pass away and leave bequest gifts, the most common approach is to create organization constituent records with the name "Estate of [person's name]." The records are usually given an *Estate/Trust* constituent code.
- Common examples of the *incorrect* use of constituent codes when the field is used for its intended purpose include:
  - *Donor and Major Donor*. The purpose of this field is donor type as defined earlier, so these options add nothing. "Donor" is not a type of donor and "Major Donor" reflects the size of the constituent's giving, not what type of person or organization the donor is. In addition, these values would be difficult to maintain. The Raiser's Edge will not add or update them when a gift is entered because this is not the intended use of this field.
  - *Prospect*. This is not a good constituent code whether you define Prospect as "someone who has never given" or add the code to indicate someone is a prospect for a specific purpose, such as a planned giving or a capital campaign. If it means "never given," The Raiser's Edge is not designed to update it because that is not the purpose of this field—"Prospect" is not a type of donor. Look at the Gifts tab to see if the constituent has ever given. To indicate the constituent is a prospect for a specific solicitation, enter that information elsewhere in the record based on a number of considerations to be discussed in this chapter and Chapter 6 on major gifts fundraising.
- Constituent codes have dates that should be used. For example, The Raiser's Edge can report on historical board giving for those who were on the board five years ago, not just the historical giving of those who are on the board today. Direct your staff to add a **Date From** whenever a new constituent code is added. Also, they should add **Date From** and **Date To** for the most important constituent codes in your system, such as Board Member and Former Board Member.

There are numerous additional details that could be mentioned here because constituent codes are intended to be as foundational to the setup and use of The Raiser's Edge as campaigns, funds, and appeals. Because constituent code is repeatedly an option when filtering mailings and reports and a category to use when running reports, you as the fundraiser should have a solid understanding of how these codes are used in your system. If you are not able to get the donor type filtering and reporting you need, talk with your database staff.

Note: Other Terms for Constituent Code

The Raiser's Edge also refers to Constituent Codes as Constituency Codes and Constituencies. These terms all refer to the same thing.

Addresses Tab

Beginning with the Addresses tab, the remaining tabs are almost exactly the same for individuals and organizations. Whether you are an individual or institutional fundraiser, the concepts will mostly be the same.

The Bio 1 and Org 1 tabs show the preferred address for the constituent—for individuals, where the person prefers to get his or her mail, and for organizations, the main address of the organization (remember, the mailing address for an organization with a contact person is in the contact's record to be discussed in the upcoming Relationships section). The Addresses tab shows the preferred address again, but it is the same address displayed in two locations. This tab also contains the constituent's other addresses, including:

- Additional current addresses such as Home, Business, Vacation, Mailing, and Second Home.
- Branch and subsidiary addresses for an organization.
- Former addresses: when doing address updates in The Raiser's Edge, best practice is to save former addresses to help with prospect research and to avoid "finding" the old address and entering it again.

While on the topic of addresses, you should note that addresses have more functionality than you might think. As a fundraiser, you might want to use the following capabilities:

- Each address stores who added it, when it was added, who last changed the address, and when it was last changed. Consult this information if there are questions about the accuracy of the information.
- If you question the source of address information, there is a field for storing the source that your data entry staff can use.
- The Raiser's Edge supports seasonal addresses for your wealthy donors and "snow birds" who divide their time among multiple homes but should be mailed to year-round.
- For users with constituents outside your own country, addresses can be printed directly from The Raiser's Edge in the format appropriate for each country. For example, U.S., Canadian, U.K., Australian, and European addresses all have different formats but can be printed in the same mailing with the fields, lines, and structure appropriate for each destination country.

Also make sure that you and your staff understand the differences among a single bad or old address, a "lost" constituent, and constituents who do not want mail. Entering these distinctions incorrectly is a common mistake that results in serious mailing problems. The most significant concern is removing good prospects from your mailings resulting in no further gifts from the constituent. Ensure that your staff understands the various fields for the different purposes.

Definition: Lost

"Lost" constituents are usually defined in the context of The Raiser's Edge as "those for whom we do not have a current mailing address." It correlates with the **Has no valid addresses** field, and that is how the term is used in this book. Others, however, define "lost" as having no current contact information whatsoever, including mailing addresses, phone numbers, and e-mail addresses.

Because there are a number of details about addresses and they play such an integral role in the successful use of your database, it is not uncommon for address updates to be centralized. It is important that if you and other staff who are not primarily data entry staff want access to change address information yourselves that you learn these details, more details than included in this chapter. Otherwise I recommend e-mailing address updates to your database staff and allowing them to make those changes.

Addressees/Salutations Tab

"Addressees" and "Salutations" are the terms used in The Raiser's Edge for the versions of names to use when addressing people in mailings. The addressee is the full form of the name that shows up on labels, envelopes, the inside address of letters, and on reports. The salutation is what appears after "Dear" at the beginning of a letter.

Individual constituents have an Addressees/Salutations tab (shown in Figure 2.4) while organization constituents do not. However, organization contacts, as discussed in the next section, have addressees and salutations so their names can appear correctly on the mailings they receive on behalf of their organizations. Because "addressees and salutations" is a mouthful to read and say, we often abbreviate them to "add/sals."

Whenever name information is taken out of The Raiser's Edge for mailings, reports, and exports, your database staff should always use the add/sals. For example, your merge letters should *not* look like this:

Title FirstName LastName
[Address]
Dear Title LastName:

Instead, they *should* look like this:

Addressee
[Address]
Dear Salutation:

The purpose here is to recognize that, in relationship-based fundraising, *we should call people what they want to be called and not force their names into formulas.*

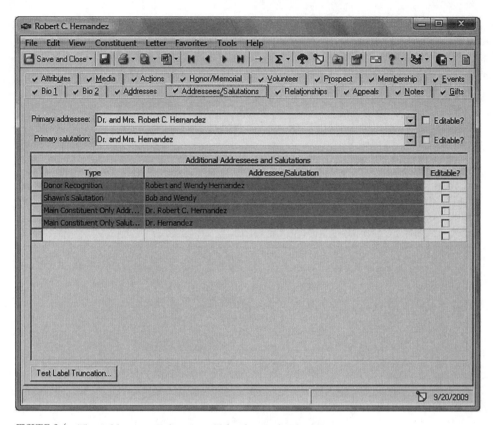

FIGURE 2.4   The Addressees/Salutations Tab of an Individual Constituent

Do not send me mail as "William P. Connors." I prefer "Bill Connors." But do not send my colleague Charles mail to "Charlie" or "Chuck"—he prefers "Charles H. Smith III." Although the "Mr. and Mrs. Robert Hernandez"-type format might work for many of your constituents, spouses and partners with different last names usually prefer a "Mr. Robert Hernandez and Ms. Wendy Figueroa" format. If Wendy is your board member, it should probably be "Ms. Wendy Figueroa and Mr. Robert Hernandez." What if the constituent abbreviates the first name and uses a full middle name, such as R. Michael Lane?

Add/sals allow us to accommodate these and other variations. This is not just an internal database matter. These are data entry values that your constituents are going to see and notice. It is important that you understand add/sals and guide the data entry staff correctly.

The **Primary addressee** and **Primary salutation** fields that appear at the top of the tab are the name versions that will be used most of the time. You should help define a procedure for your organization about how these should be constructed in general, knowing that a variety of situations will require exceptions.

■ Should the spouse or partner be included? Most organizations do include the spouse or partner.

- How formal should they be?
  - Should the addressee include titles (prefixes), middle initials, or suffixes? Should it be:

    Mr. and Mrs. Robert C. Hernandez, Jr., or

    Mr. and Mrs. Bob Hernandez
  - Should the salutation use titles and last names or first names and nicknames? Should it be:

    Mr. and Mrs. Hernandez, or

    Bob and Wendy (some would say the more proper format is "Wendy and Bob")

The most common approach in past years has been to use the more formal "Mr. and Mrs. Hernandez" format for salutations. I am increasingly seeing the less formal "Bob and Wendy" used, however. In Austria, the protocol tends to be very formal, while in Sweden, they often do not even bother to enter titles (prefixes) because the add/sals are so informal. Pick the format that is right considering the nature and age of your constituency and the culture of your organization.

In addition to the primary add/sals, there are **Additional Addressees and Salutations** that can be added. These are fields that can play an important role in working with your constituents. Additional add/sals allow you to create formats of the names that are different than those needed for the primary add/sals. The most common types of additional add/sals are:

- *Donor Recognition*. When the constituent expresses an interest in appearing in the annual report or donor wall under a name format different than the primary addressee, use this option instead.
- *Shawn's Salutation*. In this case "Shawn" is the name of the executive director or head of development who signs some letters. This additional add/sal is added when the primary salutation is formal (e.g., Mr. and Mrs. Hernandez), but Shawn knows some constituents and wants them addressed in the mail merge as she would address them when writing to them personally (e.g., Scooter, Bob and Wendy).
- *Main Constituent Only Addressee and Main Constituent Only Salutation*. These are used when the primary add/sals include the spouse or partner but, for the mailing, you only need to address the main person. Examples of this would be when the main person is a board member, a volunteer, or a contact at an organization.

These values need to be added to your database if they, or versions similar to them, are not available in your system.

Additional add/sals only need to be entered if they are different than the primary add/sals. When pulling the add/sal information, The Raiser's Edge will allow your database staff to say, "Use the X additional add/sal if the constituent has one, otherwise just use the primary add/sal."

Relationships Tab

The Relationships tab in The Raiser's Edge allows you to store the relationships your constituents have that you want to remember as a fundraiser. There are six kinds of relationships stored on this tab. They work similarly for both individual and organization constituents.

Relationship Type Examples

Relationship Type	Examples for Individual Constituents	Examples for Organization Constituents
1. Individual	Spouse or partner Family: children, parents, siblings, others Friends Colleagues Financial, investment, and legal advisors	Contact person Employees Board members Program officers
2. Organization	Places of employment Other nonprofit groups with which they are involved Religious affiliations Professional affiliations	Subsidiaries Parent companies Groups and members of groups, such as chambers of commerce and school districts
3. Banks/Financial Institutions	Used for recording direct debit details for gifts paid by withdrawals from checking and saving accounts.	
4. Education/Schools	If you are an educational institution, your school and the graduation and degree details for each degree. For all users, including educational institutions, any other level of educational attainment you wish to record.	(This kind of relationship does not exist for organization constituents.)
5. Assigned Solicitors	The person or people assigned to this constituent to manage, cultivate, or solicit the constituent for gifts.	
6. Fund	The funds in your system this constituent is related to, typically as a donor who established a named fund or a beneficiary of a specific fund, such as student scholarship recipients.	

To avoid confusion, you should know that the key relationships discussed on the Bio 1 tab are stored here. The buttons on the Bio 1 tab are simply shortcuts to the most important relationships. When you see those relationships here, they are not duplicates. Those relationships include:

- The **Spouse** or partner
- The primary alumni record with the **Education** button
- The primary place of employment from the **Business** button
- The primary **Bank** used for direct debits (although most U.S. organizations unfortunately do not use this)

These key relationships are found on a large cross-section of constituents in the typical database. Although I have provided a number of examples of relationships in the table above, most of the other kinds of relationships are used only for your most important prospects such as board members and major donor prospects.

Your discretion and leadership as a fundraiser is required to decide when there is sufficient value to spend the time doing the data entry for relationships. Much of fundraising, certainly major gifts and institutional fundraising, is all about relationships. If you do that kind of fundraising, this will be an important tab to consult when developing cultivation and solicitation strategies.

On the toolbar of the constituent, there is a button that looks like a tree. This is the **Relationship** button.

Clicking it will show you how this constituent is related to other constituents, who those constituents are related to, and so forth, as shown in Figure 2.5. Think of this as the "six degrees of separation" view of your data, helping you identify strategies for opening doors and including other constituents in your cultivation strategies for the constituent.

CONSTITUENT AND NONCONSTITUENT RELATIONSHIPS   The people and organizations represented in relationships can themselves be constituents. In these situations, the Relationships tab links the two constituent records together. Alternatively, the relationship can be recorded in the constituent without giving the relation its own

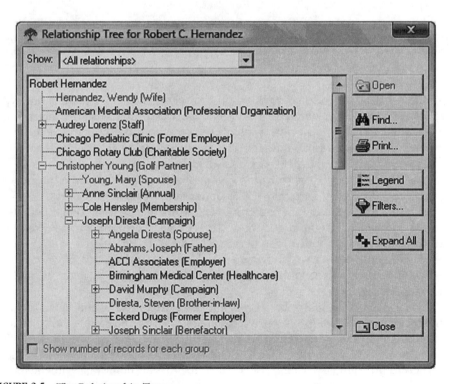

FIGURE 2.5   The Relationship Tree

constituent record if it does not need one. For example, if two of your board members are friends outside of the board, you can link their two records together using the Relationships tab. To record the name of a major gifts prospect's five-year-old son, enter him as a nonconstituent relationship directly on the Relationships tab of the prospect—the son certainly does not need his own constituent record.

You can tell whether a relation is a constituent when you open the relationship: if there is an ID number, the relationship is a constituent; if there is no ID number, the relationship is not a constituent.

Tip: Opening Linked Constituents

When two constituents are linked as relationships, you do not need to do a new search to open the constituent record belonging to the relationship. You have two options:

1. You can right-click on the constituent's name on the Relationships tab and choose **Go to** to open the relationship's constituent record. (Double-clicking opens the relationship record, not the relationship's constituent record.)
2. If the relationship record is open so you can view the details of the relationship, you can click on the **Go to** button on the toolbar to open the constituent.

CONTACTS   If you work with and raise money from organizations, there is one type of relationship that is important for you to understand: Contacts. A contact is an Individual Relationship in an organization's record who is the primary person who represents the organization. Although contact functionality in The Raiser's Edge appears in several places, the primary consideration as to who should be marked a contact is *who receives the organization's mail.* If you raise money from businesses, corporations, or foundations, you need to understand this critical concept.

Contacts for The Raiser's Edge are not necessarily the most important people at the organization, such as the president or CEO. Contacts are certainly not everyone who works at the organization. The person who should be marked a contact for an organization is the person whose name should appear on the letter, envelope, and label when you want to send the organization a solicitation, newsletter, invitation, annual report, or any other mailing.

To make an individual relationship into a contact, add a checkmark to the **Contact** checkbox in the lower left of the screen as shown in Figure 2.6.

Some organizations in your database may have more than one person who receives its mail. To accommodate this situation there is a **Contact type** field. Best practice is to use "Primary" as the contact type for organizations that only have one contact person and for the main contact who receives most of the organization's

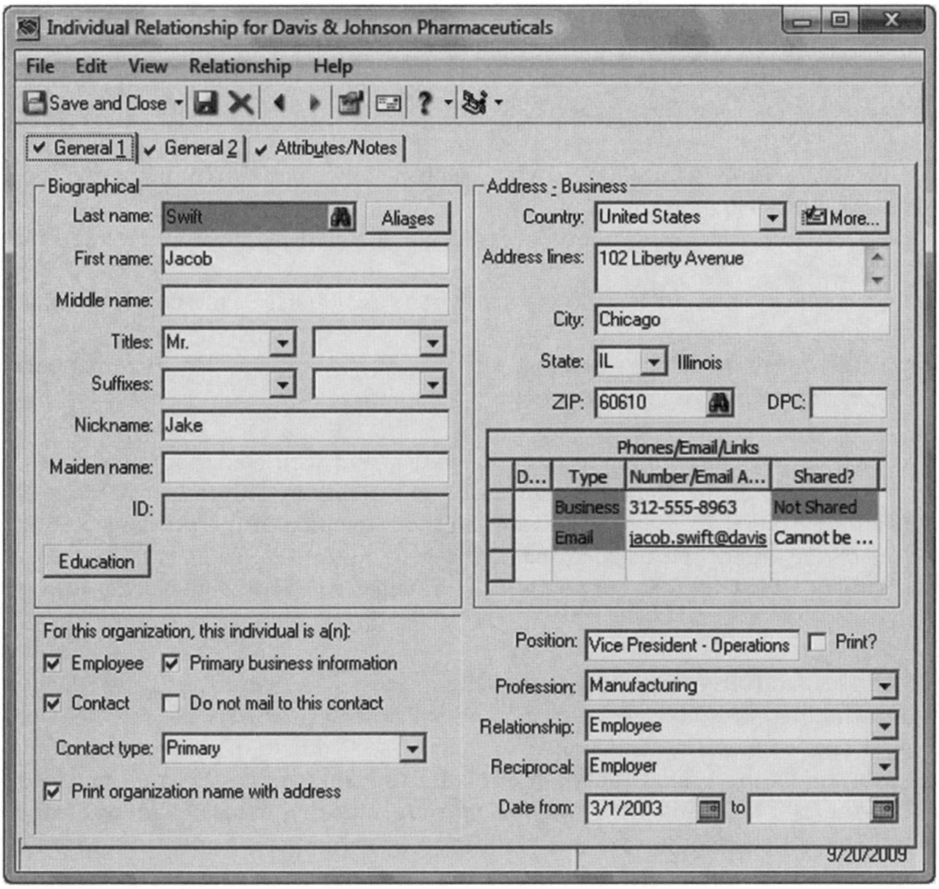

FIGURE 2.6 A Contact for an Organization

mail. It is highly recommended that you try to limit each organization to one contact to make your mailings simpler.

If an organization truly has more than one person who gets the mail, you as the fundraiser must work closely with your database staff to help them understand who receives what type of mail at the organization. You need to coordinate setting up your database's options for the **Contact type** field. The key concept to consider for contact types is that they should be *the types of mailings you do.* "Secondary," "President/CEO," and "Program Officer" are *not* good contact types and will not help your office get mailings out to organizations correctly. Good contact type examples include:

- *Event.* Sometimes specific event types are helpful.
- *Volunteer.*
- *Fundraising.* Typically the Primary contact is the fundraising contact, however.

These examples are mailing types so that when you do an event invitation, for example, you can say, "For organizations receiving the invitation, the event contact should get this instead of the primary contact if the organization has an event contact." You can also choose to include both the event and primary contacts in the mailing as we discuss in Chapter 4. The best way to determine the appropriate contact types for your organization is to:

- Identify which organizations in your database truly should have more than one person receiving their mail.
- Understand how contacts are selected when doing mailings as discussed in Chapter 4.
- Identify for those organizations what type of mail each of the contacts should receive.
- Try to develop contact types that represent these mailings and such that each contact person is assigned only one type.

There is one more important point to understand with contacts. Every contact must have at least the **Primary addressee** and **Primary salutation** fields filled out on the General 2 tab of the relationship. As discussed in the previous section, these are versions of the contact's name that will be used in mailings. If these two fields are not filled out for your contacts, their names will appear incorrectly in your mailings.

ASSIGNED SOLICITORS   "Solicitor" is the term used in The Raiser's Edge to identify those who help you manage, cultivate, and solicit your prospects. (In the U.K. version of The Raiser's Edge they are called "Canvassers" due to the alternate meaning of "solicitor" in the United Kingdom.) This functionality applies to both individual and organization constituents, whether you are pursuing a major gift or a large grant. This is important to understand for major gifts fundraisers and is discussed in Chapter 6 on major gifts and grants.

Appeals Tab

The Appeals tab in both individual and organization records is quite simple: it shows what mass solicitations the constituent has received, whether or not the constituent has given in response to them. Any time you generate a direct marketing appeal (direct mail, telemarketing, or e-mail request that asks for a monetary response), your database staff should be adding the appeal to this tab for the constituents who received it.

This includes newsletters, magazines, and annual reports with a contribution envelope and invitations for fundraising events. Mailings that do not generate gifts should be recorded as actions as discussed in that upcoming section.

Adding the appeals is done globally, not record by record. Very little data entry is done on this tab. It is simply a place to store the history of mailings for your use. The Raiser's Edge calculates how much the constituents have given to the appeals automatically.

Typically, the only data entry done on this screen is to use the **Response** column for telemarketing when the prospects do not give and provide an explanation why. The **Response** column is usually not filled out for any other situation.

The data on this screen can be used to identify the constituents that are repeatedly asked but do not give. You can then modify your approach or remove them from future mailings.

Notes Tab

Both individuals and organizations have the Notes tab (shown in Figure 2.7), and you should get to know it well: this is a tab that fundraisers should use themselves. It is simple to use if you understand its intent: *Notes are for information that is not date- or time-specific and does not go on another tab.*

- Good examples of note information include:
  - *Biographical background of constituents.* Where they grew up and family interests and activities.
  - *Wealth information.* How they acquired their wealth, where is it held and who manages it, information that might indicate liquidity, and availability for funding a gift.
  - *Communication preferences.* The date, source, and reason for solicit codes (e.g., Do Not Solicit), the **Is inactive** and **Requests no email** checkboxes, and other such information.

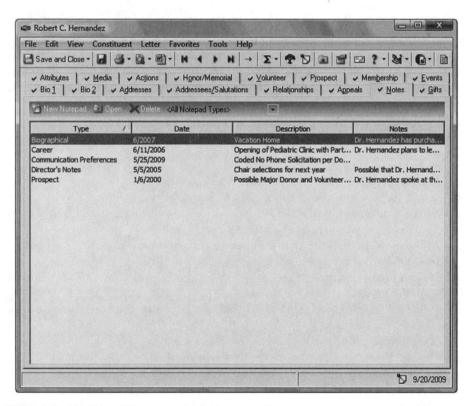

FIGURE 2.7   The Notes Tab

- *Death information.* The source to back up the checkmark in the **Deceased** checkbox on the Bio 1 tab. Some organizations will copy and paste obituary information in the note.
  - *Fundraising strategy.* Your cultivation and solicitation plan, participants and rationale for pursuing a major gift.
- Date- and time-specific activities like meetings, phone calls, e-mails, and mailings should be recorded on the Actions tab. Those activities might provide information like that discussed earlier that should be entered on the Notes tab, but all details about the interaction itself should be entered in the action. Do not use notes to record contact history.
- Notes also should not be used for information that has a more specific and appropriate place to go in The Raiser's Edge. For example:
  - The following information belongs on the Relationships tab:
    - ○ Children and other family names and ages
    - ○ Other organizations with which the constituent is involved
    - ○ Financial, investment, and legal advisors
    - ○ Education history, even if your organization is not a school
  - If your copy of The Raiser's Edge has a Prospect tab in the constituent record, most of the constituent's giving interests, support of other organizations, financial assets, and your major gifts fundraising plans and activities go there instead.

If you are out of the office and away from access to your organization's copy of The Raiser's Edge, it might be most efficient to type call report notes into a Word document or into an e-mail and send them to a data entry person to put into The Raiser's Edge for you. If you are in your office or otherwise have access to The Raiser's Edge, you should enter the notes yourself into The Raiser's Edge. It is easy once you understand what belongs in notes as we just discussed.

ENTERING NOTES   The steps to add note information:

1. Open the constituent.
2. Click on the Notes tab as shown in Figure 2.7.
3. Look at the tab to see if there is already a note of the type you need to enter your new information (if the note types in your system are not perfectly clear to you, consult your database administrator). Then:
   - If there *is* a note of the type you need already on the constituent's record:
     - Double-click on that existing note to open it.
     - Find the appropriate place in the note to enter your information as shown in Figure 2.8.
     - Press **F5** on the keyboard so The Raiser's Edge can add your name, today's date, and the time.
     - Enter the information you wish to add to the note.
     - If necessary, update the note's **Description** field to make it a more meaningful summary of what the entire note now entails.
     - Click **Save and Close**.
   - If there is *not* yet a note of the type you need:
     - Click the **New Notepad** button to start a new note.

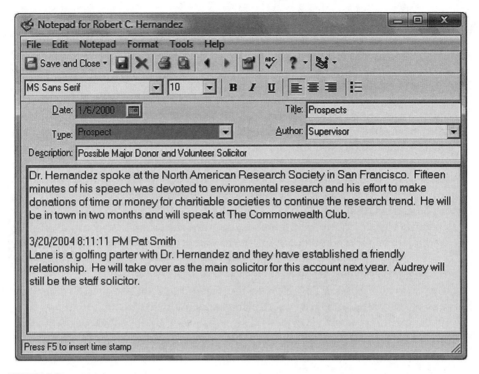

FIGURE 2.8   A Note

- Select from the **Type** field the best way to classify the information you have to enter.
- In the **Description** field enter a brief summary of your note.
- Enter the note.
- Click **Save and Close**.

See how similar this is to sending an e-mail and how easy it is?

You will find it easier when you read and print notes if the note information has been broken out by type. Add new notes and add to existing notes by appropriate type, not just one long, continuous note entry.

Within a note, you see the standard formatting options you are used to in Word and Outlook. Spell-check and printing are available as well.

Gifts Tab

Due to the importance and depth of functionality regarding gifts in The Raiser's Edge—this is a fundraising system, after all—the Gifts tab is discussed in its own chapter, Chapter 3. Chapter 3 is also written for you as a fundraiser, addressing what you need to know to understand the information on the Gifts tab and how to work with your database staff to query and report on giving correctly. There is also a short discussion about the life cycle of a gift from opening the mail to handing off to accounting for those responsible for managing the staff that does those tasks. Chapter 3, however, is not about gift entry.

Definition: Query

"Query" is used as both a noun and a verb in The Raiser's Edge. (It is also used as both in everyday English, though more in British English than North American English.) In The Raiser's Edge:

- "query" with a lower-case "q" and used as a noun is the function in The Raiser's Edge in which we create lists or segments of constituents based on how their Raiser's Edge fields are filled out. We rarely do anything to all the constituents in the database at once; we usually do processes in groups of records. A query defines and includes the constituents for each group. For example, to send a mailing from The Raiser's Edge we usually write a query to create the group of constituents that we want to receive the mailing based on their giving, constituent codes, event history, membership transactions, and so forth. A query is used to specify the criteria and save it for future use.
- "query" with a lower-case "q" and used as a verb is merely the process of creating and running a query.
- "Query" with a capital "Q" refers to the Query page in The Raiser's Edge, the place in the software where queries are written and stored.

Attributes Tab

The Attributes tab and its purpose is one of the most common causes of calls to Blackbaud customer support. But, in fact, its purpose is simple: attributes are *your organization's place to add new fields to your copy of The Raiser's Edge*. It is really that simple. This tab is for those things your organization needs to track for which there is not already a field in The Raiser's Edge. Your database administrator simply adds the new field here.

For example, in my early days training Junior Achievement offices, I used to say, "The Raiser's Edge tracks everything but shoe size." During one of my training sessions, someone raised their hand and said, "We need to track shoe size!" I scratched my head and asked why. The office did a high-end golf tournament and gave golf shoes in the goody bags for the golfers. Because there is not a shoe size field in The Raiser's Edge, we added "Shoe Size" as an attribute to track it.

There is nothing that is "supposed" to be on this tab. Blackbaud has anticipated the common field needs for fundraising and put them on the other tabs. The Attributes tab is for that information that is truly unique to your organization. Good examples of its use include:

- A "Mailings To Send" attribute: the solicit codes and other options remove constituents from mailings they are not supposed to get. Use this attribute to add someone you want to get a mailing for which they do not yet qualify. For example, use this to send your newsletter to a new major gifts prospect with no donation history.
- At the Greater Bay Area Make-A-Wish Foundation, we use attributes to record the specific information we need for wish children.

- The Marines' Memorial Association needs to record the branches of service and conflicts served for its military members. They have one attribute defined for each.
- Often, attributes are used to record information from the database you converted from, such as the date added to that database, the person who added the constituent to that database, and last changed date and user.

Do not use attributes to store historical information such as old committees or events attended. That should go to the Actions tab. Attributes should be focused on current information.

Also, avoid creating attributes for a clever idea for a new type of data to record that gets used once or twice and then forgotten:

- When you have an idea, discuss it with your database administrator to determine if that data already has another place it belongs.
- If you decide to add an attribute, document the attribute. Define exactly what the attribute means, how it is to be used for both data entry and data output purposes, and whether it has a limited life cycle. Store this documentation on your network in a place where it can be easily consulted.
- Proactively work with your database administrator to identify and remove old attributes that no longer serve a purpose.

Media Tab

The Media tab in The Raiser's Edge does not refer to television, radio, or the print media. It is not referring to public relations. "Media" is used in the technical sense of the term to mean *electronic files you want to associate with the constituent*. Examples include:

- Word documents that are letters and proposals to your constituents.
- Excel spreadsheets that are proposal budgets.
- PDFs of signed grant and gift paperwork and newspaper articles about constituents.
- Selected photos of constituents.

The Media tab should be used with your biggest and most important prospects and donors. This is not a full document storage system and is not intended for images of every check, reply device, and letter sent and received.

The files can be either added into The Raiser's Edge or just linked to locations outside The Raiser's Edge. It is important that you coordinate with your database administrator and IT staff the use of this function so that the files are managed correctly for you to access them when you need them.

Actions Tab

The Actions tab is for your *interactions with constituents*—your meetings, phone calls, e-mails, and mailings that are important enough to keep record of, as shown in Figure 2.9. This is true whether you initiate the interaction or the constituent does. For example, this is where call reports go for major gifts officers.

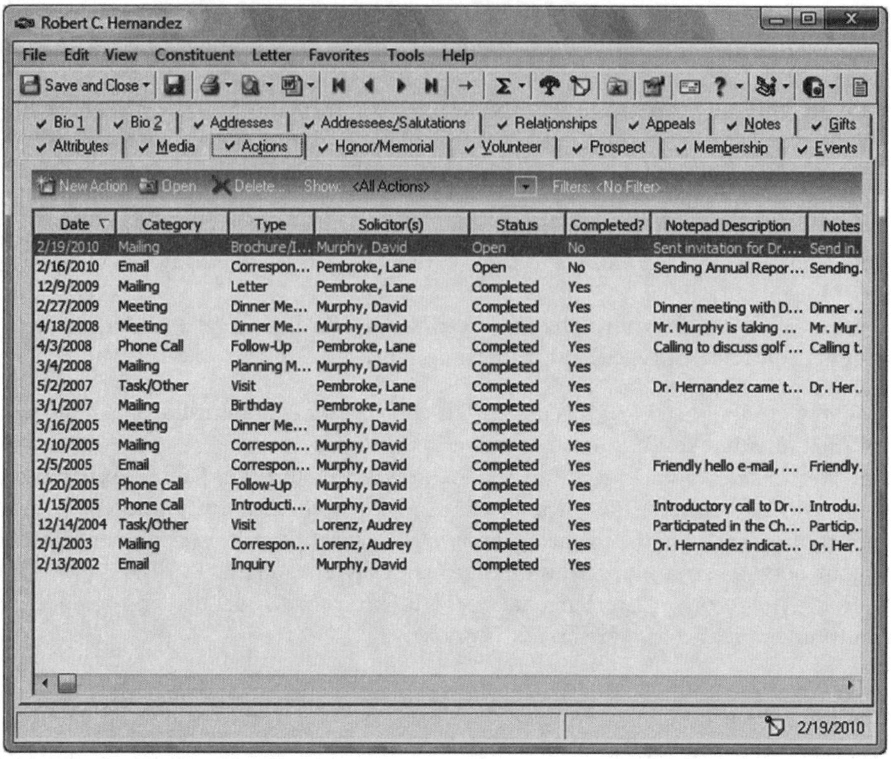

FIGURE 2.9 The Actions Tab

Actions are such an important part of The Raiser's Edge that they are their own record type, accessible directly from the Records and Home pages. They also have their own category of reports on the Reports page of The Raiser's Edge. Actions have their own attributes (user-defined fields) and notes. If you believe fundraising is based on relationships, this is where you record the interactions you have had and need to have in the future.

Future actions can be scheduled. The Raiser's Edge can then remind you when you need to prepare for and do them.

For vice presidents of advancement and directors of development who are taking a "sales management" approach and want to quantify their staffs' activities, actions are the way to do that.

You can generate letters from an action, and The Raiser's Edge will save the Word document in the action for permanent reference. Single e-mails can be generated to constituents from The Raiser's Edge. The database can automatically save copies of the e-mails in actions.

Other uses of the Actions tab that you might see in your system that are appropriate include:

- Mass mailings that are not requesting a monetary response and therefore do not go on the Appeals tab. Newsletters, magazines, annual reports, and donor recognition event invitations are included here. They can be globally added when the mailing is done, just as with appeals.

- Event attendance and volunteer participation are often recorded here for those who do not have the optional modules for these activities.
- Actions can also be tasks that are done with the constituent record. You should be careful not to overuse actions for this purpose, but actions can be used to indicate processes that need to be done on the constituent record or that have been done. For example, large organizations with prospect researchers sometimes use actions to indicate a prospect research request and its fulfillment. Some organizations use actions to indicate maintenance on the record, such as merging a duplicate constituent into the record.

ADDING ACTIONS   Actions are a powerful tool in The Raiser's Edge, a tool that all fundraisers should understand and even use themselves. If you use e-mail on a computer in your office and are comfortable doing so, actions are easy to learn to enter and use yourself. You should use The Raiser's Edge to manage your interactions with your constituents rather than an external calendar program that will leave no record in the constituent's file of that interaction. If you use Microsoft Outlook, The Raiser's Edge can integrate the action so that it appears in your Outlook calendar to help with scheduling and reminding.

Here are the steps to add an action:

1. Open the constituent with whom you did or will have the interaction. Actions go in the constituent's record, not yours.
2. Click on the Actions tab as shown in Figure 2.9.
3. At the top of the tab is a **New Action** button. Click it. (If this button does not work for you, talk to your database administrator to get security rights to do this.)
4. You should now have a new, blank action on your screen, similar to the completed screen shown in Figure 2.10.
5. Click on the **Category** for the kind of interaction you had or will have with the constituent. Except for "Advocacy" these should be self-explanatory. You do not need to use "Advocacy."
6. Click on the down arrow for **Action type** and select the option that best describes the action. If none of the options seem to apply, talk to your database staff about which to select or to add a new option. Your database staff should supply you with a list of action types and their definitions.
7. Enter the **Action date.**
   - The simplest way to do so is to click on the calendar next to the field and select the date. You can also simply type in the date in the format month/day/year such as 3/1/10. (Users outside the United States might use a different date format. Follow your country's standard.)
   - If the action is completed, enter the date the action was done.
   - If the action is something to be done in the future, enter the date the action should be done. This is not the date you want to be reminded to get ready for the action, but the actual date the interaction will occur with the constituent.
8. **Start time** and **End time** are optional fields. Enter them only if they are required, such as a meeting or phone appointment scheduled for a specific time. Enter the time in these fields by entering the time followed by "am" or "pm."

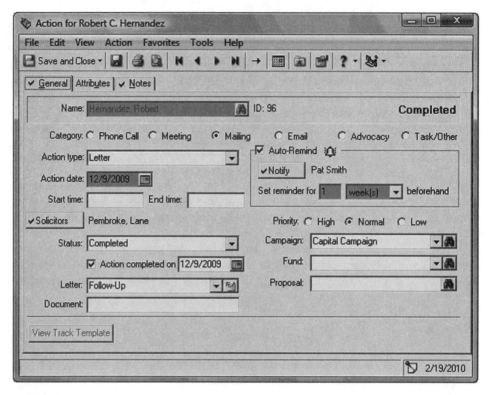

FIGURE 2.10   An Action

9. The **Solicitors** button is used to indicate who is going to do the action with the constituent. Usually this will be you. Click on the **Solicitors** button. In the white box, type your first and last name as they are entered in your own personal constituent record in The Raiser's Edge. Click the **OK** button. If you do not see your name now next to the **Solicitors** button, have a conversation with your database administrator. This can be resolved quickly so that you do not have this problem again.
10. If the next field on your screen is **Status,** talk to your database administrator about how this field should be used at your organization.
11. The next field is a checkbox preceding the words **Action completed on.**
    - If the action occurred in the past, click on the box to add a checkmark. Update the date to the right to indicate the actual date the action was completed.
    - If the action is not yet completed because you are still working on it or because it occurs in the future, leave the box unchecked.
12. The next field below **Action completed on** will vary based on the category you just selected. The field could be named **Phone, Location, Letter,** or **Email.** This field is not required. Click on the down arrow and select the appropriate value if you wish.
13. If this action is complete or you do not need a reminder to do it, continue with step 14. If this is an action that will occur in the future and you want The Raiser's

Edge to remind you to do it, click on the box to the left of **Auto-Remind** to add a checkmark to it. Continue with the following bullets.

- Click on the **Notify** button.
- Use the arrow buttons in the middle of the screen to move from the left side to the right side of the screen those users who should be reminded to do this. This should probably include yourself and might include other users as well, such as a support staff member who will help you prepare.
- If Microsoft Outlook is installed on the computer, specify whether you want to be reminded to do this action in just The Raiser's Edge or in both The Raiser's Edge and Outlook. I recommend not choosing just Outlook.
- Click **OK.**
- In the two fields following **Set reminder for,** specify how far in advance of the action date you want to be reminded to prepare for this action. The first box is for the number and the second box allows you to select "day(s)," "week(s)," or "month(s)." The smallest reminder period is one day.

14. Set a **Priority** if you find that helpful. Most users do not use this function, however.
15. Find out from your database administrator whether your organization uses the **Campaign** and **Fund** fields for actions. Most organizations do not use these fields for actions.
16. If you are adding the action to an organization, the next field will be **Contact**. Click on the down arrow to select the contact representing the organization in the action. If the correct person is not available in the list, the contact can be added on the Relationships tab.
17. If your organization has the RE:Search® optional module (your constituent records will have a Prospect tab if so), the next field is **Proposal.** If this action is related to funding for a proposal or major gift opportunity (discussed more extensively in Chapter 6), select the constituent's proposal to which this is related.
18. At the top of the New Action screen is a tab named Attributes. Talk with your database administrator to find out if you should use this tab. It is most likely you should not.
19. There is also a tab for Notes. This tab works exactly the same way as the constituent Notes tab we discussed previously. It is important to remember to reserve use of the action Notes tab to notes *just about the action.* Information about the constituent, even information found out in the course of conducting the action, goes in the other constituent tabs where it will be more easily accessible long term. Reserve the action notes for preparation, outcome, and follow-up notes about the interaction itself.
20. When you are done with the action, click the **Save and Close** button on the toolbar.

Congratulations, you have just added an action. As with many things, it takes longer to describe how to add an action than to do it. Do this a few times and you will be doing it quickly from that point on.

UPDATING ACTIONS   Updating actions is even easier.

The action can be accessed from the constituent's Actions tab as shown earlier in Figure 2.9. Just go to the tab and double-click on the action. That will open it.

If you are using the Action Reminders on your Home page (talked about more in Chapter 7), clicking on the blue hyperlink for the action's date will open the action.

With the action open as shown earlier in Figure 2.10, you can change anything about it. The most common changes that users like you would make include:

- Updating the date and time if the action is going to be done at a different date and time than originally scheduled.
- Modifying the **Auto-Remind** settings.
- Reading and adding to the notes.
- Marking the action completed. When an action has been done, you should mark it as completed so the system knows it has been done. Otherwise, The Raiser's Edge will continue to remind you. Also, your database administrator will follow up with you about old actions that appear to have not been done yet.

Constituent Tabs for Optional Modules

All of the tabs we have discussed thus far are included in all copies of The Raiser's Edge. Not every function we have discussed is included, but every tab is. (For example, every organization has Education relationships but only educational institutions with the optional RE:Alum® module have primary alumni records.)

The next set of tabs to discuss only appear in your constituent records if your organization has bought the corresponding modules. Blackbaud makes these modules optional so your organization only needs to buy, pay maintenance for, and train on the functionality that you use. Some modules are for specific types of fundraising while others are modules that you can eventually grow into as your needs justify the added functionality.

It is easy to add a module of The Raiser's Edge to your copy: simply contact your Blackbaud account representative, sign the purchase agreement, get the "activation key" from customer support, and have your database administrator enter the key. The module will then appear in your copy of The Raiser's Edge the next time you log in.

These modules are tightly integrated into the core components of The Raiser's Edge. When you add them, they provide more tabs, fields, and output capabilities to the functionality we have already been discussing. You do not have to go to an entirely different place in the software to use them. For example, the Events module still uses the constituent record functions we discussed in this chapter. The module adds a tab to the constituent records that you can use to link the constituent to event participation. The module then adds the event fields in Query and event reports to Reports.

There are some other modules, like RE:Alum, which do not add new tabs but do add new functionality. These modules will be discussed in later chapters as they apply. Let us now discuss the optional modules that add an additional tab to the constituent record.

Honor/Memorial Tab

If your organization gets a large number of gifts "in honor of" or "in memory of" people and organizations, the Honor/Memorial tab helps handle those gifts correctly. This is the RE:Tribute® module. It is most commonly used by hospices and hospital foundations. If your organization only receives a handful of tribute gifts each year, you can probably manage them by using gift attributes (discussed in the next chapter). But if you have an extensive tribute-giving program, this module helps your staff:

- Link gifts to the tribute constituent so the tribute information shows up in the gift tab and the gift information appears in the tribute person's record.
- Generate letters and reports to the family members.
- Generate lists and reports for internal and public purposes, such as newsletter and annual report listings.

This tab in a constituent's record indicates that *gifts are being received in honor of or in memory of this person*. This tab does not list the giving by this constituent. It sets up the constituent so when others give in honor or memory of this person the gifts can be linked to this person. It can be used with organization constituents but is most frequently used with individual constituents.

You can use this tab to quickly see who has given and how much has been given in tribute to this person. The tab is designed to allow more than one tribute for a person, such as someone who first has gifts given to your organization in celebration of their birthday and then later in honor of their retirement. For the correct statistics and gift details at the bottom of the tab, be sure to first click in the screen above on the particular tribute whose results you want to see. For those new to the fundraising profession, it is okay to tell tribute constituents and their families who gave and the *total* amount received, but we never reveal how much each donor gave.

Volunteer Tab

The Volunteer tab is for the RE:Volunteer® module and helps your department or organization manage extensive volunteer details and participation. You could use it in your fundraising department to track event volunteers, volunteer fundraisers, and office volunteers. Your organization could use it to track program and administrative volunteers. Although the tab is included in organization records, it is primarily used with individual constituents.

The tab is divided into a number of different screens, each of which is listed along the left side of the tab. They include options to:

- Categorize your volunteers for querying and reporting purposes; usually, volunteers are categorized by the type of volunteer work they are doing (event, program, office).
- Indicate what skills, experience, and trainings they have that will be helpful when volunteering for you, such as technical skills, language abilities, and medical training.
- Record important medical information such as tests and vaccinations, and note special needs to accommodate such as wheelchair access or the use of an assistance dog.
- Track when the volunteer is available and what they have expressed an interest in doing.

- Track the details of what volunteer assignments they have been given, such as role, date, and location.
- Track time sheets to record the completion of volunteer assignments and the hours contributed.
- List awards received for their volunteer service.
- Record requirements and contact information for "mandated" volunteer activity, such as that required by schools and courts.
- Track a summary of hours volunteered broken out by a variety of factors such as fiscal years.

The module also adds a new record type to the Records page: Jobs. Jobs are the volunteer needs, roles, and positions your organization has. The job records allow the volunteer manager to set up and indicate the need. Later she can link the constituents who are volunteering to meet that need to the volunteer position.

If you have a few volunteers or limited information you track about your volunteers, this module probably has more functionality than you need. If your department or organization has a full-time volunteer coordinator, however, you should consider using this module. Typically, volunteers are going to receive many of your organization's mailings, are donors and planned giving prospects, attend events, and have other reasons for being in your fundraising database. Managing all of their activities, including volunteer participation, is a natural fit for The Raiser's Edge, and the fewer databases your organization has the better.

Prospect Tab

The Prospect tab is part of the optional module for The Raiser's Edge called RE:Search, a play on the word "research" given the tab's purpose of supporting the major gifts process. This tab exists on both individual and organization records and should unquestionably be used with both types of records:

- For individuals, this is the tab for managing the person as a major gifts prospect.
- For organizations, this is the tab for managing your grant proposal and application process for corporations and foundations.

The tab is named "Prospect" because it reflects the two primary roles that the prospect research team plays in a fundraising operation:

1. Research the prospect's capabilities and interests in giving.
2. Track the prospect through the cultivation and solicitation cycle to help the fundraisers ensure that each identified prospect receives the proper attention.

This does not mean your organization needs to be large enough to have a prospect researcher on staff to use this module. It merely explains the naming of the tab and its purpose.

Major gifts fundraising and grant proposal tracking do not require this module, but supporting that work is this tab's purpose. Whether your organization has this module or not, see Chapter 6 for a more detailed discussion of using the Prospect tab and The Raiser's Edge for major gifts and grant fundraising.

Membership Tab

The Membership tab is part of the RE:Member® module for organizations with membership programs such as those at museums, zoos, aquariums, public television and radio stations, and some performing arts groups. Some colleges and universities also use it to manage their alumni associations.

This module is used most extensively for individuals. However, it also works well for the corporate membership programs these types of organizations offer.

The primary functions of this module include the ability to:

- Record join, renewal, and expiration dates.
- Create and assign membership categories with names, cycles, and benefits.
- Indicate and properly handle memberships given as gifts, such as a grandmother buying a grandson a science museum membership for his birthday.
- Generate membership cards for the constituent and other people in the membership.
- Track the use of and benefits available for the membership cards, including the built-in ability to scan the cards at the front gate and gift shop.
- Generate renewal notices and manage the renewal cycle.
- Report on statistics regarding number of members and upgrade and downgrade movements.

This module is not needed for:

- Grouping your donors into categories based on their cumulative giving. There is a standard report we discuss in Chapter 7 that does that for you based on giving data alone.
- Direct mail programs that make their appeal to "become a member" that is simply a way for the donor to feel greater affinity and participation with the organization. These organizations and solicitation approaches do not require the functionality needed by the typical membership programs mentioned previously.

If you work in the development department of an organization that has this module, the preceding information is probably sufficient for your needs. If you would like to know more, however, or if you work in membership at an organization with this module, see Chapter 5 for a fuller discussion of membership in The Raiser's Edge.

Events Tab

The Events tab is part of the optional module for The Raiser's Edge named RE:Event®. The module adds another record type—called the "Event" record—to The Raiser's Edge beyond those we have discussed thus far.

The Event record is where an event itself is set up. Extensive details can be recorded there, including dates, pricing, budgeting, sponsors, registrants, guests, seating, checklists, and notes.

The Events tab in a constituent applies to both individual and organization records. Although all of your event attendees and most of your event participants will be individuals, organizations often serve as sponsors of events.

The Events tab in a constituent's record serves only one purpose: to link the constituent as a participant in the event record. On the constituent Events tab you can:

- See the events the constituent has participated in.
- Add the constituent to a new event (if you have the security rights).
- Open and see the participant details for previously linked events.

Managing events in The Raiser's Edge is discussed in more detail in Chapter 5.

Tools for Fundraisers

The Raiser's Edge provides a significant number of tools within a constituent record to meet the variety of needs of you and your staff. This brief section highlights the additional functions that should be helpful to you as a fundraiser.

Tabs with Lists

Many of the tabs in a constituent record are lists of items, such as the Gifts tab, which is a list of gifts, and the Actions tab, which is a list of actions. These tabs can be modified to make those lists more useful so you do not have to open each item in the list to see the details you are interested in each time. This includes the following tabs:

- Addresses
- Relationships
- Notes
- Gifts
- Media
- Actions
- Honor/Memorial (for tributes)
- Job Assignments and Time Sheets on the Volunteer tab
- Financial Information, Proposal, and Ratings on the Prospect tab
- Membership
- Events

If you right-click on the white area of these tabs, there are two options that let you change what is displayed on these tabs:

1. *Legend.* This allows you to color-code items in the list so the list communicates more information when you look at it on the main screen. For example, on the Relationships tab, the spouse or partner can show up in bold blue and contacts can show up in bold red.
2. *Columns.* You can change the default columns of data that appear on the tab by choosing this option. Simply select the option and:
   - Move from the left side to the right side those fields you want to see.
   - Move from the right side to the left side those fields you do not want to see.
   - Use the arrow buttons to put the fields in the order you want to see them.
   - Click **OK.**

The **Columns** option is particularly helpful considering that The Raiser's Edge allows you to maximize the constituent record to fill your entire computer screen so you can see as much as possible. You can change the width of the columns by simply dragging the right side of the column heading to the width you want.

Explore the other options that are available by right-clicking on a tab as well. There are a number of options, and many will be helpful.

One other tool for tabs with lists: if you open one of the items, such as a note, action, relationship, or gift, and want to see the other items on the tab, you do not have to close the item to open the next one. Use the buttons in the shape of arrows on the toolbar to easily and quickly move forward and backward among the items.

◄ ◄ ► ►

Home Page

As noted in our kitchen analogy in the previous chapter, The Raiser's Edge has many functions. You can place those things that you do most frequently on the Home page of The Raiser's Edge because it is *your* home page. This page will have your name on it, and it belongs to you. It is not your organization's home page for The Raiser's Edge. On this page, you can put links to those things you like to do in The Raiser's Edge most frequently.

You can add links to constituents. If you are working with a particular set of constituents frequently, and would like to have quick access to them, click the **Favorites** button on the toolbar when each constituent record is open. This will put a link on your Home page to the constituent.

You can also work with your database administrator to put a query (a list) of your constituents on your Home page rather than linking them all one by one. For example, those carrying a portfolio of major gifts prospects should consider doing this.

More ideas for the Home page are discussed in Chapters 6 and 7.

Multiple Records

The Raiser's Edge allows you to have more than one constituent record open at a time. You do not need to close a record to open a new one. Simply move the open record out of the way and open the second record the way you normally open a record. Then you can switch between them or put them side-by-side on the screen to compare them.

Profiles

If you need a hard copy or PDF of anything you see in a constituent's record, you can easily print any combination of tabs in a report. For example, you might want:

- The entire constituent record on a report to take home or on the road to review in preparation for a personal visit with a constituent.
- A slightly less complete version of the report to give to a volunteer helping you call on the constituent, such as a board member, which leaves out highly sensitive or potentially confusing data the volunteer does not need to know.
- A printout of the constituent's entire or selected giving history.
- A hard copy of the constituent's contact information, such as preferred address, phone numbers, and e-mail addresses.

Each of these needs is easily met from within a constituent record. Simply click on the menu bar and choose **File, Preview.** Then select one of the following options:

- Constituent Profile
- Individual Profile
- Organization Profile

If you are not sure where to look or the options you need are not available, work with your database administrator to set them up for you. If you need copies for multiple constituents, work with your database support staff. Your staff can more quickly generate these profiles for you from Reports than your doing them one at a time in each constituent's record.

■ ■ ■

There are a number of other options and functions available from the constituent record's menu bar and toolbar. If you enjoy the database and want to learn more, I would encourage you to explore these options. Those options I have highlighted here are the most important functions in the constituent record that fundraisers should know to make The Raiser's Edge easy to use.

Summary

The Raiser's Edge can store a significant amount of information about your constituents. You, as the fundraiser and perhaps the manager of the fundraising department, need to provide the primary guidance to your staff about what to record. You need to determine what will provide future value.

As the old adage goes, "garbage in, garbage out." You will suffer the consequences if the data is not entered correctly. And to get accurate and meaningful data out of The Raiser's Edge, you need to work with your database staff to provide the fundraising direction about what you need.

Although you do not need to be versed in the nuances and intricacies of each data entry step in The Raiser's Edge, it is necessary that you understand what data the system stores, critical terminology that it uses, and the important concepts behind some of the data entry procedures. The concepts in this chapter should prepare you for this.

■ ■ ■

The value of this constituent data for us as fundraisers is to raise money from these people and organizations. Now let us discuss gifts, the result of all your hard work.

CHAPTER 3

Gifts and Giving

G ifts. They are the result of all those hours we put into raising money. It is so nice when our efforts pay off, donors say "yes," and gifts arrive in the daily mail. It is rewarding to see the checks and progress toward our goals.

But the work does not stop there. The gifts need to be recorded in The Raiser's Edge so they can be acknowledged and receipted to the donors, perhaps tribute families notified, and the money posted to accounting for deposit. We need reports on the gifts for staff and board. We use the giving history of our constituents to make decisions about future contacts with them and create development strategies.

Past giving is so critical to fundraising, in fact, we discuss gifts and giving in this chapter prior to the chapters oriented more specifically to raising gifts. Understanding how to do fundraising with The Raiser's Edge requires understanding how previous giving has been entered.

Most fundraisers do not need to understand the details of gift entry, so this chapter does not focus on that. What fundraisers *do* need to understand about gifts in The Raiser's Edge are:

1. How to look at the Gifts tab (shown in Figure 3.1) and Gift Summary of a constituent and understand the information.
2. How to communicate with the database support staff so that lists and reports contain the right constituents based on giving history and show the particular gifts and totals you want to see.

This chapter discusses gifts in The Raiser's Edge with these two objectives in mind.

Whenever you work directly with The Raiser's Edge or ask your database staff to give you any information about gifts or donors from the database, you should provide the following direction so you get meaningful, accurate results:

- The gift date range of interest (e.g., this fiscal year)
- The gift types of interest (e.g., cash, pledge, stock/property) and details associated with each (e.g., Include pledges and payments? Use stock/property donated date and amount or sold date and amount?)

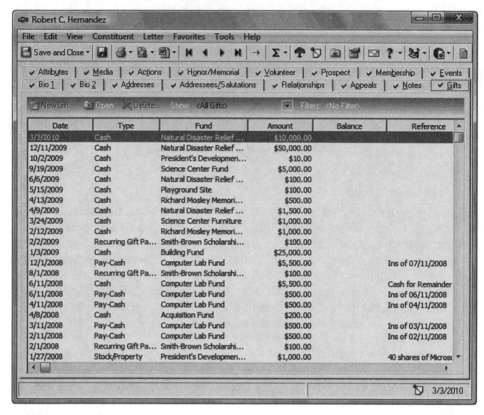

FIGURE 3.1   The Gifts Tab

- Amount ranges (e.g., more than $1,000)
  - Whether those ranges are based on a single gift or cumulative giving (e.g., those who have given at least one gift of at least $1,000 or those who have cumulatively given at least $1,000).
- Campaign, fund, and appeal filters to apply
- Who should get credit for gifts that have been soft credited
- Who should get credit for matching gifts
- Name display for anonymous donations

In fact, these options are so pervasive and critical to getting you accurate results that you should write these down, photocopy the list, or dog-ear these pages. Consider this a checklist to use from this point forward. This chapter explains the concepts behind the items in this list and other gift fields that you should understand and that you may wish to include when requesting gift information.

The chapter ends with an overview of gift processing for the fundraisers who are responsible for managing the staff that does those activities.

Note: Security Rights to Gifts for Fundraisers

Although we discuss security in The Raiser's Edge more in Chapter 8, it should be noted that typically fundraisers should be given only View rights to gifts. They should not have Add, Edit, or Delete rights. This should be true regardless of your management position or your technical ability. It is not a reflection on you personally or a broad statement about the capabilities of fundraisers. The reason for this approach is twofold:

1. There are a large number of details to understand to add and modify gifts properly in The Raiser's Edge given the program's sophistication and the many ways the data is used after it is entered. Unless your job includes day-to-day gift entry and you learn and follow all the procedures, you should not be able to add, edit, or delete gifts. Let your employees who specialize in these tasks do them so you can focus your training and work on fundraising.
2. It is not good financial control procedures for a person who raises money to be able to add, edit, or delete gifts. Your accounting staff, treasurer, and auditor prefer that fundraisers not have these rights if you want The Raiser's Edge to be taken seriously in your organization as a trustworthy repository of gift information. Restricting rights helps prevent fraud and maintains the details necessary to post with accounting, to reconcile, and stay reconciled.

Although the senior fundraiser who manages the database administrator should have access to the master password for the database, no fundraiser, including that manager, should add or change gifts. If you see a mistake, let the database administrator or gift processor know so it can be fixed. This chapter assumes you have full view access of all gifts and gift information, but only view access.

Gift Types

Understanding gift data in The Raiser's Edge begins with understanding "Gift Types." These types are built into The Raiser's Edge, defining not only information about what kind of gift you have received but also the functionality The Raiser's Edge makes available to manage the gift. There are seven types of gifts:

1. Cash
2. Pledge
3. Stock/Property
4. Gift-in-Kind
5. Other
6. Recurring Gift
7. Planned Gift

All organizations that use The Raiser's Edge have the first six types. Planned Gift as its own gift type is only available if your organization has the RE:PlannedGiftTracker™ optional module (RE:Legacies™ in the United Kingdom).

Gift types are built into The Raiser's Edge and cannot be added to, deleted, or renamed.

This section briefly defines each gift type. More detail about the roles and nuances of each gift type that affect fundraisers is discussed in the sections later in this chapter.

"*Cash*" is used in The Raiser's Edge in the accounting sense of the term. It applies to the gifts you receive that are made by check, credit card, direct debit from checking and savings accounts, currency (bills, notes, and coins), money order, or direct transfer to your bank accounts. This is by far the most common gift type.

A *Pledge* in The Raiser's Edge is a commitment to give you something of a stated value in the future. A pledge has a total amount to be paid specified as well as a payment schedule.

In The Raiser's Edge, a pledge is considered a gift—it is one of several types of gifts. Some other fundraising databases make a distinction between pledges and gifts. If you previously used one of those databases, be careful to understand that in the terminology of The Raiser's Edge, pledges are gifts.

The third gift type is *Stock/Property*. These are gifts you do not want to keep but instead plan to sell and use the proceeds. Stock refers to shares of companies that you are able to sell through a stockbroker. Property refers to real estate, artwork, jewelry, and other such items that your institution prefers not to keep and use but to sell.

A *Gift-in-Kind* is a gift of something other than money that the organization plans to keep and use. Examples are furniture, equipment, program supplies, and gift certificates.

There is a gift type in The Raiser's Edge named "*Other*." This is rarely used, and if your organization does, you should do so cautiously. Other is typically used in two ways:

1. Because most organizations using The Raiser's Edge do not have the RE:PlannedGiftTracker module, it is used for planned gifts.
2. Although the donation of services is not tax-deductible, it still benefits your organization. Other can be used, if your organization wishes, to record the monetary value of those services so the donor can still be thanked and recognized.

Recurring Gifts in The Raiser's Edge are the result of the good work of Canadian, British, and Australian fundraisers' monthly donor programs. This approach has been used by some organizations in the United States, but the extensive recurring gift functionality in The Raiser's Edge is due to the extremely high level of monthly donor activity in these other countries. A recurring gift in The Raiser's Edge is a *commitment*, typically monthly, to make a donation to your organization. It is not the receipt of any money, it is merely the commitment. It is different than a pledge because a recurring gift is open-ended. A pledge has an end date and a total amount promised. A recurring gift has neither—the money continues to be donated until the donor contacts the organization and says "Please stop." These types of gifts are popular in online giving programs.

It is possible to set up a recurring gift so the donor sends you the money each month. The best way to set up a recurring gift program, however, is to collect and record either credit card information or bank information. Each month—or other interval you agree on—your staff then uses The Raiser's Edge to charge the credit card or debit the account.

Finally, *Planned Gift* is a gift type available for those who have the optional module for the purpose of tracking these gifts. This type should be used for the planned gift commitment and intention, not the cash proceeds of a planned gift. The proceeds, when received, are still cash gifts.

These are the seven basic gift types that are available to your staff when they add a new gift. As we continue in this chapter, we discuss how this list of gift types expands as gifts are used in the system.

Whenever you request information that shows gifts or is based on giving, such as a list of donors, you must specify what gift types you want included. Over time, fundraisers and their support staff develop a mutual understanding of what is typically desired. Until that time, be careful to explicitly state what you do and do not want included when you request information from The Raiser's Edge.

Gift Tabs and Concepts

As with constituents, there is so much information in The Raiser's Edge for gifts that the data has to be organized on tabs. When you open a gift from the constituent's Gifts tab, you get a screen that itself has several tabs as shown in Figure 3.2. The number of tabs and the names of the tabs vary based on the type of gift you have opened and the modules your organization has purchased.

The tabs in a gift provide a variety of functionality, some of which you should understand conceptually. Because Cash gifts are the most common gift type, we discuss the tabs in the context of that gift type. A later section in this chapter highlights the tabs and functionality the other gift types use that are different than those used for cash gifts.

Gift Tab

Not to be confused with the Gifts tab on a constituent record (shown in Figure 3.1), the first and most important tab when a gift is opened is the Gift tab (shown in Figure 3.2). There are a number of important fields on this tab for fundraisers to understand.

GIFT DATE Make sure that your staff has a correct and consistent way of assigning the **Gift Date**. This is not just a data entry issue. It is a decision that affects the period in which the gift is reflected in your reporting. It also affects your legal responsibilities with tax authorities for the gift's tax-deductibility if you choose, as most organizations do, to print the gift date on the acknowledgement letter.

Most organizations use the date the gift was *received* in the office. Ensure that gifts that arrive at the beginning of a month are consistently entered to reflect your organization's policies for indicating fiscal month and year. Also, be sure that gifts that arrive in early January are properly credited to the correct tax year according to the rules of the Internal Revenue Service (IRS) or your country's laws.

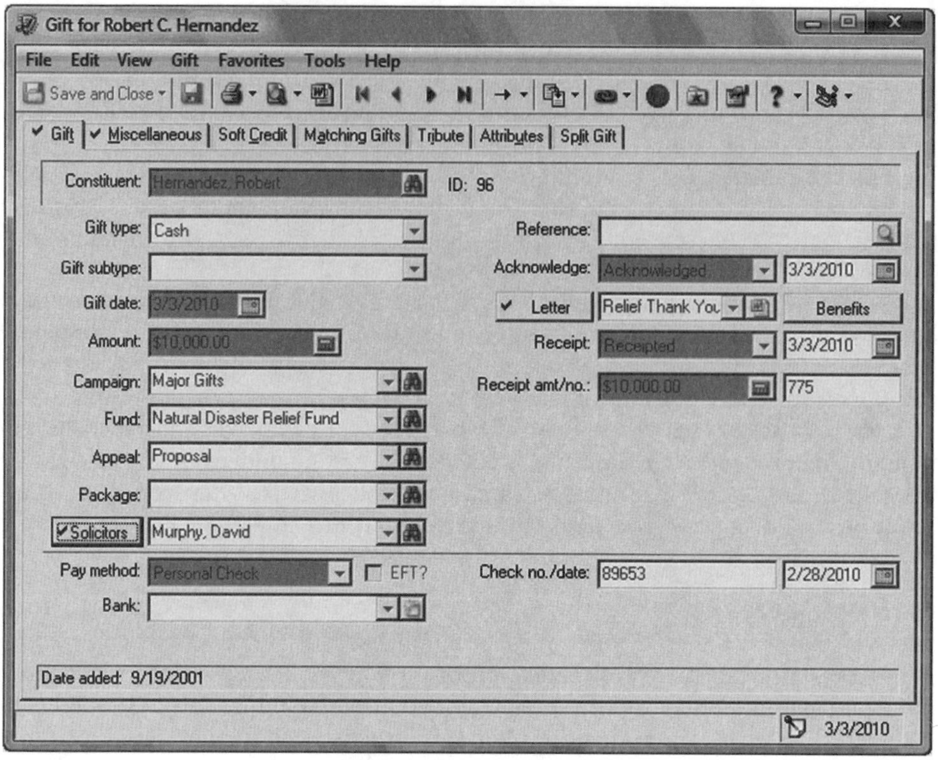

FIGURE 3.2   A Gift Record

For these reasons, the date on checks and the date of data entry are generally not good dates to use for the gift date.

CAMPAIGN, FUND, APPEAL, AND PACKAGE   The **Campaign, Fund, Appeal**, and **Package** fields on every gift are the most important reason for understanding the concepts discussed in Chapter 1. Although campaign, fund, and appeal uses appear throughout the constituent record (e.g., the constituent Appeals tab), the four gift fields for campaign, fund, appeal, and package are their most important uses in The Raiser's Edge.

The data entry step for these fields is easy: one just clicks on the drop-down list and selects one of the choices available. The values that are available for your data entry staff to choose are what are important. These values in these fields are going to determine the choices you have for reporting and querying on gift information. Campaign, fund, and appeal filters are just one of the items in the list at the beginning of this chapter for providing direction for output, but it is one of the most important.

Not only do you want reporting and filtering options that are meaningful to you, you want options that are easy for data entry staff. You do not want your gift entry staff making management-level decisions how to classify each gift you receive or asking you for coding direction for every gift. By this stage of data entry, the campaign, fund, and appeal options should be so well thought out and defined that it is obvious to anyone in your department how to code gifts at the point of data entry.

- Campaign should be the big picture categories for senior level reporting.
- Fund is typically what program or purpose the money is for.
- Appeal is the particular ask that resulted in the gift.
- Package is the specific version of the ask the constituent received.

Every gift must have a fund while the other fields are optional based on your organization's policies. Most organizations also make **Campaign** and **Appeal** required fields as well.

SOLICITORS   The **Solicitors** field (in the U.K. version, "Canvassers") allows you to record who was directly responsible for raising a gift. This is usually reserved for major gifts and telemarketing. Multiple solicitors can be assigned to a gift, and you can apportion credit for the gift as you wish through an **Amount** field for the solicitor. It is not necessary to fill out the **Solicitors** field to measure a fundraiser's performance if the person is responsible for the entire campaign, fund, or appeal. You can use reporting on those categories to evaluate performance.

REFERENCE   The **Reference** field is important and helpful to you as a fundraiser. This field is for short notes. It can help you by:

- Appearing on the constituent's Gifts tab so you do not have to open the gift to see specific details.
- Appearing on many of the standard gift reports included in The Raiser's Edge.
- Being available to merge into acknowledgement letters.

It is most typically used for:

- Short descriptions of stock/property gifts (e.g., 50 shares of IBM).
- Short descriptions of gifts-in-kind (e.g., brunch for two).
- Pledge and recurring gift payment details (The Raiser's Edge adds this information automatically indicating which installment the payment paid).

Long notes should be entered in the Notepad fields on the Miscellaneous tab.

ACKNOWLEDGEMENT DETAILS   "Acknowledgement" letters are thank-you letters sent to donors for their gifts. The **Acknowledge** fields show you if an acknowledgement letter was sent, the date it was sent, and the name of the form letter that was sent to thank the donor for the gift.

RECEIPT DETAILS   With one exception, the **Receipt** fields are typically no longer used in the United States. Organizations include the required tax information and language in the acknowledgement letter, usually as a footer. However, in other parts of the world, especially Canada, this information is of much greater importance and details such as if a receipt was generated, the date it was generated, and the receipt number can be viewed here.

The receipt field that is used in the United States is the **Receipt amount**. This field defaults to the gift amount, but it needs to be changed when a gift is not fully tax-deductible. The receipt amount is the amount that *is* tax-deductible. Because this situation typically occurs in the context of special events, see the discussion for recording special event money in Chapter 5. However, this situation also occurs when sizable premiums are offered for direct mail and other contributions. If this happens at your organization, ensure that your data entry staff fills out the **Receipt amount** field correctly and includes it in acknowledgement letters appropriately.

Miscellaneous Tab

This tab contains several important fields:

- **GL** (General Ledger; in the U.K. version, Nominal Ledger) **Post Status** and **Date**: If you are in advancement services or otherwise work with posting to and reconciling with accounting, these fields are critical.
- **Marketing Source Code, Mailing ID**, and **Finder Number**: Important if your organization has the Blackbaud Direct Marketing product.
- **Notes**: If the gift needs more detailed narrative to explain something, such as greater detail about a gift-in-kind, this is where those details are located.
- **Gift is anonymous**.

The most important concept on this screen for fundraisers is the **Gift is anonymous** checkbox. If your organization gets anonymous donations and you want to use The Raiser's Edge to properly handle them, understand that:

- If you know who gave the gift, the gift should be entered into the constituent record of the donor's name. This allows you to use the gift for any decision making or communication directly with the donor. Do not have the gift entered into a constituent named "Anonymous."
- If the donor wants all future giving to remain anonymous, there is a **Gives anonymously** checkbox on the Bio 1 and Org 1 tabs, in the lower right corner of the screen, to automatically add a checkmark to the **Gift is anonymous** checkbox on all future gifts when they are entered. Ensure that it is being used for your anonymous donors.
- The Bio/Org 1 checkbox is not retroactive. Any previous giving in the constituent's record will not be affected by changes to the checkbox on the Bio/Org 1 tab. Obtain the donor's intent for previous giving and have the **Gift is anonymous** checkmark added manually for previous gifts as necessary.
- Gifts will only show as anonymous in reports if that option has been selected by the person *running* the report. Note the emphasis on "running"—this is based on the person running the report, not the person who set it up. Anonymous gifts can show on reports in one of three ways:
  1. As "Anonymous."
  2. With the donor's name plus an asterisk (*) to tell internal staff the name of the donor but warn the gift is anonymous.
  3. With the donor's name and no indication it was given anonymously.
  Ensure with your database administrator the User Options of all people running these reports are properly set.
- Only reports from *Reports* have these options. Lists of donors pulled by *Query, Mail*, and *Export* show the donor's name with no indication of the donor's desire to remain anonymous unless that gift field is specifically pulled as well. (We talk more about Reports, Query, Mail, and Export in future chapters.)

The purpose here is to alert you of these considerations so you can work with your staff to respect your donors' wishes and avoid upsetting the donors and jeopardizing future contributions.

Soft Credit Tab

Soft credit is the ability in The Raiser's Edge to *give more than one constituent credit for having given a gift*. We do not want to enter a gift into more than one constituent record because doing so would double-count the money. However, there are some situations where more than one constituent might need credit for a gift. Examples include:

- *Spouses and partners each with their own record who give a joint gift*. We want each person's Gifts tab to reflect the gift.
- *People who own their own businesses and give a business check*. We might want to put the check in the organization's record. Because the person owns the business, it is appropriate to show the gift as part of the person's giving on his or her Gifts tab.
- *People who give through personal foundations and donor-advised funds*. We might want to put the check in the organization's record because it is the legal donor. Because it is the person's money, and the person most likely directed the donation, we might also want to see the gift as part of the person's giving.

This is not merely a data entry technicality. This is an issue that requires fundraiser direction and understanding when viewing and requesting gift information.

The data entry is easy: the gift is merely entered as usual in the "hard credit" constituent record. On the gift's Soft Credit tab, the gift processor then simply links the gift to one or more other constituents and specifies how much of the gift amount to apply as soft credit. With that, the gift now appears on those other constituents' Gifts tabs.

Tip: Identifying Soft Credits

See the section on page 62 in Chapter 2 on "Tabs with Lists" for how you can use the Legend function to highlight and identify soft credit gifts on a constituent's Gifts tab.

It is important that soft credits *not* be used in the following ways:

- *Solicitor activity*. You should never soft credit people because they *raised* or helped to raise the money. Soft credit functionality is for those who have *given* the money. Use the **Solicitors** field on the gift's Gift tab to indicate who raised the money. This is true whether applying it to staff, board, or even corporate executives who may have strongly influenced the giving decision—if the money is from the organization and the executive does not own the company, the person may be the solicitor of the gift but not a soft credit recipient.

- *Linking other constituents to gifts.* The soft credit function uses linking to assign soft credit recipients, but that is not the sole meaning of soft credits. Do not use soft credits to associate or link other constituents to a gift. *If* you are going to use soft credits, it is best to reserve the meaning of this function to *shared participation in the giving of the gift*—period.

In all cases of gift output, such as queries and reports, you and your database staff will be presented with three options for the handling of gifts that have been soft credited. The gifts can show up on the report for:

1. Just the constituent who received the hard credit and no soft credit recipients.
2. Just the soft credit recipients and not the constituent that received the hard credit.
3. Both the hard credit and soft credit constituents.

Because there can be more than one soft credit recipient on a gift, options 2 and 3 can result in the same money being reported more than once. Financially-oriented reports should, therefore, have the first option selected. But development reports, especially recognition lists and reports, might appropriately use any one of the three options.

This is an important concept for fundraisers to understand because they provide direction to gift entry staff as to whom to soft credit, look at the Gifts tab of constituents, and provide direction about how to retrieve gift data for lists and reports.

"We *might* want to put the check in the organization's record..."? "*If* you are going to use soft credits..."? The challenge with soft credits is that there is no "type" of soft credit. For The Raiser's Edge output, all soft credits are the same. We must pick *one* of the options for handling soft credits on a report when we run it. We cannot say, "Use option 1 for certain soft credits and use option 2 for others." For example, the following situation illustrates the difficulties of reporting using soft credits:

Soft Credit Report Challenge

Situation	Typical Hard Credit Constituent	Typical Soft Credit Constituent	Which Credit Preferred on the Report
Spouses and partners each with their own constituent record	The main, most important person, the head of household	The less important, non–head of household record	Hard Credit Constituent, the most important record and person
Individual with a family foundation	If the check is written from the foundation, most users would be inclined to enter the donation in an organization constituent record for the foundation	The individual or family whose foundation it is, who was the original source of the funds, and who directed the distribution	Soft Credit Constituent typically, the individual or family, since the family foundation is often just a tax-favored way of giving and not of primary fundraising interest

Raiser's Edge reports cannot currently handle this request, such as for an annual report for donor recognition. You get *one* of the following three options for *all* gifts to be included in a report:

1. Only hard credit constituents
2. Only soft credit constituents
3. Both hard and soft credit constituents for each gift

This issue has been addressed in The Raiser's Edge version 8, discussed more in Chapter 8. Until you are able to upgrade to that version, we must address this reality with soft credits to avoid many organizations' difficulties with this challenge.

Fundraisers and database staff need to think through how various situations should be handled so gifts are entered into the system the way you need them to come out. The best solution is to limit the use of soft credits in your system. Similar to our discussion in Chapter 2 about what people and organizations should be constituents, the same concepts apply here. Let us not mindlessly follow the mantra that "the name on the check has to be the hard credit constituent." We can generate tax-authority accurate acknowledgement letters without making our database more complicated than it needs to be.

In the previous soft credit challenge example it is fine to soft credit the spouse or partner. For family foundations, however, there is a spectrum of the size and significance of those foundations. They are not all the Bill & Melinda Gates Foundation. Most, in fact, are not much more than glorified checking accounts, set up by donors because of the favorable tax treatment. They are legal entities on paper with a checking account behind them but no staff. The prospect for us is the individual or family; they want to be recognized by their own names, not the foundation's; they should get the mailings as individuals, not the foundation; and it is the people you are going to approach for the next gift, not an unrelated program officer. For these situations, it is best to just use the Name on Check strategy discussed in the previous chapter to ensure a correct acknowledgement letter and to ensure minimal headache in using The Raiser's Edge afterward.

Note: Other Perspectives on Hard and Soft Credits

In fairness to you and your database staff, it should be noted that there are many people, including people I respect, that would vigorously argue that the name on the check should, in most cases, define the hard credit donor and constituent record. While I understand their perspective and their rationale, I have too often seen in my consulting work challenges with fundraisers, database staff, and use of The Raiser's Edge specifically with constituents with hard credit gifts that should not get mail, are not prospects, and are of no direct interest to the organization once the initial gift acknowledgement letter has been properly generated. I believe the approach I have suggested, for the reasons given, is the best, but your organization should define its own policy within the guidance of a variety of professional perspectives.

When you do decide to use soft credits, you and your staff should create a chart such as that used in the "Soft Credit Report Challenge" that includes columns for the situation, who receives the hard credit, who receives the soft credit, and for each output situation, which reporting soft credit option will be selected. Make sure that all situations are consistent for the output options or you will not be able to generate that output directly from The Raiser's Edge.

Matching Gifts Tab

The Matching Gifts tab allows your gift entry staff to note if individuals' gifts will be matched by their employers. "Matching gift" in The Raiser's Edge refers to company matches of employees' giving, not challenge grants in which a donor promises to match additional money you raise.

In addition to the seven gift types introduced earlier in this chapter, there is another: Matching Gift Pledge. You see this in The Raiser's Edge as "MG Pledge." "MG" in The Raiser's Edge always means "matching gift," never "major gift." This pledge represents that your organization has received the matching gift paperwork from the employee and your staff has submitted it to the matching gift company for payment.

Matching gift pledges and their payments show up in both the records of the organization that is giving the money and the individual whose gift is being matched. The pledge and payment are only entered and exist once, but they are displayed in both locations. This is to give credit to the organization actually providing the money and the person whose personal gift made the match possible. (Although matching gifts work like soft credits in this regard, they are not soft credits, and soft credit functionality should not be used. Confirm this with your staff.)

Output options for gifts in The Raiser's Edge always include a matching gift section. You need to specify who gets credit for the matching gifts included in the output:

- Only the person whose personal gift enabled the matching gift.
- Only the company that is actually providing the gift.
- Both the person and the company.

There is no "right" answer to this option. You need to evaluate it on a case-by-case basis for each output. For example:

- For financial reports where the totals matter and you might need to reconcile with accounting, it is best to give credit to the company that made the gift.
- For donor recognition reports in which individuals and companies are listed together, it is probably best to give both credit so they each feel appreciated for their efforts.
- For an annual report donor list that only includes individuals, select the option to give credit to the person.

- For an annual report donor list of matching gift companies, select the option to give credit to the company.

This functionality was built around the traditional matching gift forms that employees collect, mail to you with their contribution, get completed by your staff, and forwarded to the company for payment. It was not originally intended for today's electronic workplace giving programs in which companies automatically send matching gifts with the employees' contributions from their paychecks. Your gift entry staff may or may not be using this function for those matches.

Tribute Tab

The Tribute tab will only be present if your organization has the RE:Tribute optional module for The Raiser's Edge discussed in Chapter 2. The gift's Tribute tab is used to link the gift to the person in whose honor or memory the gift has been given, to indicate which family member(s) should be notified of the gift, and to record when those notification letters were sent.

Attributes Tab

Attributes for gifts have the same purpose as attributes for constituents: to give your organization the ability to add new fields to the database. The most common use of gift attributes is to trade tribute information for those organizations that do not have the RE:Tribute module.

Split Gift Tab

The Split Gift tab allows your gift entry staff to apply one contribution to more than one campaign, fund, appeal, or package. For example, one of your corporate supporters decides to make one gift to you for the whole year and gives a $10,000 contribution, $5,000 to support their favorite program and $5,000 toward your annual gala, which raises unrestricted support. One gift of $10,000 should be entered into The Raiser's Edge, but the gift should be "split" on the Split Gift tab so that each fund can receive its proper credit.

Although occasionally necessary, it is best to avoid "splitting" a gift in the sense of entering one contribution as two gifts into The Raiser's Edge. This will create complications with the acknowledgement letter and the donor's statistics such as number of gifts, largest gift, and average gift amount.

Functionality by Gift Type

Most of the tabs and fields are the same for all gift types. This section will highlight the functions and terms specific to the gift types other than Cash so you can understand how they are handled in The Raiser's Edge.

Pledge

A Pledge in The Raiser's Edge is a commitment to give you something of a stated value in the future. Pledges are most typically paid via Cash gifts but can be fulfilled through stock/property gifts and gifts-in-kind.

When entering a pledge in The Raiser's Edge, it is best to set up a payment schedule—how much will be paid by each due date. The Raiser's Edge can accommodate single due dates such as a pledge on February 1 to be paid in full on July 1. It can also handle multiple installments such as a $50,000 capital campaign pledge to be paid at $2,500 per quarter over the next five years.

The Raiser's Edge can generate pledge reminders for the donors to help you collect the money. When the donor pays on the pledge, the payment, which is also a gift, is applied against the pledge so that the pledge's balance can be reduced.

When you look at a constituent's Gifts tab you might see "Pay-" included in the **Type** column, such as "Pay-Cash." "Pay-" in front of any gift type simply means that gift was used as a payment against a pledge. "Pay-Cash" is typically a check used to pay a pledge while a "Pay-Stock/Property" is a pledge payment by stock.

The Raiser's Edge also accommodates write-offs. If the donor notifies you that the pledge will not be paid, or you make such a determination yourself due to non-payment, a write-off can be entered in the pledge to reduce its balance. Write-offs can be for the entire pledge balance or a portion of the pledge balance. If you have a large number of pledges that need to be written off, such as unpaid telemarketing pledges, there is a tool your database administrator can use to globally write off these pledges for you.

When you provide direction for lists and reports on gifts, you need to be specific about what you want to see regarding pledges. Pledges have multiple amounts and dates:

- Date of the pledge and the total amount pledged
- Dates when the pledge payments are due (called "installments" in The Raiser's Edge) and how much is due each time
- Dates of the payments and the amounts paid
- A running balance

When you say you want "all donors of $1,000 or more this fiscal year," how should pledges be handled?

- Should the full amount of the pledge be counted regardless of its payment status? Does $1,000 pledged but nothing paid count as a "$1,000 donor" to you?
- Or do you only care about cash in the door? Should The Raiser's Edge ignore the pledges and count only outright cash and stock/property gifts and pledge payments?

This is not a question of "right or wrong." Each organization needs to determine its own approach. That is a decision fundraisers must make instead of leaving it up to database staff.

What *is* wrong, however, is to count both the pledge and its payments in giving totals because this is double-counting. This is a common mistake, so work with your staff to ensure that it does not happen. The Raiser's Edge will never default to such a situation but users can change the default settings so that it can happen. Occasionally there are instances where you do want to consider both pledges and payments. For example, you want to know anyone with any gift activity this year. That could be defined as either made a pledge or paid on a pledge and thus the staff would have to change the default settings to look at both gift types.

The tabs for pledges are about the same as those for cash gifts with the following noteworthy differences:

- On the Gift tab there is a **Send reminders** checkbox to indicate whether your staff should generate reminder notices to the donors. There is also a **History** button so you can see what reminders have been sent.
- There is an Installments/Payments tab so you can see what installments have been scheduled, what payments have been made, and what write-offs have been applied.

Payments can be made over time and be intermixed with other gifts on the constituent's Gifts tab. Write-offs do not appear on the Gifts tab. If it is not clear when looking at a constituent's Gifts tab how the pledge got to its current balance, simply open the pledge by double-clicking on it and look at the Installments/Payments tab.

Stock/Property

The third gift type is Stock/Property. These are gifts your organization does not plan to keep but wishes to sell to use the cash proceeds.

In addition to noting the kind of gift, this gift type has the functionality to record:

- Both the date on which the item was donated and the date it was sold.
- Both the value on the date it was given and the amount for which it sold.

You can tell whether a stock/property gift has been noted as sold in The Raiser's Edge because the gift type will include "(Sold)."

When a stock/property gift is sold, the amount paid to the broker can be recorded as well. This enables you to calculate the final net value of the gift to your organization. When you run reports from The Raiser's Edge, you need to specify which amount for these gifts you want to see:

1. The original value of the item on the day it was donated.
2. The amount the item sold for.
3. The amount the item sold for minus the broker fee, the true financial impact the gift had for your organization.

Most development reports, especially recognition reports, would use the first option, the original value when it was donated. The second and third options, however, have their place, such as when you want to understand how much a capital campaign has truly raised in terms of cash to construct a building.

You will find the constituent's Gifts tab and gift reports more useful for stock/property gifts if you have your gift entry staff use the **Reference** field to enter a short summary of what was donated, such as "50 shares of IBM" or "vacation home in Aspen, Colorado." This field is typically used in the acknowledgement letters for stock/property gifts because it is best practice not to assign a financial value for these gifts in acknowledgement letters. The Raiser's Edge can accommodate this as we discuss in the last section of this chapter. Longer descriptions of the item, such as the exact address, age, condition, terms, and other details of the donation of the vacation home in Aspen should be discussed in the Notepad fields on the Miscellaneous tab for the gift.

Gift-in-Kind

A Gift-in-Kind is a gift of something other than money that the organization plans to keep and use.

Items donated for silent and live auctions would, by definition, seem to be stock/property gifts because they will be sold. However, it is common practice to use gift-in-kind for these donations. It is usually not worth the effort to record the amount each item sold for in The Raiser's Edge.

Most organizations try to assign a **Value** for the gift-in-kind (amount is labeled "Value" for gifts-in-kind). They do their best to find the fair market value, either from the donor or through third-party research. It is best practice to enter an amount in this field so you can make a distinction between a donor of $20 tickets and one who gave $20,000 worth of building supplies for your capital campaign. The amount in this field is for internal purposes only and should not be printed in the acknowledgement letter. The value can be left at $0 if no reasonable determination can be made or the gift is "priceless."

Gifts-in-kind should be assigned to your campaigns, funds, and appeals. Consider these gifts when asking for reports—does your organization count the donation of a gift-in-kind toward a goal? Be careful not to double-count auction items by first counting the donation of the gifts-in-kind and then counting the cash received from their sale. This is often handled by putting gifts-in-kind in their own funds. It can also be addressed by filtering the output by gift type.

As with stock/property gifts, it is best practice to put a short description of the gift-in-kind in the **Reference** field. Use the description instead of an amount in the donor's acknowledgement letter.

Other

There is a gift type in The Raiser's Edge named "Other." Use it carefully. In my consulting work, I often see Other being used for donations by check, credit card, and electronic transfers because users take the word "Cash" too literally for the gift type. You want to ensure that is not being done at your organization.

Other is typically used in two ways:

1. *Planned Gifts.* Because most organizations using The Raiser's Edge do not have the RE:PlannedGiftTracker module, Other is used for planned gifts. Proceeds from a planned gift, such as a check received from an estate due to a bequest, should be entered as cash gifts—your organization received a check in this instance. But if you set up a charitable gift annuity or are notified that your

organization has been made the beneficiary of someone's will, life insurance policy, or trust, Other can be used to record the planned gift on the Gifts tab. This is desirable because the Gifts tab is the place one should look for gifts, including planned gifts.

2. *Donation of Services.* Although the donation of services is not tax-deductible, they still benefit your organization. Other can be used, if your organization wishes, to record the monetary value of those services so the donor can still be thanked and recognized.

The **Gift subtype** field can be used with Other to define the planned gift vehicle or use of Other. Do so carefully because this is a field that affects The Raiser's Edge's integration with accounting.

Recurring Gift

A Recurring Gift in The Raiser's Edge is a commitment, typically monthly, to make a donation to your organization. There is no established end date.

This functionality is extremely robust in The Raiser's Edge because organizations in Canada, the United Kingdom, and Australia raise significant portions of their contributions this way and process tens of thousands of these contributions each month. In the United States, this fundraising approach has been slower to catch on in the broader industry. It has been practiced for years by environmental groups; children's organizations that help feed and educate poor children, usually internationally; and Christian organizations that support missionaries. These programs are typically called "monthly giving programs" or "sustainer programs."

Almost every day, representatives of environmental groups can be found in my neighborhood standing on the street corners of the commercial blocks. They are from British-based, for-profit organizations working with U.S. and international nonprofits asking those passing by to sign up to make a monthly gift. The more traditional way to recruit these donors in the United States is by targeted direct mail and online appeals.

The Raiser's Edge will support one-time credit card charges using the standard functionality. However, if your organization implements a full-scale monthly giving program, you need to have the RE:EFT™ (Electronic Funds Transfer) module, which will allow you to fully use recurring gifts as well as do direct debits from checking and savings accounts.

It should be safe to store credit card and direct debit information in The Raiser's Edge. It is certainly safer to do so than storing the information in hard copy or spreadsheets. Blackbaud has modified The Raiser's Edge so it meets the credit card industry's Payment Card Industry Data Security Standards (PCI DSS). Direct debit information is encrypted in the database. The data's safety is contingent on your organization's database being on the latest update and good security practices being in use, however. If you store or wish to store credit card and direct debit information in The Raiser's Edge, discuss this with your database administrator and follow the recommendations discussed in Chapter 8 and provided by Blackbaud.

Recurring gifts also have functionality called "amendments," which allow you to conduct upgrade campaigns with your recurring givers. For example, each January you send tax notices to recurring givers because you have not sent a thank-you letter for each month's gift. In the thank-you letter, you might ask donors to consider increasing the amounts of their monthly gifts. If they do not respond, you just continue to charge the amounts you had been charging. But if they agree, you "amend" the recurring gifts to indicate the new, higher amount.

It is important to understand that a recurring gift is a commitment, similar to a pledge. It is not the actual receipt of money. When the money is received, it will be a cash gift because it will be money that can be deposited and spent. Unlike a pledge, the recurring gift does not have any meaningful total amount because it is, by definition, open-ended. The recurring gift amount is the amount to be charged or debited monthly. Be careful when including recurring gifts in any of your giving analysis. The presence of an active recurring gift can identify active monthly donors for you, but including it in total giving will usually result in nonsensical results. The payments to recurring gifts have a gift type of "Recurring Gift Pay-Cash" after your gift entry staff enters them as cash gifts and then applies them to their recurring gifts. These are the gifts you should include in giving totals.

A recurring gift has two additional tabs.

1. The Transactions tab shows you each of the cash gifts collected from this recurring gift.
2. The Amendments tab shows you the amendments that have been made to the recurring gift.

Planned Gift

Finally, Planned Gift is a gift type available for those who have the RE:PlannedGift-Tracker optional module. The purpose of this module is to track planned gifts, putting them in your database with other gifts to include these gifts and their donors with all of the activities done in The Raiser's Edge. This module interfaces with PG Calc's planned giving software Planned Giving Manager and GiftWrap and does not attempt to replace the functions of this or other planned giving software.

A gift of this type modifies the tabs so:

- The bottom of the Gift tab in the gift's record has details about the planned gift vehicle.
- A Planned Gift tab is added to the gift to track further details necessary based on each vehicle option, such as rates, terms, and other beneficiaries.
- A Realized Revenue tab is added that shows the cash gifts received as a result of the planned gift.

These gifts do not post to accounting from The Raiser's Edge. If they need to be booked by accounting, you will need to notify the accounting department directly with the planned gift's details.

Adjustments

There is one other process associated with gifts you should be aware of—the ability to "adjust" a gift. Although The Raiser's Edge is not an accounting system, it is a feeder system, part of the accounts receivable process, for accounting. It contains the gifts that are entered in the accounting system.

An adjustment in The Raiser's Edge is not merely opening a gift and changing it. An adjustment is a modification to a gift that leaves an audit trail on those fields that are important to keep in synch with accounting: the gift amount and fund.

This adjustment is usually done without affect to you as a fundraiser. However, you might open a gift and see an Adjustments tab. Or you might look at a constituent's Gifts tab and see a $0 gift. It is generally best practice not to delete gifts, so if a check bounces it is adjusted to $0 and an explanation noted.

Tip: Changing Gifts

Want to win kudos from your accounting colleagues, the board treasurer, board Finance committee, and the auditors? Want them to believe The Raiser's Edge is a system they can trust? Put the following practice into place at your organization.

Once a gift has been saved and reported to accounting, it can only be changed in two ways:

1. Use the standard Adjust function if the change is to gift amount or fund.
2. Edit and change the gift but add a gift note. The note goes on the Miscellaneous tab with a type of "Gift Modification." The note should explain the change.

The rule of thumb is that the gift must never have a different **Last Changed by** name than **Added by** name or **Date Last Changed** than **Date Added** without an adjustment or note to explain the difference.

In The Raiser's Edge version 8 more functionality will be in place to track the user and date of changes.

Constituent Giving Totals

The Gifts tab is an excellent tool for viewing the details of a constituent's giving. You can see the constituent's:

- Most recent gifts
- Giving to particular campaigns, funds, and appeals
- Gift details

But this is not an effective approach for getting totals or seeing patterns.

To view the constituent's giving totals, click the **Summaries** button on the constituent toolbar. It is the Greek capital letter "S" (Σ, or Sigma), which, in math and science, is the symbol indicating to "sum," or for our purposes, to "total."

$$\Sigma$$

Summaries in The Raiser's Edge are functions every fundraiser should know. They are easy to use and will let you review and analyze your constituents' giving without being dependent on someone else.

When you click on the button, a screen will appear with four tabs of filter and formatting options. If you click on each of the tabs, you will see the relevance of most of the concepts we have been discussing in this chapter. Typically for the constituent Gift Summary we do not want to apply any filters because we want to see the constituent's entire giving.

There are two settings on the Format tab you might wish to change, however:

1. *Show decimals.* Remove the checkmark for **Show decimals.** This will remove the cents from the summary, reducing the amount of detail on the screen.
2. *Show blanks instead of zero amounts.* If you choose to add a checkmark for this option, cells will be blank rather than showing $0.

When you change any of the settings, The Raiser's Edge will remember them. You might need to reverse some of them the next time you use this function if you have changed any of the filter criteria.

After clicking **Finish**, the Gift Summary will calculate and then appear as shown in Figure 3.3. The information is in "real time"—gifts entered moments ago will appear in the summary. Most of the fields and options on the screen are self-explanatory, so let us just discuss those areas that might not be so self-evident.

- If you double-click on the First, Latest, or Greatest gift information, The Raiser's Edge will open that gift so you can see the details.

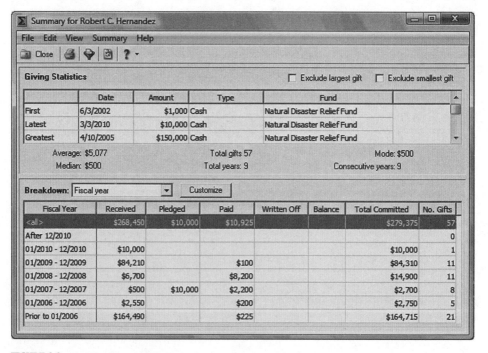

FIGURE 3.3   A Constituent Gift Summary

- As a reminder:
  - **Average**: All the gift amounts added up divided by the number of gifts.
  - **Median**: When all the gift amounts are listed from largest to smallest, the one that falls in the middle. If there is an even number of gifts and no gift is in the middle, the middle two are added together and divided by two.
  - **Mode**: The gift amount most frequently given. If there is more than one, The Raiser's Edge will display "Multiple Modes."
- All Giving Statistics are calculated based on the gift types included in the filters. A pledge and its payments are each separately counted as gifts and affect all the statistics.
  - For example, if a constituent only has a pledge of $200 and one payment thus far for $100, the Summary screen will report two gifts, an Average and Median of $150 and No Mode.
  - When the final payment of $100 is made on the pledge, the Summary screen will show three gifts, an Average of $133, and a Median and Mode of $100.
    In the next version of The Raiser's Edge, summary statistics are user configured. You will be able to include or exclude specific data elements in calculations so that how a number is derived will be much more transparent to you.
- There are checkboxes available to remove the largest and smallest gifts if you are concerned that they may be skewing these statistics. For example, one planned or "ultimate" gift may not be representative of the constituent's other giving.
- In the lower half of the screen, use the **Breakdown** option to view the constituent's giving in many different ways: by campaign, fund, appeal, calendar and fiscal year, and gift type.
- To get the "lifetime giving" amount, use the top row of the breakdown and the **Total Committed** column. By default The Raiser's Edge includes pledges in this amount regardless of their payment status (it does not duplicate payments). It does remove written-off amounts, however. In the two examples above, the Total Committed is shown as $200 for both.
- Experiment with the **Customize** button next to the **Breakdown** option to change the way the data is displayed. If you prefer, the data can be displayed in a graph rather than a table.
- The toolbar has a **Print** button if you want a hard copy of this data. There is also a **Filter** button that returns you to the previous filters screen if you wish to apply filters that you did not initially anticipate.

This screen is supposed to be used interactively. You can continually change the options to get new and different perspectives. Do not feel you need to set your options for this screen and then only get that view each time you use it. You can continually change the filters, **Breakdown**, and other options even while analyzing one constituent's giving.

We discuss reports that show multiple constituents' giving, in detail and in total, when we get to Chapter 7 on reporting.

Understanding Gift Processing

This section is a high-level overview of gift-processing procedures as they relate to The Raiser's Edge. The purpose is to help you ensure that the right tools are being used the correct way in The Raiser's Edge so your gifts are processed as quickly and accurately as possible. If you are a manager in the fundraising department, or the database or gift entry staff report to you, this section is particularly relevant to you.

Each organization has its unique needs. Size and resources affect the gift-processing procedures. But in summary, the most common steps for gift processing with The Raiser's Edge include:

1. Mail is opened by a staff member other than a fundraiser.
2. Other gift information, such as online donations and lockbox reports, is obtained and prepared for gift entry.
3. Gifts are grouped as needed for posting in accounting and speed of data entry into The Raiser's Edge.
4. Each group of gifts is totaled on an adding machine, and the adding machine tape is included with the batch.
5. Each group of gifts is entered into The Raiser's Edge by using the Batch page.
6. After the batch is committed, a report is run that shows subtotals of the batch by fund.
7. Checks are photocopied.
8. Original checks and batch paperwork are given to accounting for deposit and entry into the accounting software.
   - Accounting confirms that the gift information matches the reports and makes one general ledger entry for each subtotal by fund in the batch.
9. Development files copies of the checks and reports along with other documentation that came with the gift.
10. Development generates acknowledgement letters to the donors.
11. Development generates notification letters to the family members for tribute gifts.
12. Fundraisers check dashboards and reports in The Raiser's Edge when they wish to see the day's gifts and their effect on fundraising metrics.

Let us discuss this process in a little more detail. We focus on the concepts and tools that the fundraisers managing the staff responsible for this process should understand to take greatest advantage of their investment in The Raiser's Edge.

Batch Preparation

Gift information to be entered into The Raiser's Edge comes in a variety of ways:

- Each day's mail.
- Downloading contributions directly into The Raiser's Edge from Blackbaud RE:NetSolutions™, NetCommunity™, and Sphere™.
- Downloading reports and files from other online applications.
- Downloading reports from lockbox services, such as banks.
- Information already in The Raiser's Edge in pledges where payments are due, recurring gifts that need to be processed, and recurring batches that need to be reprocessed.
- Accounting or HR with information about employee payroll giving.
- Files or reports with the previous evening's telemarketing results.

This gift information needs to be put into groups for entry into The Raiser's Edge. Although gifts can be added directly to the constituents' Gifts tab, the best way to do gift entry is in the Batch page of The Raiser's Edge. The batch screen is like a spreadsheet where staff can do the gift entry as quickly as possible without having to click on tabs, buttons, and fields. Staff can enter the gift details as fast as they can type across the screen. It is also faster because default values can be set so they do not have to be selected for every gift being entered. This screen is not technically the same as a spreadsheet because the gift entry staff can only enter values that are appropriate for the field—a date cannot be entered into an amount field, for example.

Entering gifts by groups, called "batches," by using the Batch page is wise for two reasons:

1. It is a much faster way to enter the gifts because there are a large number of tools available in Batch to expedite gift entry. This is a widely used part of The Raiser's Edge, and Blackbaud has developed significant functionality in this area.
2. It creates a permanent grouping of the gifts that can be used to track them through the entire gift-processing cycle, from entry into The Raiser's Edge, to depositing, posting to the accounting software, and monthly reconciliation.

It is most efficient for an organization for the accounting staff to enter gift information summarized by fund for each batch into the accounting software. Accounting staff should not reenter every gift. Gifts need to be batched based on the following two criteria:

1. *The requirements accounting has for deposits.* All gifts in the same batch should be deposited together. Gifts need to go to the same account in the accounting software. For example, if your checks are deposited to a separate bank account than your credit card gifts, checks and credit cards should be entered in separate batches.
2. *The fastest way to enter the gifts given the tools available in Batch.* For example, in one day you might receive dozens of checks that accounting deposits into the same bank account. If half of them are from a direct mail appeal and the other half are registration fees for an event, it is easier to divide the checks into two batches. Each batch can have the fields and defaults it needs for staff to most rapidly enter the gifts.

Although it might seem old fashioned, it is wise to run an adding machine tape for each batch of gifts once they have been assembled. This will provide a manual backup to the data entry to ensure that no gift is entered twice or skipped and that amounts are entered correctly.

Batch

Batch is a powerful tool for your gift entry staff, so they should spend the time learning it well. It allows for all the gift entry functions needed to add new gifts to the database. Batch even allows the gift entry staff to review and modify constituent data without having to open the constituent records. For example, they can compare the spelling of names, spouse information, and phone and address details from the gifts with that information already in the database. New donors can be added directly from Batch. There is generally no need to review constituent data before beginning gift entry.

Some other features of Batch:

- The number of gifts and total amount from the adding machine tape should be included when setting up the batch. The Raiser's Edge can help validate the data entry accuracy.
- Templates can be created for batches so gift entry staff do not have to set up the fields every time.
- Defaults can be specified so that common values across gifts like gift date do not have to be manually entered for every gift.
- Gifts can be linked to events, memberships, and tributes. Pledge payments can be added and linked to the pledges.

The functionality is extensive.

Batch is a temporary holding area in the database. The gifts will not appear in the constituent records or be available for queries and reports until the batch is "committed." The process of committing the batch allows the batch to be validated to ensure that the expected number and amount of gifts are present.

When the batch is committed, it is wise to print the control report and save it as a permanent record of the gifts just added. Each batch is assigned a number that will stay with the batch's gifts permanently, even if the batch is later deleted.

Posting

Posting is the process of transferring gift information to accounting. The accounting staff then enters the gift information into their accounting software. There are four ways to do this:

1. If your organization uses The Financial Edge™, The Raiser's Edge posting process can transfer gift information directly into that program with no rekeying.
2. If your organization does not use The Financial Edge, you can still use the posting tools in The Raiser's Edge to create a file to import the gift details into your accounting software.
3. You can use the posting tools to create reports by account numbers from the accounting system's chart of accounts, and accounting staff can manually enter the amounts from the reports.
4. You can use another report to show totals by fund by batch.

If your organization uses one of the first three approaches, you should give an accounting staff person security rights to set up the general ledger account numbers in The Raiser's Edge and to run the posting process. (They should only have View rights to gifts.)

However, most organizations use the fourth approach.

The batch control report lists each gift separately. You want accounting to enter the total for each fund in the batch, not each gift separately. On the Reports page of The Raiser's Edge, there is the Gift Detail and Summary Report. This report can be run based on the batch number to get the total by fund within the batch.

The totals of the summary report by fund and batch control report will be the same. Accounting will want to see this information to be comfortable that development has done the data entry correctly and the reports properly reflect the gift details. With that support, they should be able to make one entry into the general ledger for each fund in the batch.

Acknowledging

Every organization needs to thank its donors for the gifts they have given. The Raiser's Edge calls these letters "donor acknowledgement letters" and has a special tool for doing this.

One of the pages of The Raiser's Edge is called Mail. Discussed more in Chapter 4, Mail is a goldmine of resources that Blackbaud has developed specifically for the mailing needs of fundraising operations. Many organizations using The Raiser's Edge do not take advantage of this tool, so check with your staff to ensure that they are generating acknowledgement letters from Mail using the **Donor Acknowledgement Letters** function. Occasionally, there are legitimate reasons to not use this tool, but they are rare.

Like Batch, Donor Acknowledgement Letters in Mail is one of the most widely used tools in The Raiser's Edge. It is powerful. It integrates The Raiser's Edge and Microsoft Word to generate the letters. There are two capabilities in this tool of note:

1. Donor Acknowledgement Letters can perform "conditional mail merges." This ability allows your organization to set up a variety of Word documents to use for acknowledgement letters. When doing gift entry, your gift processor specifies for each gift the name of the form letter the donor should receive. The Raiser's Edge then uses that name to determine which Word document to merge for the gift. It is only one merge, but each gift is merged with the Word document appropriate for it. An example of the use of different letters is to vary them based on gift type: cash, pledge, stock/property, and gift-in-kind letters each need different text.
2. Within the Word documents "conditional statements" can be set up. This allows your letters to vary the text without needing a separate Word document for every variation. The most common use of this function is to reflect tribute information. The letter for a gift without tribute information might start with "Thank you for your gift of $50, which we received on August 14, 201X. Because of your support..." But the letter for a gift with tribute information needs to say, "Thank you for your gift of $50 in memory of Amy Wong, which we received on August 14, 201X. We have also notified the family of your donation. Because of your support..." Two Word documents are not necessary to handle this; one Word document using a conditional statement can. If your staff does not know how to use conditional statements in Word documents, this is a valuable training opportunity.

When the letters are run from Donor Acknowledgement Letters in Mail, The Raiser's Edge will mark the gifts as "Acknowledged" and will enter the date they were acknowledged. The letter itself is not stored in the gift, but the name of the form letter is. The letters from the merge can be saved in a folder on the network.

Tribute gifts require another acknowledgement process. For "in honor of" gifts, the person who is being honored needs to be notified of the donor's gift. For "in memory of" gifts, the designated family representative(s) should be notified. These letters should include the name and address of the donor but not the gift amount. A common practice has been to send tribute cards to these people. It is easier for your staff if you use The Raiser's Edge to generate letter-size notifications instead, but The Raiser's Edge can work with cards. They are set up in Word so the documents can be formatted however you wish.

If your organization has the RE:Tribute module, Mail will also include an option for **Honor/Memorial Acknowledgement Letters**. These letters are more complex to set up because there are two names (person being notified and donor), at least two addresses, possibly more than one family member to notify, and possibly more than one donor per tribute. But this is a powerful tool that once set up will make generating these notification letters easy.

If your organization does not have the RE:Tribute module, you will not have this option in Mail. I recommend storing the tribute details for the gift in the gift's attributes. These attributes can be used to generate the family notification letters using the Donor Acknowledgement Letters tool if these letters are run *first*, before the donors' letters are run, and not yet marking the gifts as acknowledged.

Daily Gift Reporting

A best practice in the use of The Raiser's Edge is that gift-processing staff do not run hard copy reports for circulation after each day's gifts are entered. Fundraisers should be logged into The Raiser's Edge and use the many tools available there to see the gifts in the system. This has the following benefits:

- It saves gift processors' time for more important things.
- It saves paper, trees, and printing expenses.
- All fundraisers can get access to the information immediately without waiting for the copy of the report to get to them.
- Fundraisers can more easily focus on the gifts they are interested in—by size; campaign, fund or appeal; donor or group of donors.
- Fundraisers can see the presentation of data that is of interest to them—for example, the major gifts officers might want to see each of the big gifts from the day but the annual fund manager and membership director want to see totals of the day's activities. Additionally, some fundraisers might like numbers and details while others want to see charts and graphs.
- Data viewed inside The Raiser's Edge allows for interaction with the system. A dashboard has drill-through capability so fundraisers can explore the gifts and donors in more detail if they wish. Queries allow for easy clicking through each gift or donor so all the details can be seen in context.

Occasionally, it makes good business sense to print hard copies and to e-mail spreadsheets or PDFs of reports. With The Raiser's Edge, however, you will want to keep that to a minimum.

For any distribution method, the best dashboards and reports to use for these purposes are discussed in Chapter 7.

Other Gift-Processing Activities

Not all gift activity is the entry of new gifts. There are other activities that fall under gift processing.

- Stock/property gifts are sold and need to be marked as such.
- Pledges need to be written off.
- Checks bounce, mistakes are found, and gifts need to be adjusted and edited.
- Occasionally gifts need to be deleted.

When these activities occur it is important that they be handled correctly and by the right staff. It is also important to coordinate these events with accounting so The Raiser's Edge and the accounting system stay in balance. There are reports on the Reports page that correlate to each of these actions to provide accounting with the hard copy backup of the activity.

Reconciling

The Raiser's Edge should be reconciled to your accounting system each month. Although it might be difficult to envision this possibility, it is happening with greater frequency. At the Greater Bay Area Make-A-Wish Foundation, we have been reconciling every month to the penny on an annual budget of more than $6.5 million.

Some people may even think this impossible because fundraising and accounting use different numbers and different standards for reporting. Understand that "reconciling" does not mean the development and financial reports will have exactly the same numbers on them at board meetings. It means that where the two systems do share data, that data has been confirmed to be the same. For example, many organizations do not book pledges in the financials until the end of the year. But we fundraisers generally count pledges in fundraising reporting. Gifts-in-kind and planned gifts might never get booked by accounting, but we might want to show them in fundraising reports. Cash and stock/property gifts, whether outright or pledge payments, however, should be reconciled. So should other gifts types that accounting also tracks.

Reconciliation should be done monthly. If all procedures as discussed here are in place, this should only take a couple of hours at most once the process is established. I recommend using a pivot report on the Reports page of The Raiser's Edge to see the month's giving by fund. Compare those totals with a report from the accounting system that shows by account the starting amount for the month, the month's batch entries, and the ending total for the month. The Raiser's Edge pivot report can be compared to this accounting report. Where a fund total in The Raiser's Edge differs from the corresponding account total in the accounting report, use the pivot report to drill into the batches to do a batch-by-batch comparison to determine what created the difference.

A few tips:

- Reconcile both the last month and the fiscal year through the end of last month. Adjustments in The Raiser's Edge can be made to gifts previously reconciled and will affect those previously reconciled periods. You need to make sure that the last month has been reconciled but also that the whole fiscal year stays reconciled.
- Do the reconciliation before accounting closes the books on the previous month. Although my experience is that mistakes are more commonly made in The Raiser's Edge than in accounting, accounting staff do make mistakes, too. It is best if any needed corrections are made to last month in the accounting software before it is closed.
- Usually, development staff does the reconciliation work. For these purposes, the accounting system is the master system and we need to ensure that our system matches theirs. There are certainly exceptions, but typically development staff does the reconciling.
- Remember the distinction between gift date and GL post date. Pull the reconciliation query for the pivot report and other reconciliation needs based on the GL post date and not gift date.
- "Reconciled" does not mean the numbers are exactly the same; it means they are the same or, where they are not, the difference is justified and explained. You probably need to have a list of "known differences" that you note each month for details that are not the same and cannot be made the same between the two systems. For example, a bounced check in the first month of a fiscal year for a gift made in the previous fiscal year will show in the current fiscal year in accounting but will show in the previous fiscal year for The Raiser's Edge. Adjustments are reflected based on gift date or the gift's GL post date in The Raiser's Edge.

Summary

As a fundraising system, The Raiser's Edge has extensive functionality to manage gifts. Fundraisers need to understand the terminology and concepts in order to provide direction to data entry staff and to request and get accurate lists and reports.

Each time gift output is requested from The Raiser's Edge, fundraisers should address the following areas:

- The gift date range of interest
- The gift types of interest and details associated with each
- Amount ranges
  - Whether those ranges are based on a single gift or cumulative giving
- Campaign, fund, and appeal filters to apply
- Who should get credit for gifts that have been soft-credited
- Who should get credit for matching gifts
- Name display for anonymous donations

The Raiser's Edge also has extensive functionality to support gift-processing needs. Fundraisers who oversee the staff who do that work should ensure that the tools that The Raiser's Edge offers to do that work as efficiently as possible are being used.

■ ■ ■

Now let us talk about how to use The Raiser's Edge to solicit these gifts by mail, e-mail, and telemarketing.

CHAPTER 4

Direct Marketing and Other Mailings

There are endless ways nonprofit organizations use mailings:

- Newsletters and magazines
- Direct mail acquisitions and renewals
- Event invitations
- Membership acquisition and renewals
- Pledge reminders
- Gift acknowledgement letters
- Annual reports

Additionally, e-mail continues to gain in use for the same purposes as hard copy mail.

The Raiser's Edge is an excellent tool for creating the lists and providing the data needed for mailings and e-mails. The challenge in accomplishing these tasks is that the fundraising needs are quite complicated.

It is common for me to see an e-mail from a fundraiser putting together one of these mailings that is a long list of, "This group and this other group should get it but be sure to leave out anyone who is X or Y or Z. And oh! Do not forget A, B, and C, too!"

Sometimes, mailings need to be segmented as well. Rather than needing one big list, the mailing requires a number of small, unduplicated groups.

To address these fundraising needs, this chapter has two purposes:

1. To identify the information The Raiser's Edge needs to produce the proper results for your communications and the issues you should consider when providing those details to your database staff.
2. Common mistakes to watch for when working with your database staff to help them ensure that you get the right results.

This chapter is not going to teach you how to generate mailings yourself. The objective is to teach you the concepts you need to know to work with your database staff to get the right results.

Most uses of the word "mailing" in this chapter apply to both hard copy mailings and e-mail campaigns. Although there are notable differences about the contact method, assembling the lists for whom to contact is similar. The primary difference to consider is whether all constituent preferences regarding e-mail communications are recorded in The Raiser's Edge.

The content of this chapter also applies to phonathons and telemarketing, processes that involve creating lists of prospects and pulling data fields necessary to make calls. This is true if you are using students or other volunteer callers and need to print phonathon forms in-house. It is also true if you need to create a data file to upload into your on-site call management software (such as CampusCall) or send the data to a telemarketing firm. And it applies whether you are asking for a gift or doing a "thank-a-thon."

■ ■ ■

Have you ever heard the expression, "How do you eat an elephant?" The answer is, "One bite at a time." Although this chapter might seem as if it provides a significant amount of detail, it simply breaks down the big process of generating your mailings correctly. The details are here because they occur in the process of doing nonprofit mailings, e-mails, and telemarketing. The Raiser's Edge has these options because they are needed to most accurately generate your mailings. If someone ignores these details, thinks they are "too much," they have not found a simpler way that is accurate. Instead, they are most likely not generating their mailings correctly and just do not realize it. So hang in there! This chapter is not technical; it simply discusses the fundraising direction your database staff requires in order to get you the most accurate mailings possible.

The examples in this chapter are primarily about hard copy mailings because they remain the most common form of communication for most nonprofits. However, the selection and output concepts apply equally to telemarketing and e-mail efforts.

Four Steps

Remember the kitchen analogy in Chapter 1? The Raiser's Edge has a number of functions to accomplish the fundraising tasks for which it is designed. How your staff decides what parts of The Raiser's Edge to use and how they use them are based on how you answer the following four questions:

1. *What is the final output format you need?* Do you need a printed product such as labels or envelopes, a mail-merged letter, some combination of the two, a file to send to a mail house or telemarketing firm, or data to pass to your e-mail program?
2. *Which constituents should be in the results?* What individuals and organizations need to be included in the output, and just as importantly, which should be left out?
3. *What fields are needed for these constituents?* Name, address, giving, and other fields?
4. *What content should be in those fields?* What version of the name should be used for the addressee? What address should be used in the address fields?

These questions frame the steps to stating the requirements for a mailing.

As your database staff work with you, they will learn your preferences. Until that time, however, it is up to you to communicate your needs and preferences. Your database staff should help in the process, reminding you of issues to think about and offering recommendations to consider. This should be a team effort. It takes both the fundraiser and the database staff to produce a correct final result—neither person can do it alone.

When you send an e-mail to your database person requesting a mailing, you should welcome and invite having them schedule a time to get together with you to discuss it. Until you master the concepts in this chapter and answer all the questions in your request, or until you and your database person have worked together long enough for them to know how you will answer these questions, it is completely appropriate for them to ask you a number of follow-up questions. This is not a sign that they are being overly detailed or do not know The Raiser's Edge. Were I to come to your office to generate a mailing for you, with my years of work with The Raiser's Edge, I, too, would ask a series of questions to ensure that I gave you the right results.

Each of the four steps includes a number of more detailed questions you should consider. The answers will determine what tools in The Raiser's Edge your database staff will use to generate your mailing. It is best if all of the questions are answered on paper first, before your database staff begins working on the mailing.

Your database staff needs to know the final objective in order to know where to begin and how to get there. For example, let us say we are located at the Empire State Building in New York City. If we want to go somewhere else, we need to know what the final destination is to determine how to get there. If we want to get to Central Park, we could walk, take a taxi, or ride the subway. If we want to get to Connecticut, we need to drive or take the train. If we want to get to Los Angeles, it is best to fly. And, if we want to get to London we could fly . . . or take a ship.

The mode of transportation is not the only detail. We need to know dates, times, budget, and travel preferences. Where we are going in Connecticut, for example, helps us determine the best driving directions. Maybe we need to make multiple stops along the way.

The point is, just as there are several ways to get from the Empire State Building to other locations, there are a number of ways to get data out of The Raiser's Edge. The best and most accurate way is determined by where you want to go and some important details along the way.

When you provide those details to your database staff, it is best to provide them broken out by the four steps listed earlier. It is difficult for database staff to receive requests like the following example, which is from an actual situation I experienced:

What we need are donors who have given a direct mail gift, full gift history, gift type, name and address, salutation field, id number.

The other thing you need to do is to pull out anyone whom we do not want to mail to—that would be people that specifically requested to not receive direct mail, or those who asked for mail only once or twice a year, board members, advisory council, VIPs, sustainers (monthly donors), staff, volunteers, deceased, bad addresses.

I know in the past we have mailed to family foundations. Aside from the family foundations, we probably should not be getting any corporate donors.

What is more useful instead is a request broken into the four steps listed previously with the additional details needed. Doing this not only makes it easier on your database staff but enables them to return your results faster and more accurately.

Let us discuss how to make a mailing request in the recommended four steps. We conclude the chapter by showing how the preceding direct mail request turned out when I applied this approach to it.

A Note to Database Administrators

Every point made in this chapter corresponds to a function in The Raiser's Edge you should consider when creating mailings. Many of them relate to the extensive functionality on the Mail page. However, the order in which the issues are raised in this chapter is what I believe to be the most logical order for fundraisers thinking through their mailings. You will need to take each answer and apply it in the appropriate tool and order in The Raiser's Edge. These questions do not apply to you in the same order, and you should not attempt to handle them all in Query.

Step 1. Output Format

The first direction you need to provide is about the final result: what is the end result you need? The typical options include:

- A standard printed result such as:
  - Labels
  - Envelopes
  - Forms
    - Pledge reminders
    - Membership renewals
    - Telemarketing call forms
- A customized printed result typically handled through a Microsoft Word mail merge. These merges can be letters or any other format you can imagine that can be created in a Word merge.
- A data file to send to a mail house, telemarketing firm, or some other company or computer program to process your data.
- Data for an e-mail program that integrates with The Raiser's Edge.

In each case, the fundraiser needs to provide details such as the following:

- What size labels or envelopes are needed?
- What should the Word merge letter say? Where is it saved on the network so the database staff can copy it into The Raiser's Edge?
- What are the requirements of the company or software program receiving the file? Should the file be in Excel or some other format? How can the file be securely transmitted to the contact person?

Detail is critical here, or significant rework could be necessary by your staff after they produce the first version. Be as specific as you can, working with any third parties such as mail houses to get the details they require. Or, provide a contact person at the third party for your database staff to communicate with directly.

Step 2. Recipients

The Raiser's Edge makes a clear distinction in its preparation of mailings among three different questions:

1. Who should get the mailing?
2. What fields are needed for that "who"?
3. What data goes in those fields?

When you provide direction to your database staff, you get faster and more accurate results if you provide direction about each of the three areas separately rather than running them all together in your request.

Let us start with the recipients, the answer to the question "Who gets it?"

The first thing you can do to help answer this question is to divide it into two parts:

1. The criteria of those who *should get it*.
2. The criteria for those who are included in the first group *but should not get the mailing* anyway (e.g., deceased, lost, do not want it).

Try to separate these two thoughts rather than running them together.

Understanding that we should indicate whom to mail to by creating two groups, the "includes" and the "excludes," let us discuss the details you should be thinking about when communicating those needs.

Note: Specialized Mailings

There are a number of mailings that fundraising offices do that are specialized to particular tasks and data needs. The Raiser's Edge has special functions just for these tasks (as shown in Figure 4.1) that make the process of identifying who needs to be included much easier.

They include:

- Donor Acknowledgement Letters to thank donors for their gifts
- Honor/Memorial Acknowledgement Letters to notify "in honor of" constituents and the families of "in memory of" constituents about gifts received for the tribute
- Receipts for gifts
- Pledge Reminders to collect on pledges

(continued)

(Continued)

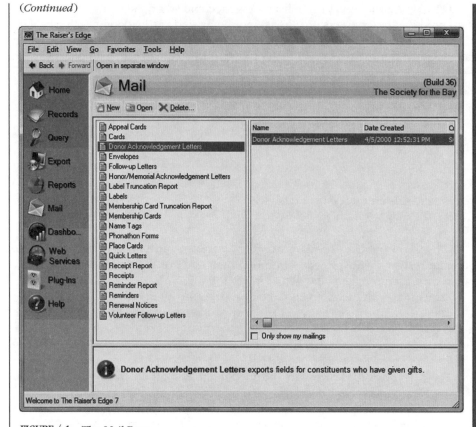

FIGURE 4.1   The Mail Page

- Recurring Gift Reminders to collect on monthly donations
- Membership Cards
- Membership Renewal Notices
- Volunteer Follow-up Letters
- Phonathon Forms for in-house telemarketing campaigns

Most of the discussion in this chapter applies to these specialized mailings, as well. You still need to specify the output format you want, who should and should not receive them, and what data is included in them. However, work with your database staff to understand the built-in functionality these tools have to most easily identify who needs to receive these mailings.

Those to Include

Organizations rarely mail to every constituent in their databases. Whenever I have encountered an organization that does, and we have talked through the situation, they have changed their approach. Unless your organization is small and new, it simply does not make economical sense to send mailings to every constituent in The Raiser's Edge.

For example, a few people a staff member met at a networking reception five years ago expressed interest in your organization and were added to the database. They have been mailed to for five years but have never given, participated in an event, joined the membership program or volunteered. It is probably time to stop wasting printing and postage expenses on them.

Because we do not mail to everyone, we need to define criteria for who should receive each mailing. The answer might be short and simple or long and complex, but this section discusses the questions you should think about. I often refer to this group as the "includes."

INDIVIDUALS AND ORGANIZATIONS The first question to answer is simply: Do you want both individual and organization records to get the mailing if both record types meet the criteria? Most mailings do go to both record types, but there are occasional exceptions.

TYPICAL CRITERIA FOR INCLUSION The typical considerations in determining which of those individuals and organizations should receive the mailing include the following criteria:

1. *Constituent codes*. What types of constituents should be included? For newsletters and annual reports, for example, we typically want to include board members and former board members. Constituent codes are common in mailing criteria. Review the list of codes for their application to each mailing. Be certain to separate the codes to be used for inclusion purposes and exclusion purposes.
   - Be clear when expressing constituent code criteria whether you just want constituents for whom the code currently applies or those for whom the code ever applied. For example, former board members should still have the "Board Member" code, with a **Date To** supplied. If you say "include board member constituent code," do you mean just current board members? Or do you mean anyone with that code, so former board members are included as well?
2. *Giving*. Should donors or nondonors be included in the mailing?
   - Be sure to check the list noted at the beginning of Chapter 3 to clearly define exactly what gifts count toward the criteria.
   - Also be sure to review the other gift concepts covered in the chapter. There can be many reasons and many ways you might want donors to be included in a mailing such as major donors; monthly donors; previous donors to a certain campaign, fund, or appeal; donors with a pledge balance; or a constituent with a planned gift intention even if that planned gift had to be entered as $0.
   - Be careful with the use of "last gift" criteria. The Raiser's Edge can query based on "first gift," "last gift," and "largest gift." Remember, as discussed in Chapter 3, the many types of gifts in The Raiser's Edge. Too many times I have seen annual fund directors and direct mail consultants put in their criteria "last gift was last year" in the search for lapsed donors. If someone donated a gift-in-kind or bought an event ticket this year, would that exclude them from your lapsed appeal for direct mail? If someone's gift last year was a gift-in-kind or event ticket, should that qualify them for your direct mail lapsed appeal? Avoid the use of "last gift," and be more specific: first define in your inclusion criteria the gifts, using the checklist from Chapter 3, which would

qualify someone to get the mailing. Then, in your exclusion criteria, list the giving criteria that would remove someone from the group. For example:

Includes: Constituents with a cash gift to a Direct Mail appeal (list them) within the dates of July 1, 2008, and June 30, 2009.

Excludes: Constituents with a cash gift to a Direct Mail appeal (list them) since July 1, 2009, or any other cash, stock/property, or pledge gift of $500 or more since July 1, 2009.

This approach intentionally ignores other gift activity such as gifts-in-kind and event tickets that might be irrelevant for this purpose and produces a more accurate result for a lapsed donor direct mail appeal.

3. *Event participation.* Does attendance at a previous event or registration for a future event qualify the constituent for the mailing?
   - Make a distinction between event participation and event contributions. If your interest is in event sponsorship and registration fees or purchases at events, use the giving criteria checklist noted in Chapter 3 for these gifts.
   - There can be event participants who are not constituents, they are merely entered into the event record in The Raiser's Edge and do not have their own constituent records in the database. Define whether those event participants should be included in the mailing, or just people and organizations important enough to have their own constituent records.
4. *Membership activity.* Should members be included in the mailing?
   - Define the membership programs or categories that qualify for the mailing as all might not be applicable.
   - Define whether you want active, lapsed, and dropped members included.
5. *Volunteer involvement.* Should volunteers be included? All of them, from across the organization and all time? How do you want to define them—based on constituent code, volunteer type, assignments, time sheets?
6. *Prospect information.* Should major gifts and other prospects get the mailing? These criteria include the **Prospect Status** and **Prospect Classification** fields if you use the Prospect tab/RE:Search module or other fields such as attributes if you do not. Newsletters, magazines, and annual reports are great cultivation tools. Perhaps you want prospects to receive them regardless of any other information in their records, including a current absence of giving history.
7. *Attributes.* Are there certain constituent attributes that define who should be included? Depending on how your organization has set up your database, there could be several attributes to consider.

One example given in Chapter 2 for attributes is a "Mail To Send" attribute. The intent of such an attribute is to include constituents in your mailing who do not yet meet any of the previous criteria but should get the mailing anyway. This attribute should *not* be used to mark everyone to get the mailing, it should be used for the exceptions, those constituents who do not yet meet any of the previous criteria but should get it anyway. One good example for using this attribute is for prospects who do not yet have a giving history but who should receive the mailing as part of a cultivation process. Another good example is constituents who contact you and ask to be put on lists, such as someone who has not yet attended your gala but hears about it and wishes to get an invitation to the next one.

One potential problem with this approach is that your organization could begin mailing to these constituents over and over without a response, thereby wasting your organization's resources. To avoid this, it is suggested that you and your staff enter a date on the attribute when it is added and use the attribute **Comments** field to note the full name of the person who added the attribute and the reason. If you use this attribute for a mailing, it is important you do the following each time you create the mailing:

- Work with your database staff to run a query for everyone who has the attribute for that mailing. Review the records that have the attribute, the date, and the reason, and determine whether you still want to keep mailing to those people. For example, if you have invited someone to your gala at their request for three years and they still have not attended, perhaps you should no longer send it to them given the cost involved. You can delete the attribute from the constituent or you can add a date filter for this attribute to the mailing criteria.
- Remember to put in your inclusion criteria a reminder for the database staff to include anyone with this attribute. If necessary, also note the as-of date so uses before that date are no longer considered.

Potentially, any field in a constituent's record can be used as criteria to define who should get your mailing. The criteria listed are the most common criteria used.

COUPLES Another consideration for mailing criteria applies just to individual constituents: If the spouses or partners each has a record, should there be two copies of the mailing sent, one to each person, or only one copy sent to them as a couple? At this stage, do not worry about the name on the mailing, just whether you want one or two copies sent to members of couples who each have a constituent record.

The answer to this question depends on the kind of mailing you are doing. Most solicitations, event invitations, newsletters, and other mailings are sent to the head of household record with both constituent names listed. However, some mailings to volunteers, for example, might require one copy to each volunteer. Mailings to alumni, when each spouse or partner is an alum, might also require sending one copy to each.

USE OF "AND" Another point to consider when writing down your inclusion criteria is to be clear about how much of the criteria the constituent has to meet. Do they just need to meet a part of the criteria, or do they need to meet all of it? For example, we might say, "I want board members and donors of $1,000 or more." Does that mean you want "board members who have given $1,000 or more" or "all board members *plus* everyone, board member or not, who has given $1,000 or more"?

The word "and" in logic—and your staff are using logic in The Raiser's Edge to make mailings happen for you—means that *both* conditions must be true. We often use "and," however, to list different groups we want that constituents only have to be in one of to be included. Make sure your staff knows when someone has to meet multiple criteria and when they only have to meet part of the criteria. One easy way to do this is to put multiple criteria that have to be met in the same paragraph. Separate criteria, any one of which needs to be met, should each be in its own paragraph.

CONFUSION WITH OUTPUT   A final point to remember: most people, including fundraisers and database staff, who are new to this process make a common mistake of mixing *criteria of who should receive the mailing* with *the output fields that are needed in the mailing*. This can make it more difficult to get the results you are looking for. In your mailing request, be sure to separate what has to be true about the constituent and what you want to see about them. What you want to *see* goes in steps 3 and 4.

For example, do not include name information in this step. People's names will have no bearing on whether they get the mailing. Save that for Step 4. The same is usually true about address details. Occasionally, a mailing is done based on geography, but typically the address does not need to be handled until Step 4, as well.

SEGMENTS   There are times when fundraisers do not want one large group of mailing recipients. Instead, the mailing needs to be segmented so that each subset gets a different version of the mailing. This is done most often with appeals. This section discusses handling of the typical needs for segmentation in The Raiser's Edge.

The segment the constituents receive and give to is usually recorded as a package within the mailing's appeal code.

Different Constituencies and Donor Sizes   Organizations often send end-of-year or holiday direct mail appeals in which they want to vary the letter depending on the recipient's role with the organization and previous giving. For example, the segments they need look like:

- Current board members
- Former board members
- Major donors
- Smaller donors
- Lapsed donors
- Volunteers

There are two challenges in preparing such a mailing:

1. Creating each segment.
2. Ensuring no one is in more than one segment. For example, a board member could easily meet the current board member, major donor, and volunteer criteria. That board member should not get three letters, however.

The Raiser's Edge can accommodate this need. It is among the more sophisticated uses of the software, so your staff might not be familiar with it. Direct your staff to contact Blackbaud customer support if this need seems difficult for them to meet.

Tip: Segmenting Tool

If your database staff talk about having to "merge a lot of queries" to make the segmentation happen, they are probably doing it the hard way. Make sure they use the Segment tab in Mail. You do not need to use this tool yourself; simply mention it to them in advance if you think they might not be familiar with it. Blackbaud customer support can help if necessary.

Do the following to provide direction for a mailing to be segmented:

- *Define the inclusion and exclusion criteria for the entire mailing.* As a simple example, excluding deceased and lost constituents applies to the whole mailing and not to particular segments.
- *Identify by name and criteria what makes each segment unique.* Do not restate the larger inclusion and exclusion criteria. Also, do not include "but not . . ." criteria to leave out the other segments. That is understood. Simply define what makes each segment unique. For example, a "current board member" segment should be self-explanatory. The major donor segment will need to be defined using the giving criteria noted in Chapter 3 based on what you and your organization define as a major donor.
- *Sort the segments from most important to least important.* The Raiser's Edge will include constituents in the first segment in which they apply. It will not repeat a constituent in subsequent segments even if the constituent meets a later segment's criteria.

With this detail, The Raiser's Edge can produce a segmented mailing without much more effort than a nonsegmented mailing. This is also the approach to use when segmenting for telemarketing purposes, such as having students call alumni based on matching majors or extracurricular activities.

Different Packaging If the purpose of your segmentation is to test a control and a comparison piece to see which produces better results, The Raiser's Edge can help you with that, as well. In summary, you and your staff need to:

- Run the mailing process in The Raiser's Edge to determine the number of records that should receive the mailing. Your database staff should run the mailing through the entire process, not just create the queries, to get an accurate number.
- Use the "Random sampling" tool in Query to select a random sample of the mailing recipients based on the number you specify. This number will probably be half of the total number, but The Raiser's Edge will need you to specify the specific number, not a percent. Assign this query to the test group.
- Create another query for those who should receive the mailing but are not in the test group. These are your control subjects.
- These queries can then be used independently to generate each segment or can be joined using the Segment tab in Mail.

Expenses incurred for appeals can be recorded at the package level. If one package is more expensive than another, such as one offers a premium the other does not, you can record the expenses for the packages in The Raiser's Edge. The reports from The Raiser's Edge will show you not only the gross revenue from each package but also the net results.

RFM Segmentation   There are three ways to do Recency, Frequency, and Monetary Value (RFM) segmentation, typically used for direct mail purposes.

1. Use the same procedure outlined previously for "Different Constituencies and Donor Sizes" if your RFM segments are sufficiently few enough to warrant the effort to create one query for each segment.
2. Use the Blackbaud Direct Marketing™ program, which interfaces with The Raiser's Edge and allows for greater direct marketing functionality, including more sophisticated RFM segmentation.
3. Provide the data from The Raiser's Edge unsegmented and with the detailed fields necessary for your direct mail consultant or mail house to do the RFM segmentation for you. Be sure your staff includes the constituents' IDs with the data so the database administrator can import back into The Raiser's Edge the appeal and segment data to the constituents' Appeals tabs.

Those to Exclude

Once you clearly define the entire group of constituents you would like to receive the mailing (the "includes"), make a list of the criteria that excludes a constituent from receiving the mailing even if they meet the include criteria (the "excludes").

These criteria should be stated in the positive, not in the negative.

For example, do not say in your include criteria "I want all donors from last year who are not dead and are not lost." Separate the inclusion and exclusion criteria. The inclusion criteria in that statement is "I want all donors from last year," which should be defined with more detail about exactly what "donors from last year" means—see the list in Chapter 3.

A separate list of exclusion criteria, stated in the positive so it is as clear as possible to everyone, would then be, "Take out anyone who is: Now deceased or has a checkmark for **Has no valid addresses**."

Breaking the process into a list of include criteria and a different list of exclude criteria also makes the process easier. You only need criteria for removing records for those that might meet the inclusion criteria. You do not need to worry about trying to remove people who are not going to be picked up by the inclusion criteria.

Exclusion criteria take precedence over inclusion criteria. Be clear to your staff if there is any reason for which you would not want someone excluded from the mailing even if they meet the exclusion criteria. This is rarely done and makes the mailing more difficult to prepare. The point is to understand that unless you and your staff handle it otherwise, there are no exceptions: anyone meeting the exclusion criteria will not get the mailing.

TYPICAL EXCLUSION CRITERIA   The typical criteria to consider in determining which individuals and organizations should not receive a mailing include:

1. *Those who cannot get your mailing.*
   - Those who are deceased
   - Those who are marked as **Has no valid addresses** (a checkbox on the Bio 1 and Org 1 tabs)
   - Those who are not marked as **Has no valid addresses** but do not have any good addresses.

   In The Raiser's Edge, it is a manual step to mark constituents as not having a good address in their files. Your data entry staff might mark an address as bad based on returned mail, get distracted by a phone call, and forget to mark the constituent as no longer having any good addresses. When running mailings, The Raiser's Edge can remove these constituents based on the presence of only bad addresses even though the record has not been marked as lost.

   The natural inclination will be to say "Of course I want to remove those without a good address from my mailing." But this is not always the best approach. There are situations to consider when providing direction to your staff on this issue:
   - If you are giving the data in a file to a mail house that is going to run the National Change of Address (NCOA) process on your data first, you might want *to leave in* those without good addresses. The point of the NCOA process is to find lost constituents. (Be sure to also include the field indicating the address being provided is known to be old. If the mail house cannot find a new, good address for the constituent, they can then exclude the constituent from the mailing.)

Note: NCOA

In the United States, the National Change of Address (NCOA) process is a service that the U.S. Postal Service outsources to third-party companies such as Blackbaud and mail houses. They take the postcards that people who are moving fill out, enter them into a database, and then make that information available to selected third-party companies. For a fee, those companies can take your name and address data—you must provide the old address, not simply a name—and, if they find a match, can give you the new address.

Beginning in November 2008, this process or a similar address updating process must have been done to your data within the past 95 days to get the best rates for bulk mailings. Blackbaud has a product that will do this for you in The Raiser's Edge or you can use other companies' services. Three points of caution, no matter whose product you use, to ensure the integrity of your address data is not compromised:

1. Work with your mail experts to determine which addresses to update and which to ignore (or at least test first). There are a number of codes that

(continued)

(Continued)

indicate the type of move and level of name match, and you do not want to update The Raiser's Edge with every single result returned from this process.

2. The data is typically returned in CASS-certified format, which is the most efficient format for the post office but least attractive in letters. The data is in all capital letters, there is no punctuation, and much of the information has been abbreviated. If your staff imports the data in this format into The Raiser's Edge, all your letters will show the address in that format. Work with your staff and NCOA vendor to get the addresses in better shape for letters generated from The Raiser's Edge. Your mail house will be able to CASS-certify the addresses again later when you give them back for bulk mailings where that format does not matter.

3. Work with your staff to ensure they process the updated addresses correctly. You will probably be fine if the staff processes the changes by hand, but this can take a long time. Importing the updates is quicker, but what might seem a simple task actually has some important nuances to consider in keeping the old and new address information. There are possible effects on the phone, e-mail, and web information as well.

- Remember that the step of *who* to include is a separate consideration of *what* data to include. It is possible to include in a file the constituents without good addresses but to include them without an address or with the **Has no valid addresses** indicator. Running your file this way gives you an opportunity to see those you would like to mail to based on the previous inclusion criteria. You can then determine whether further research on these lost constituents is merited. You can run a draft version of the file this way and wait to exclude these constituents when you run the final file to produce the mailing.

- You could also include those with no valid addresses if the mailing is so important you want to try anyway or if you do not trust the accuracy of the data entry on this point. Of course exercise extreme caution with this approach as it could result in a large amount of returned mail and unnecessary expense.

2. *Those who have requested not to receive your mailings and those your organization has decided to no longer mail to despite meeting the criteria.*

- *Inactive constituents.* As noted in Chapter 2, understand how this checkbox is used in your database as it has no standard meaning in The Raiser's Edge. I have repeatedly encountered organizations with no consistent use of this checkbox. Do you really want to take these constituents out of consideration for your mailing? Discuss this with your database staff.

- *Solicit codes.*
  - Look at your codes in this field carefully to decide whether each code in the list should be added to the exclusion criteria. It is important that your organization have written documentation that defines each code carefully so it is entered and used in data output properly. Remember a simple code misunderstood and entered could remove a large donor from a mailing and end the donor's contributions. For example, what does "Do Not Mail" mean? Does this truly mean this person never wants to ever receive any hard

copy mail from your organization ever again? What does "Do Not Solicit" mean? Did either of these codes ever get quickly slapped onto a constituent because the constituent complained about too much direct mail but never meant you could not ask on a less frequent basis? This is by no means merely a data entry issue. These codes remove your prospects and donors from cultivation and solicitation processes. Make sure everyone in your organization understands each code and review the lists of the constituents to whom they have been applied to make sure you agree.

- There are generally two styles of solicit codes, and they can be confusing. Make sure you think through each code when applying them to mailings.

  The first is in the style of "Do Not..." or "No..." such as "Do Not Send Invitations" or "No Direct Mail." *Select these codes for the mailings that are mentioned in the codes.* Pick "No Direct Mail" for your exclusion list if the mailing is a direct mail piece, for example.

  The other common style is "...Only" such as "Newsletter Only." *Select these codes for the mailing you are doing that is not mentioned in the code.* For example, pick "Newsletter Only" if the mailing is a direct mail piece but not if it is the newsletter.

- *Requests no e-mail.* This is a checkbox on the Bio/Org 1 tab. The Raiser's Edge will exclude these constituents automatically if you are using Blackbaud RE:NetSolutions or NetCommunity to send the e-mail. If you are preparing a file for another program, you need to include this in your criteria.

- *Attributes.* In the previous generation of The Raiser's Edge, version 6, the **Solicit code** field did not exist. The right way to do what is now handled by Solicit codes was to use an attribute to exclude constituents, typically called "Special Mailing Types." Many organizations never transferred that data to Solicit codes in version 7, so the data is still in attributes. Some organizations intentionally decided to leave this information in attributes because attributes have dates and comments for notes that Solicit codes do not. Understand your system so you can use the proper field.

  As with the "Mail To Send" attribute, you should review the constituents that have these codes before each mailing, especially those particular to the mailing, to determine whether to leave the code on the record and whether to add a date filter to the attribute in the mailing criteria.

Tip: An Important Word about Solicit Codes and "Mail to Send" and "Special Mailing Types" Attributes

It is important that these fields only be used when *there is no other field that communicates to include or exclude the constituent from the mailing.*

- *Do not use these fields for everyone to receive or not receive the mailing.* Your mailing should be based on a variety of criteria, and these fields should only be used for the *exceptions*, not as the sole determinant for inclusion or exclusion.

(continued)

(Continued)

- *Do not use these fields to handle the mailing needs for records that are already marked with the aspect that dictates the mailing procedure.* For example, do not add a "No Direct Mail" solicit code for all your monthly donors. Exclude these donors specifically on the active recurring gift information in their records. When donors are no longer monthly donors, they can go back into the direct mail process without someone having to remember to remove the "No Direct Mail" solicit code. Do not add solicit codes because someone is a board member, major donor, or major donor prospect—exclude them based on their constituent code, actual giving history or a prospect status or classification. Similarly, do not add someone to the "Mail To Send" attribute because they are a board member or prospect; use the constituent code or prospect status or classification, respectively, instead in the mailing criteria.

It is important that these fields be used exclusively for one-time, specific requests by the constituent or staff and are not otherwise indicated by any other field in the constituent's record.

Other mistakes to avoid when coding records for mailings:

- Do not mark an entire constituent record with Do Not Mail because one address comes back undeliverable. Otherwise when you get a new address for this person they still will not get mail from you because they have been marked as Do Not Mail. In this case the *address* should have been marked as bad, not the constituent.
- Make sure to enter the code at the appropriate "level." For example, is it a specific gift or set of gifts that should not receive gift acknowledgement letters? Then mark those *gifts* in the **Acknowledge** field with "Do Not Acknowledge." Or is it the constituent that should truly never receive acknowledgement letters? Only then add a solicit code of "No Acknowledgments."
- When adding these types of codes, always note who entered the code and why. The "who" should always be identified by full name, not just initials (e.g., who was "SW" six years ago and why should we care what codes she added if we do not know who she is?). For solicit codes record this in a constituent note, for attributes use the attribute's **Date** and **Comments** fields.
- Although it is important that we respect donor wishes, we do not want to "shoot ourselves in the foot" by overreaching with our codes and taking previous donors out of the prospect pool. If possible, ask the donor exactly what they want. Assign the code with the least effect that honors the request. For example, do not assign a "Do Not Mail Anything" code to a donor who says "take me off your list" on a returned direct mail piece. Try to confirm, but the constituent might have meant "only send to me one time a year" or "no more direct mail," not necessarily "I never want to hear from you again."

3. *Those who are too important or not appropriate to receive the particular mailing.*
   - *Constituent code.* Board members should not be solicited through direct mail. You might not want to send event invitations to foundations.
   - *Prospect status.* Major donor prospects perhaps should not be getting direct mail solicitations. Should someone about to be solicited for a large major gift even get your newsletter or annual report in the mail? Perhaps hand-delivery of these items is a terrific opportunity for further personal cultivation.
4. *Giving history is often used to exclude records from mailings.* It is common to have some giving requirements in the include criteria and other giving history in the exclude criteria. In fact, this is the best example where fundraisers get confused or make confusing statements in their criteria. Is the point of the giving in your criteria to note who should be included or who should be excluded? Be clear about this. For example, I often hear "...and do not include tribute donors." Does that mean, "When determining whom to include, do not consider tribute gifts—the constituent must have other gifts as well"? Or does that mean, "Take out of the mailing anyone who has made a tribute gift, even if they have other gifts, too"? The first interpretation would be put with the inclusion criteria while the second interpretation would be put with the exclusion criteria for the mailing and could yield different results.

   Common reasons for using giving history to exclude constituents for mailings include:
   - *Major donors should not receive it, such as direct mail solicitations.* It is much easier in The Raiser's Edge to exclude major donors from a mailing by considering them in the exclusion criteria than to define the inclusion criteria as "donors who are not major donors." For this reason, it is easier to think in the positive (not a bad way to live, either). Try to avoid the use of "not." Your inclusion criteria should be who *to* include. Your exclusion criteria should be who *to* exclude. Of course, each organization should and can define in The Raiser's Edge what constitutes a "major donor" using the giving criteria noted in Chapter 3.
   - *The constituent has already given to the appeal cycle.* If your organization does an annual cycle of gift renewal appeals, those constituents who have given no longer need to receive the mailing. It is easier to say, "take out those who have already given"—stated in the positive—in the exclusion criteria than "only include those who have not yet given" in the inclusion criteria.
   - *The constituent gave too recently to ask again already.* You might not want to send a solicitation on top of a gift just received.
   - *To remove active monthly donors.* Typically a benefit of being a monthly donor is not receiving every direct mail piece. Be clear about whether you want only Active recurring givers or those on Held status as well.
5. *Those outside your country.* For most mailings the expense of international postage is too much to justify including foreign constituents.

As with the inclusion criteria, be clear about the use of "and." Typically the exclusion criteria are a list, and if a constituent meets any *one* of the criteria the constituent is excluded from the mailing.

FURTHER CONSIDERATIONS FOR ORGANIZATIONS   There are two other considerations you need to make about organizations:

1. *Should organizations that do not have contacts receive your mailing?* There are two approaches to this question and you need to pick one that is right for you and your constituents.
    - *Yes, include organizations with no contacts.* We have some small businesses in our database that will qualify for this mailing, and it is okay if they receive this mailing because we are comfortable the mail will still be received and read even without a contact person's name.
    - *No, take out organizations without contacts.* If the organization does not have a contact person, do not include them in the mailing because the mailroom will not know what to do with the mailing and will throw it away.

        You can make different selections for this option between the draft and final versions of your mailing lists. Including organizations without contacts in at least the draft version of the mailing list will give you the opportunity to see who you might be missing if you exclude these organizations.
2. *If the contact for an organization also has his or her own constituent record, and the contact's individual record will also be qualifying for the mailing, do you want the contact to get one or two copies of the mailing?* If one, for which record? This is a common situation for organizations with a local mission that raise significant funds from organization donors and the contacts also give or volunteer personally. I have experienced this at both Junior Achievement and the Greater Bay Area Make-A-Wish Foundation. There are three options to answer this question:
    - *We will send a copy to each record.* Most likely the contact's personal record uses a home address and the organization record uses the contact's business address. The contact will understand that we are sending one copy home for their personal use and one copy to them at the organization for the organization's use.
    - *We will only send one copy, and it will go to the contact's home address.* Our personal relationship with the person is more important and mailing home will more likely result in a response.
    - *We will only send one copy, and it will go to the contact's work address.* The affinity is greater to the organization than to the contact personally.

Step 3. Fields

After specifying who should receive your mailing in terms of include and exclude criteria, you need to indicate to your database staff the data you need for the mailing. The next step is to list the fields that are needed.

The fields vary greatly based on the mailing type. For example, a newsletter to be mailed from a mail house might only seem to need:

- Name
- Address

A file to be sent to a direct mail consultant where RFM analysis will first be performed and giving history reflected in the mailing might require quite a few more fields.

At this step, you should just make a bulleted list of the exact fields your mailing needs. Be as specific as possible. Think through the following three needs:

1. The fields that will be printed directly onto the mailing.
2. The fields that are needed to do analysis for creating the mailing, such as gift details.
3. Other fields needed to properly manage files of data that are used outside The Raiser's Edge.

This last point is particularly important because it is the one most frequently overlooked. You need to coordinate this with your database staff. For example:

- Every list ever generated from The Raiser's Edge should always contain the **Constituent ID** field.
  - Many potential needs can arise later for which the file is almost useless if it does not have this ID. This includes bringing updates back into The Raiser's Edge, either to the constituents' records or indications to whom the mailing was sent.
  - As often as possible, the Constituent ID should be printed on the mailing itself so returned mail can be processed quickly by your database staff.
  - Print the Constituent ID on all reply cards so they can be processed as quickly and accurately as possible by your staff as well.
- If the file will be run through the NCOA process or a phone update process, the file should contain what are called "Import IDs" for the addresses and phones so that they can be properly updated when the data is returned. Work with your database administrator on this. Your role is to help the database administrator understand what will happen to the data after the list is generated and whether there is any possibility the data might be returned for update into The Raiser's Edge.

Name

When doing mailings from The Raiser's Edge, you should not ask for First Name and Last Name. The Raiser's Edge uses addressees and salutations for mailings. This ensures that each person is referred to in the format that is appropriate for them and which they prefer.

A mailing that does not include a letter such as an event invite, newsletter, or annual report should just have a field for:

- Addressee

A mailing that includes a letter should have fields listed for:

- Addressee
- Salutation

If a file is going to be created for review in Excel prior to generating the final mailing, you can also include in your request a field called **Sort Key**. This field allows you to properly sort your data alphabetically, which you cannot do with addressees. This field is in the format of last name, first name, middle name, and an internal ID number. For organizations, it contains the sort value (the value after the backslash) of the organization name followed by an internal ID. You want this field, not separate **Last** and **First name** fields, to alphabetically sort your data from The Raiser's Edge in Excel.

Address

One of the reasons for needing to know the output format of the file is for your database administrator to know how to prepare the address. If you are doing a mail merge inside The Raiser's Edge, the address field might simply be:

- Address

When doing mail merges in The Raiser's Edge, the program can create and format the entire address block as one field.

When working with mail houses and generally any computer program that requires a file, however, you want to break the address into its separate parts. A better list of fields for your mailing would look like:

- Address Line 1
- Address Line 2
- Address Line 3
- Address Line 4
- Address Line 5
- City
- State or Province
- ZIP or Postal Code
- Country

The Raiser's Edge allows up to five lines for each address. Although it is rare to have a five-line address, because The Raiser's Edge allows it, you should always request all five lines to ensure that you have a complete address. If lines three, four, and five are empty, those columns can be deleted later. But do not make this assumption until you check.

There are two other fields that are missing from the preceding list that are necessary for mailing but are not part of the address fields:

- Position
- Organization name

These fields should always be included in any address block. They are needed to handle two situations that probably occur in every mailing:

1. Individuals who have a preferred address that is a business address
2. Contacts at organizations

These fields will only be filled out with data if both:

- The mailing address for the person is a business address.
- The **Print** checkbox for each of these fields in the business address has a checkmark.

Thus, having included these fields for people who are getting their mail at home will not be a problem. In mail merges, these fields will be empty and Word will pull up the address lines so no gaps are left. In a file, these fields will just be left blank.

We will specify which address should go into these fields in Step 4 regarding field content. But include these fields in your list of fields so they are available for those getting mail at a business address.

Summary

You can see that even a simple mailing has more detail than simply "name and address" if you are doing the mailing correctly.

For example, a simple newsletter file for a mail house should probably include:

- Constituent ID
- Addressee
- Position
- Organization name
- Address Line 1
- Address Line 2
- Address Line 3
- Address Line 4
- Address Line 5
- City
- State or Province
- ZIP or Postal Code
- Country

A simple mail merge letter to be produced by a mail house in which the only variables in the letter are the name and address should have these same fields plus:

- Salutation

Step 4. Field Content

Once you have a good list of the fields you need for the mailing, the final step is to go back through each field in your bulleted list and define exactly what data should go in each field. You should do this with each field, but the main fields to consider for this purpose are the name, address, and gift fields. Apply the same concepts to any field for which a constituent can have more than one value.

Name

Your mailing file is going to have at least one field for Addressee and perhaps another for Salutation. But these are just the field names, the places in which to put the constituents' names. That information alone does not define the format of the name to go in them.

You need to specify the formats of the name to use for individual constituents and for contacts at organizations. These are different options and usually different selections are appropriate.

INDIVIDUALS   The most common option to use for individuals is **Primary addressee** and **Primary salutation**. The purpose of these specific fields is to be the option that is most commonly selected for mailings.

If the mailing should be addressed to just the main constituents, however, you should state that when explaining the contents for these fields. This will allow your staff to select the "Main Constituent Only Addressee" for those constituents that are married or partnered but have been given this additional addressee for needs like this (their primary addressee will include the spouse or partner name). For those constituents who are single, your staff can use the primary addressee.

If the mailing is a letter that is going to be signed by someone for whom an additional salutation has been set up, let your database staff know that as well. This will allow them to pull the personal version of the salutation for that staff person rather than apply the broader primary salutation. For those constituents without the personalized version, they can then use the primary salutation.

Your staff does not have an unlimited number of name options to apply to groups in your mailing. What they can do is say to The Raiser's Edge for the addressee field, "Use the X addressee type if the constituent has it otherwise use the Y type." The same is true for salutations. Typically the primary addressee and salutation are used in the X position (and Y does not matter). When not in the X position, primary addressee and salutation are always used in the Y position.

CONTACTS   The situation for contacts is slightly different because contacts can have their own constituent records and be married or partnered in those records. In that circumstance, their primary addressee and salutation is often not the first format needed because these formats might include the spouse or partner. We usually do not want a spouse or partner included when sending mail to a contact at an organization in their role as that contact. Remind your database staff of this situation to help them select the correct format for contacts for your mailing.

Address

In the previous section, we talked extensively about the address fields. These fields provide the locations where the address data will go, but we need to further define what address to put into those fields. The preferred address is not necessarily the address to use. The considerations are different for individuals and organizations.

INDIVIDUALS   Provide answers to the following questions for your staff:

■ If the person receiving the mailing has a seasonal address, should the mailing be sent to that address if it applies? I would recommend "yes"—if someone has taken the time to do this data entry then it indicates it is important to follow it.

  • If you answer this question "yes," as I recommend, you then need to provide the date *you expect the mailing to arrive in the constituents' mailboxes*. This will enable your database staff to indicate that date in The Raiser's Edge so The Raiser's Edge will pull the right address based on the seasonal setup of addresses.

■ If the person does not have a seasonal address, to which address would you like the mailing sent? I would highly recommend you use the preferred address. It is generally unwise to say specifically "home" or "business," even for event invitations. For most individual constituents in most nonprofit organizations' copies of The Raiser's Edge, the preferred address will be the home address. If a constituent has taken the time to notify you they prefer to receive their mail at work and your database staff has set up the constituent's record accordingly, it is best to honor that wish. However, if you need to do otherwise, The Raiser's Edge will accommodate mailing to addresses other than the preferred.

Note: Address Selection by Mailing Types

It is possible in The Raiser's Edge to set up a constituent with more than one mailing address and then indicate for each address what kinds of mail should be sent to each address. However, this is advanced functionality that few organizations need and it is best to avoid its use unless absolutely necessary.

■ If the person does not have any good addresses that meet the criteria you have specified, but you decided in your selection criteria to include these constituents in the mailing anyway, indicate what The Raiser's Edge should do:

  • *Leave the address fields empty*. This is a good option if you have time to review the data before the mailing. You can determine whether to invest time to find the addresses for these constituents or change your Include criteria above to remove these records from the mailing. Use this option for draft versions of the file but not for the final version of the file.

  • *Print an address anyway even if it is noted as a bad address in The Raiser's Edge*. You can specify which address to use but the preferred address would be the natural choice. This can be a viable selection if the file will be sent to a mail house for NCOA processing, the mailing is so important you want to try anyway, or you mistrust the accuracy of the address data entry in this regard and wish to give it a shot.

  If you wish to exclude from the mailing the constituents that do not have a good address according to The Raiser's Edge, return to Step 2 and the section on "Typical Exclusion Criteria" to note that there.

ORGANIZATIONS   For organizations, selecting what address to use for the mailing is more complicated. This is because organizations have contacts. Mailings should be addressed to the contacts, not the organizations. To be clear: it is the *organization* constituent that must meet your inclusion criteria in Step 2 for the mailing to be generated for it. Once the organization has been selected to receive the mailing, it is the *contact* to whom it should be addressed. This again reflects the distinction The Raiser's Edge makes in mailings between selecting the constituents to get a mailing and what data should be in the fields used for the mailing.

Provide answers to the following three questions to guide your staff to get the right contacts for organizations included in the mailing.

1. Should the mailing go to contacts at the organizations if they have one, or should the mailing be addressed to the organizations with no contact names listed even if the organizations have contacts? I would always suggest specifying to mail to the contacts if the organizations have them.

2. Because an organization constituent can have more than one contact, you need to answer some questions so those situations are handled correctly. This is a good example of the Pareto principle, also known as the 80–20 rule: 80 percent of your activity is driven by 20 percent of the cases. Although most of your organizations will only have one contact, there can be instances in your database where an organization does have more than one contact. They need to be handled correctly, despite the additional thought they require. In fact, if they are large and important enough to have multiple contacts, they might be the organizations most important to get right. If you know with absolute certainty that not a single organization in your database has more than one contact, you can skip this step—your database staff should know what to do. But be absolutely certain before you skip this step.

   There are two questions to think about and answer simultaneously: (1) which contacts, based on Contact Type, should get this mailing, and (2) if the organization has more than one of those contacts, should they each get a copy of the mailing or should only one?

   Your Contact Types should include "Primary" and a list of the *types of mailings* your organization does. Contact Types are needed to distinguish contacts for this very step. It is here where you choose the contact types to include in a mailing.

   If only one contact type is to receive it, just specify that type, such as "Primary." Typically, there should not be more than one Primary contact in an organization.

   If you select more than one contact type but only one contact should get the mailing, you need to specify the contact types *in order of importance* so the correct contact is selected. For example, you might have "Event" as a contact type for those organizations where the Primary contact said to work with another person for the organization's event participation. If the mailing you are now working on is an event mailing, you want to select the Event contact type to get the Event contacts. You also need to select the Primary type to get the Primary contacts for organizations without an Event contact.

   If both types of contacts get the mailing, there is no need to worry about order. But if you only want one copy to go to the organization, only want one contact to get a copy, you would put Event first and Primary second. Even though the Primary contact might be the more important person, the intent of this mailing is for an event and the Event contact takes precedence over the Primary contact for event mailings—that is why the Event contact exists.

You can select any combination and as many contact types as you want for the mailing. Just remember that you need to also specify whether all of them get it or only the first one by type. In the latter case, you need to have prioritized the list from most relevant type to least relevant.

Contact Selection by Mailing Types

As with individual addresses by mailing types, it is possible to create a list of mailing types and assign any combination of those types to contacts at organizations with more than one contact. If your needs are sufficiently sophisticated, you might have no choice but to use this function. However, this, too, is advanced functionality that is better avoided if not absolutely needed. It is easiest for data entry and output, if your business needs allow, to assign each contact a Contact Type and to manage your mailings with that.

3. If an organization in your mailing does not have a contact and you have chosen to allow these organizations to remain in your mailing in your recipient criteria, you have two choices as to what to do with the address fields.
    a. *Leave the address fields empty.* You can then review these organizations in a draft version of the data for the mailing and research contacts for each organization, decide it is okay to send the mailing without a contact name, or change the exclude criteria to remove organizations from the mailing entirely that do not have a contact name. Use this option for the draft versions of mailing lists only, not the final versions.
    b. *Print an address from the organization.* You may have smaller organizations that know how to handle your mail just fine without a contact name and you would like these organizations to receive the mailing. If you select this option you also need to specify what address for the organization to use (I recommend its Preferred address) and whether to remove the organization if no good address is found for it (I would recommend you do).

GIFT INFORMATION   Gift information is occasionally needed for direct mail files. Follow the checklist in Chapter 3 for *each* of the fields you request to ensure that you get accurate results.

The criteria expressed for Step 2 to identify recipients may be the same or may be different for the criteria you need on output fields. If gift information is used to determine who gets the mailing and gift information is included in the fields that come out, *state the gift information in each section independently*, even if that means you repeat it. Do not confuse the concepts of who gets the mailing and the data provided about those recipients.

For example, your criteria for *who* gets the mailing may be those who have given $1,000 or more in the past 12 months. However, you might like to see in the *output* their cumulative giving for the past five years to see your current large donors in greater context.

List in each location of your request the gift criteria for that section to ensure that there is complete understanding on your part and that of your database staff about what you need.

The Mailing Process

The key involvement your database staff need from you for the mailing is providing the guidance previously discussed. While undeniably many details are involved, these are all business decisions—fundraising decisions—not just database procedures.

There are a few other points for you to understand to complete the mailing process.

The Right Tool?

Because mailings are so common in nonprofits, there are a number of tools in The Raiser's Edge that your staff can use to generate them. It is not a matter of several right ways to do the same thing. There are many tools because each has been designed to support particular processes and needs. Here is a list of signs to watch for and guidance you can give your staff if they are struggling to give you the right results in a timely manner.

- If your staff keeps saying "query this" and "query that" be concerned. If they talk about more than one "merge query" be concerned. Query is *one* tool for generating mailings, one step in the process. For a mailing it should *never* be the only step in the process. The other tools staff should be using and might make reference to include "Mail" and "Export."
- If there are duplicates in your draft lists they can be the result of either true duplicate records in the database or using Query incorrectly. The key is to look at the Constituent IDs we said you should have in every file. If the IDs are different, these are duplicate constituent records you need to ask your staff to merge. If the IDs are the same, your staff is generating the list for you incorrectly—they are probably exporting directly from the Query tool when they should be exporting from Mail or the Export page.
- Just ask your staff: "What tools are you using in The Raiser's Edge to generate this mailing?" You want to hear, in order of preference
  - Mail, perhaps *based on* or using a query
  - Export, *based on* a query and perhaps even based on a query and Mail

    If your staff does not mention "Mail" with a capital "m"—the Mail page of The Raiser's Edge as shown in Figure 4.1—ask them why they are not using this tool. The Mail page should be used unless it just cannot do what is needed. If that is the case your staff person should be able to tell you what Mail does not do that is causing them not to use it, and they should be using Export with a capital "e." If you just hear "Query" they are almost certainly doing the mailing wrong.

To resolve the concern have your database person contact Blackbaud customer support. Then consider further training opportunities.

Drafts

When you need to know how many pieces of mail to expect, work with your database staff to set up the entire mailing process from beginning to end. Because each step of the process can remove and add recipients to the mailing, the safest way to get a count to order printing, postage, and supplies is to set up and run the process through all the steps. All of this setup can be saved so updating and rerunning it should be quite easy.

Work with your staff to ensure that the files produced for mailings are safely secured and distributed. In today's environment, it is inappropriate for unsecured spreadsheets with the names and addresses of hundreds or thousands of your constituents, and perhaps their giving history, to be sitting all over your network and flying all over the Internet. I recommend:

- *There should be one location on your network where all draft and final mailing files go.* They should *not* be stored in the network folder to which they apply (e.g., for the event, the newsletter, for direct mail) but in a "Mailing Files Temp" folder. Here they can be accessed by those who need them and then deleted after the need has passed, rather than sitting indefinitely on your network drives.
- *Files should never be e-mailed to you or others on staff.* They should be placed in this folder to temporarily hold the files. The staff people who need to access these files to review them can be sent an e-mail with a link or description of the location in which the file has been placed.
- *You and your staff should review the files from that location and not transfer them to laptops, home computers, or flash drives.* Although name and address information might not be as sensitive as social security numbers, it still should be carefully protected to avoid undue risk to your organization.

Ideally, you and your database staff should review the mailing data in Excel before they produce and send off the mailing or file. We have discussed many of the benefits and functions of reviewing drafts throughout this chapter.

When creating draft files:

- Choose to include individuals not marked with **Has no valid addresses** but that in fact do not have any valid addresses and leave the address fields blank.
- Choose to include organizations with no contacts and to leave the contact and address fields blank.
- You might want to include some of the fields that are included in the criteria about whom to include and exclude so you can ensure you are getting the right constituents. Be careful with this request because it can make the file large, difficult to create, and increase the security risk with its improper use. Focus your efforts instead on working with your database staff to enter the criteria correctly. There can be merit, however, in judiciously selecting fields for the output in the draft formats that are not needed for the final file to ensure the correct constituents are included.

Once you have the data in draft form, you and your database staff should:

- Review the records with no addresses and determine the best plan of action, either to update the records or change your final mailing production criteria.
- Look for duplicates by sorting on *each* field and scrolling through the records to review them. Sorting by addressee, sort key and address lines can each reveal different potential duplicates. Duplicates in a mailing can be due to the following three causes (use the Constituent ID to open records to help determine the cause):
  1. True duplicate constituents. Have your staff remove the duplicates that are appearing in mailings before working through an alphabetical list of all duplicates in the database.
  2. Spouses and partners that are not properly linked together and so the **Head of household** function is not removing one of them.
  3. Contacts at organizations that also have individual constituent records that are not properly linked to each other.
- Review the quality of the data, looking for spelling and capitalization mistakes, add/sals that are wrong, and address mistakes such as misspelled cities or mismatched cities, states/provinces, and ZIP/Postal Codes.

Two very important points about this process, however:

1. *Do not fix the data in Excel.* Fix the data in The Raiser's Edge. Otherwise you and your staff are wasting effort since the problem will still be in The Raiser's Edge and will appear the next time you mail to the constituent. Use Excel to identify the problem and then go to The Raiser's Edge to fix the problem. It is easy to keep regenerating the file once the process is set up.
   - If you as the fundraiser are reviewing the spreadsheet, add a column to the spreadsheet and put your notes there for the database staff to put into The Raiser's Edge later. Do not change the existing data in any way.
   - If the database staff is doing the review encourage them to do it in a query inside The Raiser's Edge rather than in Excel. When they find a mistake they can double-click on the record to open it and fix the record.
2. *Do not do the mailing from Excel.* Use Excel to review the data and fix The Raiser's Edge, but do printing and mail merges inside The Raiser's Edge. This helps ensure that your mailing is as up-to-date and accurate as possible, The Raiser's Edge data is kept up-to-date, and those receiving the mailing can be marked as having received it.

Final Production

When you have thoroughly reviewed the mailing data, deemed it correct, and the mailing date has arrived, your staff will produce the final mailing for you. (Remember, this process also applies to e-mail campaigns and telemarketing.) Keep the following considerations in mind:

- *Make sure your staff marks the records as having received the mailing.* Almost all mass mailings should be recorded in The Raiser's Edge. This helps you better visualize your contact history with specific constituents, see trends where you are sending too much or too little, and identify opportunities for constituents to remove from mailings due to repeated mailings with no response.

If the mailing asked for a monetary response, it should be added as an appeal. The package should also be added, if applicable, as well as the date the appeal was sent. Examples of these mailings include direct mail appeals, e-mail solicitations, telemarketing calls, and fundraising event invitations. If your newsletter, magazine, or annual report has a reply envelope for a gift, they, too, should be indicated as appeals.

If the mailing does not ask for a monetary response, the mailing should be added as an action. This typically applies to newsletters, magazines, annual reports, donor and volunteer appreciation events, and "thank-a-thons."

Appeals and actions can be globally added by your database administrator. Ensure that they use the correct query and process to add the appeal or action as typically several queries are involved in a mailing. If Mail is used to generate the mailing, some options in Mail can globally add the appeal automatically for the final mailing. Otherwise Mail can create a query of the actual, final list of who was in the mailing. The query can have fewer records than were in the mailing. The query only identifies each organization constituent once no matter how many of its contacts received the mailing.

Sometimes not all the names provided to a mail house are mailed based on further analysis or failed efforts at finding new addresses for lost constituents. Make sure that your staff knows what will happen to files sent to third parties for processing so they know whether to globally add the mailing to everyone in the file or wait to find out which names in the file actually received the mailing.

- *As with the drafts, make sure any files created such as Excel spreadsheets or mail merge documents are stored in a secure location temporarily and then later deleted.* The Raiser's Edge should be used to indicate who received the mailing, not old spreadsheets and Word documents kept indefinitely on the network.
- *Work with your staff to ensure a secure transmission of data files outside your organization.* Spreadsheets or .csv files should not just be attached to e-mails and sent. Sending an e-mail over the Internet is like sending a postcard through the mail. It can be intercepted and misused. Files should be password protected and ideally transmitted by hand or through secure ftp procedures (see your IT staff about these options).

Staff Training

A final note on the topic of producing mailings from The Raiser's Edge: the length and details of this chapter should help you understand that producing accurate mailings from The Raiser's Edge can be a complicated procedure. That complexity is not due to the software. The Raiser's Edge has this level of functionality because of the fundraising needs we have.

If your database staff struggles with producing accurate mailings for you from The Raiser's Edge, consider:

- Sharing this book and chapter with them
- Sending them to more advanced training on The Raiser's Edge
- Sending them to more advanced training on Microsoft Word merges

Reporting

If your mailing or e-mail was an appeal or event invitation, or if you are doing telemarketing, you are going to want to know how it performed. See Chapter 7 for recommended reports for tracking the progress of these efforts to see their success.

Putting This Together

You could ask your staff to create a mailing request form. Other organizations that use The Raiser's Edge have done this and there are examples of these forms on the Support section of the Blackbaud web site.

After much thought, I decided not to include a sample request form in this book for the following reasons:

- There are a number of different forms available already on the Blackbaud web site in electronic format where they can be easily copied, modified, and used if you wish to have a form.
- A form to cover everything discussed in this chapter would be quite long and detailed. Such a form is probably not necessary depending on the experience of your database staff. Your staff probably knows to assume certain decisions and so any form should be customized based on the needs and knowledge of your specific staff.
- This process should be a discussion, not merely the exchange of a form for data. The fundraiser asking for the mailing should meet with the person responsible for generating it.
- A form, especially one that might get filled out by hand, is not the best way to keep a history of the request and how it was fulfilled.

I have successfully generated dozens of mailing requests for all the purposes discussed in this chapter at the Greater Bay Area Make-A-Wish Foundation. I never felt the need to create a form there. Those needing mailings would send me an e-mail with an outline of their request and then we would meet to refine it. This has worked well for this organization. Larger organizations might need a form to help manage workflow for database staff, but it is unlikely an extremely long form would get filled out completely or entirely correctly—the person asking for the mailing and the person generating it from The Raiser's Edge still need to talk, if not meet face-to-face.

The best and easiest approach is to create a Microsoft Word document each time you need a mailing that has not yet been documented this way. Simply divide the document into the following six sections:

1. Brief explanation of the name, need, and purpose of the mailing.
2. Detailed explanation of the output format needed.
3. Inclusion criteria explained in detail.
4. Exclusion criteria explained in detail.
5. Segment list and criteria prioritized and explained in detail if applicable.
6. Field name and content needed. First make a list of each field needed. Then go back and explain for each field the content required for each field.

Create the Word document with these sections using this chapter and book as your reference about the details you need to communicate.

Provide this Word document to your database staff person who will create the mailing for you in The Raiser's Edge. That person should then use this document in two ways:

1. As their guidance from you on what needs to be created.
2. As the document in which to further record the exact steps and processes by which this mailing was created.

There is more discussion in Chapter 8 about the importance of policy and procedure documentation for The Raiser's Edge. In a well-run fundraising operation, important and complicated communications as we have discussed should not just be put together, they should be documented. The Word document you start provides an excellent tool for your database staff to continue to use as they make notes on the "how" and "why" of generating that communication. This document can then be used next month, quarter, or year when the next version of this mailing is needed. You both review the notes as to what was done last time and with significantly less effort the mailing is created again. This is especially helpful when staff turnover occurs.

A "real world" example of this type of mailing documentation is provided in Appendix C. In fact, this is the result of my work to produce the mailing originally requested by the fundraiser in the example at the beginning of the chapter.

Summary

The Raiser's Edge is a powerful tool for generating mailings, e-mails, and telemarketing lists for nonprofit organizations. It has been refined from years of use by nonprofit organizations who have given feedback to Blackbaud about the particular nuances nonprofits encounter in doing these activities correctly. So, the process to request a mailing, e-mail list, or telemarketing prospect pool requires some focused thought. However, it is possible if it is approached one logical step at a time.

In summary, the issues to think about and the four steps to walk through when asking for a mailing are:

1. Clearly explain the needed output for the mailing, the final format of the result. Merged letters, labels, a file for a mail house, or data for an e-mail program are all examples.
2. Clearly define who should receive the mailing, putting aside the data needed for the recipients and just focusing on the criteria the constituents must meet. Break this question into parts:
   - What is the "include criteria" the record must meet to be considered for the mailing?
   - What is the "exclude criteria" that would remove a record from the mailing even if they met the include criteria?
     If the mailing is to be segmented, identify the segments by inclusion criteria as well.

3. List the fields needed to completely produce the mailing. Include not only those fields that will be printed in the mailing but also the fields needed to calculate information to print, such as an ask amount, and fields needed to properly process the mailing when it is returned, such as IDs.
4. Specifically identify the content that needs to be in each of the fields, including the versions of constituent names to use and the addresses where the mailing should be sent.

As with any big project, this is much easier to accomplish if it is broken down into smaller parts and tackled one part at a time. Skipping this does not mean you have outsmarted the system, it probably means that your mailing is not being generated correctly.

Finally, work with your staff to review draft lists and get the database updated properly; protect your constituent data that is involved in the mailing process; ensure that the records that are receiving the mailing are marked as having done so; and document the entire process.

■ ■ ■

Almost all fundraising, not just direct marketing, has some work with mailings. We now turn our attention to the more specialized forms of fundraising, starting with events and membership.

CHAPTER 5

Events and Membership

Two specialized and important uses of The Raiser's Edge are to manage:

1. Nonprofit events, especially fundraising events.
2. Memberships, such as the programs found at zoos and museums.

The Raiser's Edge is probably the most widely used database program for both purposes.

Given the specific nature of these types of revenue generation activities for non-profits (often not even called "fundraising"), a chapter devoted to them is warranted. This chapter is intended for both those who directly participate in managing events and membership programs and others who wish to better understand how these activities should be conducted in The Raiser's Edge.

The Raiser's Edge can be used for events by both organizations that do and do not have the optional RE:Event module. Both approaches are discussed here. True membership programs, however, with membership cards, renewals, upgrade and downgrade statistics, gifts of membership, and so forth, require the RE:Member optional module. Membership in this chapter is only discussed in reference to that module.

Events and Membership in Context

The first and key item of note about events and membership in The Raiser's Edge is that they are fully integrated in all respects into the larger database. If you are an events coordinator or a membership manager, you should not skip the other chapters. Most of the book is for you, too.

- The money that comes in from your efforts still needs to fit in the campaign, fund, and appeal structure because you will use the reports tied to that func-tionality. Membership and specific events often each have their own funds, and appeals are the specific ways you solicit for event registrations and new members.
- Members and most event participants are constituents. You use the same bi-ographical, address, add/sal, and note fields as all other users of The Raiser's

Edge. The constituents' event and membership involvement is reflected in tabs for these purposes in the constituent records.

- Membership payments and event registration fees and sponsorships are gifts in The Raiser's Edge. They are linked to membership and event records, but this money is still recorded as gifts. You need to understand most of the discussion about gifts to ensure your data entry is done correctly and that you retrieve your financial results accurately. This is also of particular note for setting up security for gifts and for the data entry responsibility of doing the linking with the gift.
- Your mailings are done the same way as direct marketing and other communications. Event save-the-date announcements, invitations, and sponsorship letters are all generated through the same methods discussed in Chapter 4. Membership has special functions in Mail for membership cards and renewal notices, but mailings for member-only events and to get previous members to rejoin use the standard mailing tools. Chapter 4 is applicable to membership activities, too.
- There are event and membership reports, dashboard and queries, so understanding output is essential to you, as well.

Integrating these activities into the larger data management of the organization is one of the benefits of using The Raiser's Edge. You and your fellow users of The Raiser's Edge can see everything the constituent does with your organization. You also benefit by sharing tools and approaches to support and improve each other's fundraising methods.

The sections that follow focus on the event- and membership-specific functions of The Raiser's Edge. Those whose work falls in these areas, however, should keep the larger picture in mind.

Events

The Raiser's Edge can be used for events of all types, from fundraising events like galas, golf tournaments, and walk-a-thons to other events such as donor and volunteer recognition lunches.

The Raiser's Edge versus Excel

There are several reasons for managing events in The Raiser's Edge:

- Save-the-date cards, invitations, and sponsorship requests should be generated from within the system.
- Sponsor and registrant name and address information should be kept up-to-date in the database.
- Sponsorship and registration fees need to be recorded as gifts in The Raiser's Edge.
- The event itself can be prepared for and managed in the database, such as seating, meal preferences, name tags, budgeting, and the event checklist.
- Attendance at the event should be recorded in the constituent records for everyone who uses the database to know of the participation. This recording benefits event staff when mailings need to be done for the next event and the cycle starts over. It also benefits other staff, such as major gifts officers who want to know the events their prospects attended.

There is a tendency among some event staff to want to manage their event data in Microsoft Excel. This is due to their comfort with Excel and singular focus on the event. It is also more common for part-time and contract event staff. However, I highly encourage all event staff to use The Raiser's Edge as much as possible.

- Although I frequently hear, "We will update both our spreadsheet and The Raiser's Edge," this usually does not entirely happen. Someone updates one location and forgets the other. It gets busy as the event gets closer, and the work is put off. But after the event, the data cannot be found and the desire to do this work is lost. Your organization then looks disorganized to your constituents because the data in The Raiser's Edge is incorrect. Doing data entry twice is also highly inefficient.
- All event money should be recorded as gifts in The Raiser's Edge. Not only are the gift records needed for a complete donor history, this is the method used to post and reconcile with accounting. (See the accompanying note on this topic.) If money also has to be tracked in a spreadsheet, there is a good chance the data is going to get out of synch. And, again, double-entry is inefficient.

Note: Special Event Gifts

Most organizations enter all event payments in The Raiser's Edge as gift records, regardless of the tax-deductibility of the payment. "Gift" is the term in The Raiser's Edge for all money the database records. Gift functionality is not limited to only 100 percent tax-deductible charitable contributions. There is a **Gift Amount** field for the full amount received and a **Receipt Amount** field for the amount that *is* tax deductible.

For example, some organizations that sell things will record those sales in The Raiser's Edge on the Gifts tab. Organizations can distinguish this money from the more typical contributions by the fund or another field the purchases are assigned. They enter the purchases as gifts because this information further informs the organization's understanding of the constituent. For example, if someone makes a $250 purchase, they are demonstrating a high degree of interest in what your organization does and the ability to spend that amount and potentially contribute that amount.

The same is true for event monies. Even event payments that are 100 percent *non*-tax deductible are entered as gifts in The Raiser's Edge for the following reasons:

- Most event participants are not participating in our events for the entertainment value, as one choice among many competing for the attendees' discretionary entertainment budgets. Most participants are attending the event as a show of support in our organization and commitment to what we do. The tax-deductibility of the money is a tax issue with the IRS or other tax authority; it is not a representation of the attendee's interest and commitment to our organization. They chose to support our organization and give money to attend our event; their giving history should reflect this.

(continued)

(Continued)

- If you agree with this perspective and include event money in your cumulative recognition levels, The Raiser's Edge needs a gift record for the money to include it in all lists, reports, and other output.
- As with the earlier example about recording purchases, the amount spent on the event is an indication of potential interest and ability to give.
- The fundraising office typically does not have any database or financial system other than The Raiser's Edge. This is the place to interface with accounting to post and reconcile money. Therefore the money needs to go in The Raiser's Edge.

This applies to sponsorship fees, registration fees, and auction item purchases. The special event money, whether partially or fully non-tax deductible, is usually distinguished in The Raiser's Edge from regular contributions by a special fund or another field and by a receipt amount that is lower than the gift amount (a receipt amount of zero is fine). This allows us to generate the appropriate acknowledgements and receipts.

If your organization is an educational institution, there are special needs to consider in this regard so that data can be calculated correctly for the Voluntary Support of Education survey. Work with your database administrator to balance the needs discussed here and the requirements for this survey, such as establishing different funds for the deductible and nondeductible portions of a gift and splitting gifts with both deductible and nondeductible components.

- Excel is not a database. Everyone has stories of sorting data incorrectly and getting the cells mismatched for the rows. It is easy to both delete the spreadsheet and end up with multiple copies that are hard to reconcile. A spreadsheet is difficult for multiple people to use at the same time. It is easy to accidentally overwrite a cell. Formulas can be written wrong. Excel's flexibility is a two-edged sword.
- The Raiser's Edge, on the other hand, although more complicated than Excel, is a database designed for the tasks related to event management. It has functionality and reports specifically for the needs of events, such as the features that handle event seating. This function allows you to create groups of people that need to sit together as they register and assign them to tables a few days before the event.
- Participation and attendance in the event should be recorded in The Raiser's Edge because these are the best prospects to invite to the next event. It is often said, when Excel is being used, that this participation will be put into The Raiser's Edge afterward. More often than not, however, after an event everyone just wants to move on and this does not get done.

What starts as a good intention to use Excel for its flexibility and keep The Raiser's Edge up-to-date afterward rarely occurs. It is best to just use The Raiser's Edge as you go.

If, however, your organization decides to use Excel for events, you should still:

- Generate the mailings for the save-the-date cards, invitations, and sponsorship letters from The Raiser's Edge.

- Record all monies that come in as gifts in The Raiser's Edge.
- Update all biographical and address information for those already in The Raiser's Edge. You need to decide who should be entered into the database if they are not already there.
- Consider whether attendance information should be recorded in the constituent's record. Although it is likely that long-term access to name-tag names, seating locations, and meal preferences will not be needed, simply indicating that someone attended the event might be useful. Decide whether you only care about those who gave and spent money. This activity will be recorded in gifts. If you wish to record those who attended but did not give any money or make any purchases, we will discuss that in a following section.

Other Software

Although I recommend trying to avoid the use of Excel as your event database, there are other software programs that might need to interact with The Raiser's Edge for events. These programs play some of the roles discussed earlier instead of The Raiser's Edge.

AUCTION SOFTWARE The Raiser's Edge integrates with one auction package (AuctionMaestro Pro®), and other auction software packages are available. The Raiser's Edge itself does not have any specifically defined auction capabilities. The Raiser's Edge should record:

- The auction item donors as constituents and their donations as gifts (usually as gifts-in-kind).
- The event sponsors, attendees, and auction item buyers.
- The sponsorship and registration fees and auction item purchases as gifts.

The challenge of needing most of this information in both The Raiser's Edge and the auction software is not an easy one, but it is unavoidable. At the Greater Bay Area Make-A-Wish Foundation, we do not use AuctionMaestro Pro. We use a different package for auctions. Therefore we:

- Enter all auction item donors in both databases manually.
- Enter all auction item donations in the auction software.
- Enter all event participants in both databases manually.
- Enter all sponsorships and registration fees only in The Raiser's Edge.
- After the event, we export all auction item donations from the auction software and import them into The Raiser's Edge.
- We do the same for the auction item purchases.

"A-THON" ONLINE PROGRAMS Most walk-, run-, bike-, and bowl-a-thons today use one of the many online programs to allow participants to collect donations. Unless the program is integrated with The Raiser's Edge, and there are several that are, most of this detailed data should stay in the online program. This is certainly true of the donors of $5 and $10 gifts. In my experience most organizations have determined that mailing to and soliciting these donors further does not produce positive results.

Donors of particularly large gifts might be worthwhile to enter individually if you believe that further direct contact with them will result in more gifts later.

With the event participants themselves (the walkers, runners, bikers, and so forth), consider the time to enter them in the database with your future plans to communicate with them. You may wish to enter those who raised large sums of money. Consider leaving out those who appear to have only participated because of external influences, such as a coordinated company event, and will not be good prospects in the future. Balance the communications that your online program allows with your need for them to specifically be in The Raiser's Edge.

Gift data will need to be entered into The Raiser's Edge, and a strategy for doing so needs to be developed. One approach is to enter the data in lump sum in a gift in a constituent named "Anonymous." Be careful to distinguish *money raised* from *money given:* the money participants raise does not go in the participants' records. It goes in the donors' or "Anonymous" records and the participant is a solicitor if you record that level of detail.

RE:Event Module

If you have the RE:Event module, it provides you with:

- An Event record (see the Records page from the main screen)
- An Events tab on constituent records
- Event-related mailings
- Event categories for queries, reports, dashboards, and exports

EVENT RECORD TABS   The event has a record in the database just like a constituent does, as shown in Figure 5.1. The event is not just an option in a lookup field—there is too much data about the event itself that needs to be noted and managed. An event can have so much data that the event record has the following tabs:

- *General.* The primary setup of the event, with name, ID, dates, location, goal amount, capacity, and other fields. This is the primary access point for Seating, a powerful tool for the seating needs of dinners. Seating is also flexible enough to use to assign teams for events like golf tournaments (assign to starting holes) and bowl-a-thons (assign to lanes).
- *Prices.* Set up your sponsorship and registration levels (called "units") here so sponsor and registrant data entry is limited to those applicable to the event.
- *Expenses.* Enter budgeted and actual amounts by expense type so The Raiser's Edge can report how you are doing on actual expenses as compared to budget. The expense data is also used to calculate your net revenue objective to measure performance against it. You can also track vendors and money spent with them this way.
- *Jobs.* If your organization also has the RE:Volunteer optional module, this tab is available to help you set up and manage your volunteer needs for the event. For example, you could record: "I need three people to help for set up from 3 to 6 PM, two people to work registration from 6 to 7 PM, . . ."

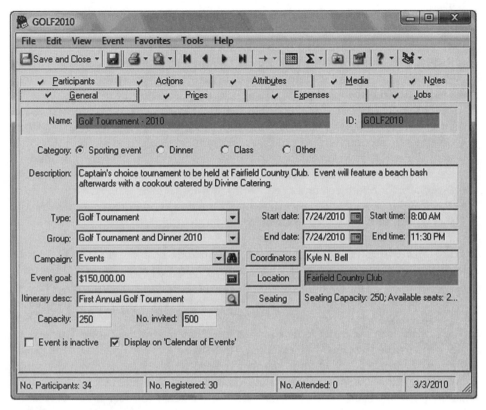

FIGURE 5.1   An Event Record

- *Participants*. Use this tab to enter your sponsors, registrants, and their guests. All details about them, from registration level to name tag and meal preferences, go here as well.
- *Actions*. Put your event checklist on this tab, and use the action functionality of The Raiser's Edge to manage it better.

Tip: Action Tracks for Events

Use an "Action Track" to set up your checklist rather than entering the checklist item by item directly on the Actions tab of an event. If you enter the items directly on the Actions tab, you need to do this again the next time you have an event. With action tracks you only set up the checklist once. You can set up several checklists, one for each event type you have. You can then assign all the actions in the appropriate action track at once to each new event. Action tracks are set up and assigned using the **Tools, Actions Tracks** menu of the main screen of The Raiser's Edge (the "shell").

■ *Attributes*. If the General tab does not provide all the fields you need for the event, you can add more here. For example, museums that offer trips create one event record for each trip and use an event attribute to specify the region for the trip. When trips to that region are offered again, a simple query finds everyone who has gone there before to invite them to go again.

■ *Media*. As with the constituent Media tab, this is not used for public relations purposes. This tab is for electronic files you wish to keep in the database about the event. Examples include the event's logo, program agendas in Word documents, program scripts, PDFs of program handouts, and so forth. Use this with discretion so your database does not get too large. It is not intended as the full document storage area for every file related to the event, just key items especially for future reference.

■ *Notes*. Write or copy and paste notes into this tab to keep further narrative details that do not otherwise have a tab in the event.

SETTING UP EVENTS   The most valuable recommendation I can provide you for events is to *set up each event in The Raiser's Edge before you do any major data entry, testing each need for the event from beginning to end*. Because events are conducted so differently at each organization, even the same kind of event, the events module in The Raiser's Edge is extremely flexible in its design. You need to decide which fields to use in what ways in order to accomplish the data tracking needs for your event.

When I worked at Junior Achievement, I tried to establish templates for the bowl-a-thons and business hall of fame dinners conducted by chapters. Even the same event within the same national organization was hard to document because each chapter did it differently. You can imagine the challenge of designing event software for the variety of events done by the entire spectrum of nonprofits in the world.

The solution to this is to:

1. Learn the software.
2. Play with the event tools to learn them better.
3. Get data entry and output examples from your last event of this type.
4. Tentatively set up the event.
5. Enter some data.
6. Test the setup for the reports and lists you need.
7. Document the procedures before you do any significant data entry, particularly the data entry procedures for participants.

Experiment with the sample database that comes with every copy of The Raiser's Edge, as well. You do not want to wait until two days before the event to figure out how to run a critical report or name tags only to discover that a key data requirement was put in the wrong field. Be sure to think about the following:

■ Do you need one event *record* for your event or more than one? For example, are the data needs different enough for your golf tournament and the dinner and auction that follow that you need two event records in The Raiser's Edge? If so, you would create one event record in The Raiser's Edge for the golf tournament and another event record for the dinner and auction. They would share the same **Group** field value, such as "201X Golf Outing." The Raiser's Edge calls this an event "group" or "grouped event."

- How do the registration units in the event relate to the campaign, fund, and appeal structure?
- Does every participant need to be a constituent, or should some simply be entered as nonconstituent participants?
- When will sponsor, registrant, and guest functionality be used?
- What entries provide most value in the widely used participant **Participation** and **Status** fields?
- Who will do gift and participant entry and in what order (gift to participant records or vice versa) so they can be linked?
- What summaries, dashboards, reports, queries, and exports should be used to give you the data you need to track your progress and preparation for the event? Chapter 7 offers some recommendations.

Events without RE:Event

If your organization does not have the RE:Event additional module, you can still use The Raiser's Edge to manage your events. Because you will not have event records without this module, you do not have the seating function and standard event reports. You will still have many of the other key elements:

- Constituent records
- Mailing tools
- Gifts
- Gift reporting and other output

To record registration, attendance, and other important details for the event participant, I recommend that you use the constituent action function if you do not have the RE:Event module. There are several ways to do this, but one approach includes:

- The action's **Category** should be "Task/Other."
- The **Action date** is the date of the event.
- The **Action type** is the name of the event.
- **Status** could contain values such as Registered, Declined, and Attended.
- The action Attributes tab can be used to define additional fields, if necessary, to track more details for the event such as meal preference.
- The action Notes tab can be used for notes such as seating preferences.

You can then use action and constituent queries, reports, dashboards, and exports to meet your output needs.

Membership

The RE:Member optional module supports organizations with membership programs such as those at museums, zoos, aquariums, public television and radio stations, and some performing arts groups. Some colleges and universities also use it to manage their alumni associations.

This module is not needed to group donors into categories for tracking donor levels or for listings in an annual report. It is also not needed for appeals that use the attraction of "becoming a member" but do not have a formal membership program. RE:Member provides functionality for joins, renewals, upgrades, and downgrades; box offices, front desks, and gifts shops where a membership card is presented for benefits; memberships given as holiday and birthday gifts; and a recurring expiration and renewal cycle.

Constituent Membership Tab

The heart of the RE:Member module is the Membership tab in a constituent's record as shown in Figure 5.2. Although the discussion here focuses on individual memberships in the examples, this tab also exists on organization constituents and is just as applicable to them.

Membership data in The Raiser's Edge is well defined, with particular terms and rules about its proper usage. This is necessary for accuracy in the important statistics that membership programs require.

Those responsible for handling membership data entry should be fully and properly trained, but the key concepts to understand about the Membership tab are discussed in the following sections.

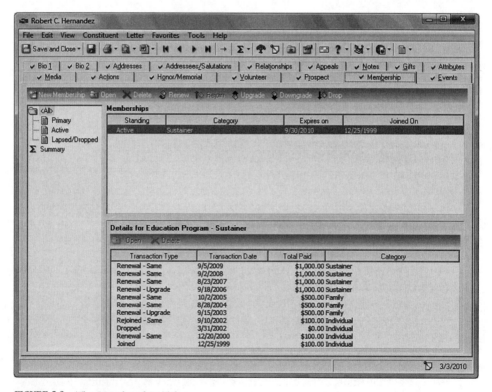

FIGURE 5.2   The Membership Tab

SUPPORT FOR MULTIPLE MEMBERSHIPS   The Raiser's Edge allows a constituent to have more than one membership. The best example of using this capability is zoos, which have the traditional individual membership program and adopt-an-animal programs. A constituent could be a member of each.

In The Raiser's Edge, membership *categories* are the usual levels we think about in regard to membership programs. Examples include Student, Individual, Family, Associate, and Patron. The categories are defined by dollar ranges and benefits.

These categories can be grouped into *programs*. A membership program in The Raiser's Edge is a group of categories for an intended audience or purpose. The categories in the program define each of the price levels for membership in the program. Typical examples include the standard programs for individuals and families; corporate and organization membership programs; and adopt-an-animal programs.

If your organization does not have multiple membership programs that one constituent could join, it is important that the database setup be marked to only allow one membership per constituent. If multiple memberships are only allowed in certain situations at your organization, you should ensure that staff clearly understand this and follow those guidelines.

To support multiple membership functionality for those who need it, however, The Raiser's Edge makes a distinction between member and membership. A member is a constituent that can have one or more memberships. This is also why there are Membership IDs in addition to Constituent IDs. The Raiser's Edge cannot force the IDs to be the same as there is the ability for more than one membership per constituent. Be careful when you and your team write queries and exports to distinguish between constituent and membership queries and exports.

STANDING   There are three "standings" calculated automatically by The Raiser's Edge. This is not an option you can change nor is any data entry on this value required. The membership standings are:

- *Active*. The constituent has a current membership, and the expiration date for it is in the future.
- *Lapsed*. The constituent's membership expiration date has passed, but the membership has not yet been dropped.
- *Dropped*. The membership expiration has passed, and after sufficient opportunity to renew the membership, it was not renewed. Dropped allows us to make a distinction between a lapsed membership that recently expired that we hope the member has just been slow to renew, and a membership long expired that has not and does not appear will be renewed. Each organization can decide how many months after lapsing a membership should be dropped.

Many organizations do not use the membership drop functionality. However, your reporting and analysis will be more meaningful if you do.

"Drop" does not mean "delete." The member and membership stay in the database. A drop is just another transaction (discussed more in the next section) to indicate that you have sent your entire cycle of renewals and the membership was not renewed. The value of this is twofold:

1. There is a qualitative difference between someone who is merely lapsed and someone who is dropped. Members often wait until after their memberships

have expired before they renew them. We may send renewals and allow response for up to three months after expiration, some organizations waiting as long as six months. When the donor sends in the membership payment, we consider this a renewal, a continuation of the existing membership. However, at some point, a lapsed membership is lapsed so long that there is little expectation of the member coming back through the usual renewal cycle. We will have to do special rejoin appeals or add these members into our standard membership acquisition appeals. When they come back, as they hopefully will, we cannot meaningfully count that as a renewal and a simple continuation of the last membership cycle. Assigning the standings of Lapsed and Dropped help us understand the membership's situation.

2. When we have dropped a member, we can use the Rejoin function if the member eventually comes back. Rejoin cannot be used otherwise. Again, our viewing and reporting becomes more meaningful when we make a distinction between those who have simply renewed and those who have rejoined after a long absence.

Dropping can be done in two ways. It can be done directly on the Membership tab (if the user has security rights) when you are told the member plans to not renew. Examples of this include the member passing away, moving out of your area, and no longer having children at home.

The more common way to drop, however, is through a global process your database administrator should run monthly. This will drop everyone who has been lapsed for the designated period of time for each membership category. There are important settings you should discuss with the database administrator to ensure that this process has the intended effect.

TRANSACTIONS   A membership "transaction" is each dated activity done to the membership. Just as a constituent can have many gifts, a membership can have many transactions.

The following membership transaction types are built into The Raiser's Edge. They cannot be changed because they are integral to the membership functionality and reporting. It is critically important that you and your data entry staff understand these types in detail. If they are entered incorrectly, they will cause serious mistakes in your reporting and they are difficult to undo, especially as time progresses.

- *Join(ed)*. This is the only option available for a new member and is started by clicking the **New Membership** button. The common mistake I see is that data entry staff does not understand the difference between a new membership and a renewal or rejoin on an existing membership. A new membership should only be added if the member has *never* had a membership in the program before. It is imperative that the data entry staff be well trained on this point and you work with your database administrator to set up the options in Configuration so The Raiser's Edge can help avoid this problem.
- *Renew(al)*. When you get payment for the next year on an active or lapsed membership, that is a renewal. The existing membership is selected, but a new transaction is added to it, called the renewal transaction, to extend the expiration date typically for another year. There are three types of renewals:

- *Same.* The membership category selected for the renewal is the same category as the previous transaction. Family category to Family category, for example.
- *Upgrade.* The membership category selected for the renewal is a more expensive category than the previous transaction. Family category to Associate category, for example.
- *Downgrade.* The membership category selected for the renewal is a less-expensive category than the previous transaction. Family category to Individual category, for example.

    If the category of the renewal transaction is not the same as the previous category, The Raiser's Edge will make the user select either upgrade or downgrade within the renewal.

- *Upgrade and Downgrade.* These options are another common source of confusion. They are important to understand for your membership reporting to be accurate. These options should only be used for *same-cycle* upgrades and downgrades. They should *not* be used for renewals. For example, a family buys a membership for the Family level online. When they get to your facility a few days later, they realize they really could use the benefits of the Associate level. They approach your front gate and ask to switch. They pay the difference and are now an Associate member. *However, their expiration date was not extended.* This is what is meant as "same cycle." This example is an Upgrade, which is not the same as a Renewal–Upgrade.
- *Drop.* Dropping was discussed in the previous section. This is the transaction that is added manually or globally when a lapsed membership has exceeded the number of months you specify.
- *Rejoin.* When a dropped membership is restarted, a new membership should *not* be added. Instead, the membership that is being picked back up should be given a rejoin transaction to make it active again and indicate the new expiration date.

■ ■ ■

The importance of understanding the concepts discussed in these sections on the constituent Membership tab cannot be overstated. None of the built-in processes for managing membership will work well for you if your data entry staff does not follow these procedures or membership staff does not understand them when pulling data.

Other Membership Highlights

Remembering that this book is intended for fundraisers and not data entry staff, and is conceptual rather than technical, there are other key points to keep in mind in managing membership in The Raiser's Edge.

- The Configuration page of The Raiser's Edge has a number of important options to set up your membership categories and manage membership activity in The Raiser's Edge. For example, this is where you specify when memberships expire and whether a constituent can have more than one membership. If you are responsible for membership at your organization, you should discuss and understand exactly how these options are set up in your copy of The Raiser's Edge to ensure that they reflect the policies for your membership program.

- The money for membership payments is considered gifts in The Raiser's Edge. They should be entered as such when doing the membership entry. All discussions in this book about good gift practices therefore apply to membership also.
- The Mail page has a tool for generating membership cards. It has a number of special features such as marking the card as printed in the membership record. You should try to use this to generate your cards.
- Also in Mail is the tool for generating membership renewal notices. This is sophisticated enough to generate the appropriate renewal number for each expiring membership. However, most organizations find it more straightforward to set up one set of parameters for membership renewal notices for each notice in the cycle.
- The Raiser's Edge does a good job handling gifts of membership. These are situations in which one person buys another person a membership, such as a parent buying a child an adopt-an-animal membership at the local zoo for the child's birthday. There is functionality to record this, but keep this added complexity in mind when creating the membership cards and renewal notices. The complexity is driven by the need, not the software, but The Raiser's Edge does accommodate it. You just need to ensure your setup of the tools recognizes this.
- The Raiser's Edge supports "joint memberships." A joint membership is when two or more constituents share the same membership. The most common example of this is when spouses and partners are on the same membership but each have their own constituent record. One person needs to be identified as the "primary" member and the membership will be set up on that constituent's Membership tab. The Membership tab of the joint member will reflect the membership as well, but it is one membership showing on two members' records.
- The RE:Member optional module adds a Scanning page to The Raiser's Edge. When the software is available at the site's entrance point and gift shop, the membership cards can be scanned using a simple scan "gun" attached to a normal computer. The Raiser's Edge will notify the attendant of the status of the membership and if desired, will mark the member's record to indicate the card has been used. This tool supports the cheaper (in the long run) and more environmentally friendly use of permanent membership cards. These are cards that include barcodes to identify the membership but do not have the expiration date printed on them.

Summary

The Raiser's Edge is a good tool for managing events, whether your organization has the RE:Event module or not. The module is sophisticated and does take some time to learn and set up. But once that has been done, you are able to reap many benefits from keeping event data in The Raiser's Edge rather than using Excel.

Membership is an incredibly robust module. Perhaps more than other modules and uses of The Raiser's Edge, it is important that membership staff understand it and ensure it is used correctly. Membership transactions build on each other year after year. Unlike gifts, which are independent transactions and can always be inserted and changed retroactively (with appropriate security rights), membership transactions cannot. The membership statistics, so important to membership and organization management, rely on this tightly controlled environment.

Both event and membership activities are tightly integrated into The Raiser's Edge. This provides benefit to those doing events and membership to be able to benefit from the work of colleagues and to use the many powerful tools The Raiser's Edge offers. It also benefits other fundraisers and staff so they can see the full picture of the constituent's involvement in your organization.

■ ■ ■

Now that we have addressed the direct marketing, event, and membership approaches to fundraising, let us turn our attention to the uses of The Raiser's Edge for major gifts and grants.

CHAPTER 6

Major Gifts and Grants

The Raiser's Edge has been designed to be your organization's *single* fundraising database. It does a great job tracking data and creating mailings for direct marketing and other mass communications. But it is also a tool that has been designed for:

- Major gifts fundraising with individuals.
- Institutional fundraising with corporations and foundations through direct asks, grant applications, and proposals.

This chapter is about how to manage these processes in The Raiser's Edge.

"Major gift" needs to be defined by amount in the context of what is appropriate for your organization. It might be $1,000, $10,000, or $25,000. For the purposes of this chapter, however, major gifts prospects are *individuals and organizations whose potential giving to you is large enough that they warrant individualized fundraising attention*. The approach might be something as simple as picking up the phone and making a one-on-one ask based on a personal relationship. Usually, it is more than that, however, and involves at least one personal visit.

You need to decide after reading this chapter which constituents deserve the level of attention and data entry this chapter discusses. There is a spectrum in fundraising approach. At one end are those only solicited by mass solicitation such as direct mail. At the other end are your largest donors whom you would only ask through a direct, face-to-face request. In between are a group of prospects and donors who are increasingly being referred to as "mid-level donors" or "middle donors."

The tools discussed in this chapter do not need to be applied in the same way to every prospect in your database who is more than a direct marketing prospect. Consider this chapter a toolbox from which you can select those tools that best meet your needs. You need to meet with your database staff to determine what you think is the appropriate level of data entry resource to manage the prospects.

This chapter has equal applicability to both raising money from people and raising money from organizations. As someone who has done both, I learned and practiced that good institutional fundraising is as much about relationship building as it is for individual fundraising. We should not simply be pulling grant applications off the Internet, filling them out, and sending them in. We should be using every opportunity to establish a relationship with the organization and its representatives.

There may be situations where there is nothing more you can do but obtain the giving guidelines and send a grant application. However, the effort involved and the size of requests even in those situations typically justify using much of this same functionality so they can be tracked.

Institutional fundraisers need to make the same judgment call about the level of effort of data entry that provides value. There are certainly plenty of organizations that can be solicited through direct mail and event invitations (typically small businesses). There are large corporations and foundations you would never approach this way. And there are those in between. Select the functionality for each group of prospects that is right for them and right for you.

All major gifts and grants fundraising should be managed through The Raiser's Edge. All prospects, contacts, interactions, deadlines, asks, and gifts should be in The Raiser's Edge. Do not track this fundraising in a spreadsheet. The Raiser's Edge is well equipped to manage major gifts fundraising with individuals, corporations, and foundations, and your institution will be best served if you use it for that purpose. (For an explanation why, see the section on the use of Excel in Chapter 5 on page 128.)

Note: Governments

The Raiser's Edge can be used to track fundraising and gifts from governments and their agencies if you wish. This is typically done if this money is raised by the development department and not by a separate "government contracts" person or group.

Once more, if you are an educational institution participating in the VSE survey you will need to be careful to code these constituents and their gifts for proper VSE reporting.

A few other notes before we begin:

- "Prospect" is used in this chapter as *those we are pursuing for a gift*. This is true whether or not they have already given. This chapter does not define prospect as "those who have never given." In fact, our best prospects are usually those who have previously given.
- "Moves management" has become synonymous with "major gifts fundraising" as the term is used by many fundraisers, but they are not the same thing. Moves Management® is an approach, a methodology, a system to do major gifts fundraising. In fact, it is even trademarked. It is one way to do major gifts fundraising. We discuss this more in the second part of this chapter.
- Although we usually make a distinction in the industry between "major gifts" and "planned gifts," many planned gift fundraising solicitations use exactly the same approach as that used for major gifts. Some planned gift prospects may receive invitations to a seminar (see Chapters 4 and 5), attend, and then let you know your institution has been added to their wills. Others will require a strategic and methodical approach to ask for or get the gift. This chapter is

equally applicable to that latter type of planned giving fundraising even though it refers to "major gifts" throughout.

- This chapter continues the approach of the book thus far to keep the discussion conceptual. The sections discuss the tools available and concepts you as a fundraiser should understand. You need to work with your database administrator to implement the details on data entry and reporting procedures.

- Finally, I am not telling you as a fundraiser how to do your fundraising. Although I was fundraiser myself, with my share of success doing it, I am not a fundraising consultant. The objective of this chapter is to explain to you the tools available for you to manage major gifts fundraising in The Raiser's Edge so you can apply them to your needs. You should develop your own major gifts methodology and system, whether you use Moves Management or another. Then integrate these tools into that system. I do not believe the "tail should wag the dog": The Raiser's Edge should not dictate how you fundraise but should support it. The methods discussed here are examples and models you can follow or modify as you wish.

What I do hope to accomplish with this chapter, however, is to encourage and help you establish and document your major gifts methodology and its use within The Raiser's Edge. Many of the organizations I have worked with just "do" major gifts and are unable to articulate any plan or process with how they do it. Other than knowing at the end of the fiscal year how much was raised, some organizations have little idea what their pipeline looks like, whether prospects are getting too little or too much contact, who has responsibility for what contact, or how the major gifts officers are spending their time. The Raiser's Edge can help manage each of these tasks, both for major gifts officers and their managers.

Note: Major Gifts Pipeline

Major gifts fundraising is a process based on the premise that it takes time to prepare and ask for a major gift. For example, it might take 18 to 24 months between the time a major gifts prospect is identified and the prospect is asked for a gift. During and after that time, the prospect is at different stages in the process. The organization is working with the prospect according to the requirements of each stage. Common stages include research, cultivation, solicitation, and stewardship.

Fundraisers and their managers need to know how many prospects are at each stage of the major gifts process. This view is called a major gifts pipeline. Prospects are entering the pipeline through identification and coming out the other end (we hope!) after stewardship for a major gift contribution. For long-term success and cash flow, fundraisers and particularly managers need to make sure that, at each stage, there are a sufficient number of prospects to ensure continual movement through the pipeline and resulting major gifts.

In truth, the process is more like a river flowing out of a lake with inlets and outlets along the way, eventually ending up with much less, but the best, water. Unlike a pipeline, there is not a continuous flow from beginning to end. But pipeline is the term used for simplicity to visualize the process of flow.

(continued)

(*Continued*)

A sample of a pipeline is shown in the dashboard panel in Figure 6.1.

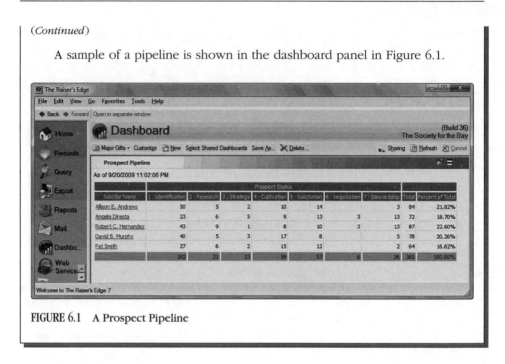

FIGURE 6.1   A Prospect Pipeline

This chapter is divided into two parts to meet the variety of needs organizations have to conduct major gifts fundraising.

1. *Basic tools*. The first part discusses the basic tools available in The Raiser's Edge to manage the core activities of major gifts fundraising. This discussion is primarily focused on the tools in The Raiser's Edge you can use to master the key elements of a small, simple major gifts practice.
2. *Life cycle of a major gifts donor*. The second part takes a more advanced and intensive approach. It outlines the typical life cycle of a major gifts prospect in The Raiser's Edge and applies the Moves Management methodology. This section relies heavily on the RE:Search optional module for The Raiser's Edge, but there are also explanations for taking this more sophisticated approach and applying it without that module.

From these two parts, it is hoped that you will select the approach that is right for your organization.

Basic Major Gifts Fundraising Tools

All copies of The Raiser's Edge, regardless of optional modules, have the following key tools for major gifts fundraising:

- Constituent records
- Relationships

- Solicitors
- Notes
- Actions

Constituent Records

A major gifts prospect and donor uses the same constituent record we have discussed in previous chapters. All name, address, phone, add/sal, and other biographical and demographic fields are the same. There is one record and one view of the constituent. This supports your major gifts work by allowing you to understand the prospect's full relationship with your institution and to benefit from others' work to update the record. It also informs other staff members' work, such as mailings, so they can include or exclude your prospects as you wish.

Relationships

Because much of major gifts fundraising is about relationships, the Relationships tab is primarily of use for major gifts prospects. We should record the relationships we already know for all constituents, especially spouse and partner names. However, there is little value in seeking out family relationships to record for direct marketing constituents, but it is essential for major gifts work.

- Individual Relationships
  - Enter children's names and birthdates or ages here so you can ask about the children when talking to and meeting with your prospects.
  - Consider adding details on past marriages, especially when ex-spouses are living, as this can add complexity in multigenerational gifts.
  - Enter the prospect's friends here so you can involve them in the cultivation process.
  - Enter the prospect's legal, financial, and investment advisors so you can communicate with them as appropriate in discussions regarding funding a major gift or setting up a planned gift.
  - Record program officers' names and phone numbers for future contacts at foundations and corporations.
  - List employees and board members of the organization who might be points of leverage in assisting with funding your request.
- Organization Relationships
  - Enter business relationships such as places individual prospects work and corporate boards on which they serve to help you monitor their wealth and to provide you topics for conversation as their companies and industries appear in the news.
  - Enter religious affiliations so you can be sensitive to religious needs, schedules, and perspectives.
  - Enter other nonprofit involvement, especially current and past board memberships, to track areas of interest and levels of involvement, identify opportunities for research on previous giving, and perhaps even note "competition" for a major charitable gift.

Solicitors

On the Relationships tab is a relationship category called "Assigned Solicitors." The most direct use of the solicitor functionality is the person assigned, whether staff or volunteer, who is going to ask the prospect for a gift. If the ask does not require a cultivation strategy and reporting on the solicitor's activities, there is no need to use this functionality. The data entry time will outweigh the benefits. Solicitor functionality is good to use when you need to:

- Know who has been assigned to the prospect; in whose portfolio does the prospect belong?
- Manage a long-term cultivation and solicitation plan for a major gift ask.
- Track the activities of your solicitors to be able to measure their performance and results.

Other uses for assigning solicitors include:

- Recording the fundraiser or prospect researcher who is the prospect manager, or "moves manager," responsible for working in the background to ensure that the prospect is kept moving through the process.
- Noting other individuals involved in the major gifts cultivation process who might not be the ones who make the ask, but are key players in the cultivation and solicitation strategy.

There is a field in the solicitor assignment for defining these roles (**Solicitor type**). There are also fields for noting the assigned date range, an expected or desired amount, and notes. A prospect could have multiple solicitors, each for a different purpose, so solicitors can also be assigned based on campaign, fund, and appeal. For example, Samantha could be assigned to Robert to ask him for his capital campaign gift, but David is going to ask him to renew his event sponsorship.

Solicitors must be constituents. A constituent is marked as a solicitor using the **Is a solicitor** checkbox on the Bio 1 tab. The **Details** button next to that checkbox allows you to:

- Assign goal amounts to your solicitors to record how much you hope they will raise or how much they have committed to raise. You can also group your solicitors into teams with this tool. We used this concept at Junior Achievement to inspire and assist board members to raise money.
- See to whom the solicitor is assigned. Keep in mind:
  - The assigned solicitor on the Relationships tab shows who is working with this constituent for a gift.
  - The solicitor **Details** button on the Bio 1 tab shows who this constituent is assigned to work toward a gift.

You can easily construct a query to get a list of prospects for each solicitor. There are also a number of standard reports that show the success of the solicitors. For these to work, however, it is important that you provide the solicitors' names to gift entry staff and the solicitors are linked to the gifts they raise.

Notes

Notes are a powerful tool for major gifts fundraising because you have the following kinds of narrative information to record:

- The giving interests and background of your prospects.
- The prospects' wealth history and its current accessibility.
- Cultivation and solicitation plans.
- Development thoughts for proposals and grant applications.

It is important that the history of interactions with your prospects and scheduled future interactions not be entered in notes; they go in actions. Information that has its own fields elsewhere in the constituent record should be stored in those fields as well, not in notes.

Actions

Of all the tools noted in this section for major gifts fundraising, actions are the most important. This is where you record:

- Phone calls
- E-mails
- Visits and meetings
- Mailings

Record these past, present, and future interactions with your prospects whether you or the prospects initiate them.

Recently, I have noticed a greater interest in tracking not just the results of major gifts fundraisers' activities—the gifts—but the activity itself. Actions are the way to do this. The Raiser's Edge has standard reports that will count actions in time periods you define, and break them out in a number of ways, including by:

- *Action solicitor*. The person doing the action with the constituent, whether staff or volunteer.
- *Action category*. The "mechanics" of the interaction as listed above (they are built into the system and cannot be changed because they determine other functionality).
- *Action type*. A list you and your database staff create to describe the purpose, intent, or details of the action.

The **Action type** field is particularly important because you will want to use it to make the reports more meaningful. A superficial "meeting" while the major gifts officer was out for dinner and a "meeting" for a face-to-face personal solicitation do not carry the same weight. Some fundraisers make a distinction between "foreground" activities, those interactions which meaningfully move the constituent further toward a gift, and "background" activities, those interactions we have that are necessary but not significant, such as sending birthday cards. The fundraisers in your organization, including fundraising management, should decide what action types are meaningful to measure. Another option is to add a new field to actions (an action attribute) where a foreground versus background-type designation can be specified.

Remember to limit the notes within an action to the details of the action itself—preparation notes, logistics, reminders, and outcome summary. Substantive findings about prospects, such as their giving and interests, and your thoughts for future cultivation and solicitation strategy should be recorded in a constituent note or "proposal" (discussed later in this chapter) rather than buried within actions. You will appreciate this effort later when you use the constituents' records to understand their current status and do not have to read back through every action's notes.

Who Does the Data Entry?

Actions are the proper place to store call reports. Should major gifts officers be entering the call reports and other action information in the constituent records themselves?

I do believe that, as much as possible, major gifts officers should be out of the office interacting with prospects and not sitting in their offices in front of their computers. For example, when a major gifts officer goes on a visit to a prospect's home or office, as soon as the fundraiser leaves, she should write her call report, even while sitting in the car in the parking lot, while all the details are as fresh as possible. If she has wireless access and a virtual private network (VPN), then the details could be entered into The Raiser's Edge. However, it is likely that the best that can be hoped for is access to a laptop computer and notes typed in a Word document or e-mail.

What should be done with those notes? There are several options:

- If there is sufficient support staff, these notes could be e-mailed to a support person who would then do the data entry into The Raiser's Edge.
- Another approach with support staff is for the fundraiser to copy the call report into the notes of an action. A query can be set up for support staff to find the action and then distribute the call report notes throughout the constituent record as appropriate.
- Without support staff, the fundraiser should do her best to enter the call report findings throughout the constituent record where the data properly goes.
- The worst case should be that the call report notes get entered into an action note without any further distribution of the information into the proper fields in The Raiser's Edge.

At a minimum, the call report needs to be in The Raiser's Edge. Hard copy–only call reports do not make sense for an organization that has The Raiser's Edge. Furthermore, The Raiser's Edge will be more useful to everyone if data is stored where it belongs rather than the entire call report just put into action notes. Each organization needs to determine for itself the balance between providing support staff to do data entry correctly and major gifts fundraisers being responsible for this task themselves.

My experience has repeatedly shown that the key determinant to success with entering the call report is the expectations and requirements put into place by fundraising management. It is understandable that fundraisers usually do not enjoy the process of making notes after interactions with constituents. I admit that even I, as a database consultant, do not enjoy the process of note taking after phone calls and visits with clients. But it is part of what we must do in order to perform our jobs well. The best success with getting data recorded in The Raiser's Edge has been at organizations where the senior fundraising manager has made it a requirement, only accepting reporting of activity directly from The Raiser's Edge: "If it's not in The Raiser's Edge, you didn't do it. Don't send me an e-mail, Word document, or spreadsheet. If I can't run a standard report from The Raiser's Edge to see your activity, I will assume it hasn't been done and evaluate performance accordingly." Some organizations even go to the extent of not reimbursing fundraisers for their expenses until a backup call report from The Raiser's Edge is supplied in addition to the expense receipts.

Regardless of who does call report data entry, all fundraisers should be required to use The Raiser's Edge in four ways:

1. If fundraisers are in the office or otherwise have access to The Raiser's Edge on their computers (such as having been provided VPN access for remote connection to e-mail and files), they should enter actions into The Raiser's Edge. Any fundraiser capable of using e-mail and being a fundraiser in these times has the ability to learn the few steps necessary to add an action and do it correctly.
2. Similarly, fundraisers should be required to add constituent notes when The Raiser's Edge is available.
3. Other types of data entry might be best left to support staff to manage—there are a number of variables in making that determination. However, all fundraisers should be able to open a constituent, review the tabs, and understand the information.
4. Finally, The Raiser's Edge makes reporting incredibly easy to access. Although it often takes some thought to set up a report so that it produces the specific information desired, the report can be saved. Additionally, it can be saved as a favorite on the Home page of fundraisers so that running the report requires nothing more than a single click, just like clicking on a hyperlink on a web page. Once reports are set up for fundraisers by database staff, they should run some of the reports themselves. (A consulting colleague shared with me that she had a client whose executive director wanted "the Friday report." My colleague set up the report, saved it on the executive director's Home page, and named the link "click on me on Fridays.")

Instructions for the first three activities were provided in Chapter 2. Fundraisers who send e-mail, use the calendar and contacts in Outlook, and open, create, change, and save simple Word documents and Excel spreadsheets, can do these easy activities in The Raiser's Edge, I promise you.

The Life Cycle of a Major Gifts Donor in The Raiser's Edge

In the previous part we discussed the tools in The Raiser's Edge that are best for major gifts fundraising. They can be used in any combination and in any order.

However, many clients have shared with me over the years that seeing these tools demonstrated in the logical order of conducting major gifts fundraising makes more sense to them.

I first presented the concepts discussed in this part in 2004 at Blackbaud's annual Conference for Nonprofits in Charleston, South Carolina, in a session titled "The Seven Stages of a Major Gifts Donor in The Raiser's Edge." Rather than just discussing the tools available, I presented one option for making something using those tools. For example, if The Raiser's Edge is a toolbox with a hammer, saw, screwdriver, pliers, and other tools, let us not just talk about what each tool does independently. Let us create a blueprint for a chair, and use those tools to create a chair.

This part is one model, one blueprint, of how to use The Raiser's Edge to manage major gifts fundraising. I was pleased to see at the 2008 and 2009 Blackbaud conferences several presentations where representatives of different organizations used the same tools to follow different blueprints and make different versions of the same major gifts fundraising "chair."

Based on your personal fundraising education and experience, what has been successful at your organization with your constituents, and the level of resources your organization can invest in this process, outline the major gifts fundraising process you wish to follow with your prospects. Fill in that outline with the details for your fundraising approach. Finish by creating a process similar to the following for how The Raiser's Edge can be used to support your major gifts approach.

Introduction to the Life Cycle

The setup and use of The Raiser's Edge for major gifts fundraising should be based on how one does major gifts fundraising. The model discussed next is based on two ways of thinking about major gifts fundraising:

1. The seven stages of a major gifts prospect
2. Moves Management

The "seven stages" are the traditional way to think about the progression of a prospect through the process, from both the prospect's and fundraiser's perspectives. No matter the number of stages or names they are assigned, prospects usually move through a similar experience when being prepared and asked for a major gift.

Some fundraisers and fundraising consulting firms have developed particular approaches with terms, concepts, and activities to help fundraisers manage this process more easily. Whether called "approaches," "methodologies," "strategies," or "methods," they are particular ways of thinking about and doing the major gifts fundraising process, of taking a prospect through the stages. We use Moves Management as an example here, but there are plenty of others to choose.

I find the two concepts used together create a powerful way to plan, conduct, and manage the major gifts process, both as a fundraiser and as a user of The Raiser's Edge.

THE SEVEN STAGES   When we visualize the major gifts process, we think of it as that—a process. New prospects ideally move through this process from beginning to end through a series of stages. Each stage identifies where the prospect is in the process and what activities our organizations should be undertaking with the prospect.

It is not your institution that is going through the major gifts process, it is the prospect. I call the process the "life cycle of a major gifts prospect." Most organizations are working with dozens to hundreds of major gifts prospects at a time, with many prospects in each stage. Fundraising managers like to know how many prospects are at each stage, allowing them to measure whether the right kind of activity is occurring at levels sufficient to ensure ongoing major gift contributions.

The number and names of stages that major gifts fundraisers use typically vary among four, five, or seven categories. A simple approach would be:

1. Identification, frequently called Discovery
2. Cultivation
3. Solicitation
4. Stewardship

An approach I learned when I worked at Brakeley Ltd., a fundraising consulting firm in London (www.brakeley.com), was to use seven stages:

1. *Identification.* Determining who is a potential candidate for the major gifts process.
2. *Research.* Whether full-scale research by a prospect researcher or information gathering using the Internet and contacts, finding information that will help to "qualify" the prospect by demonstrating whether the prospect has sufficient inclination (likelihood and interest in supporting the organization) and capacity (wealth) to make a major gift and that will help inform the initial strategy.
3. *Strategy.* Creating the cultivation and solicitation plan that will most likely lead to the largest and most fitting major gift from the prospect.
4. *Cultivation.* Collecting information from the prospect and preparing the prospect for the ask.
5. *Solicitation.* Making the ask. This is a stage, rather than just a brief activity, because a major gift ask might take some preparation, consideration, and follow-up.
6. *Negotiation.* Discussing with the prospect how best to make the gift and schedule, fund, and recognize it. The term is not meant to indicate any adversarial relationship, but instead to reflect the reality that completing a major gift might involve conversations with spouses and partners, family, lawyers, financial and investment planners, accountants, and the organization.
7. *Stewardship.* Thanking and recognizing the donor for the gift.

The process is not linear; Stewardship is not the end of the process. Once a gift has been properly thanked and recognized, the prospect may be entered back into the process at the appropriate stage to begin the cycle again. The process is a circle that once entered, continues until the prospect either passes away or is no longer able or interested in making another major gift.

A final "stage" that is necessary in this process for a database and tracking perspective is "Dropped," indicating the prospect had entered the major gifts process but has since been removed. A prospect would be removed either because the organization determined the person did not have sufficient inclination or capacity for a major gift or the prospect self-identified as not having interest.

You can define as many stages as you wish to use and name them what you want. When they are set up in The Raiser's Edge, however, your reports will perform better if the names contain the order, such as:

- 1-Identification
- 2-Research
- 3-Strategy

Continue this and end with "9-Dropped" no matter how many stages you have. This clearly indicates it is last in the order and not really a stage in the major gifts process; it is only a holding category for these constituents. Use "9" so The Raiser's Edge, and if exported, Excel, will sort them properly.

MOVES MANAGEMENT   There are several approaches that have been developed over the years by fundraisers to help more clearly define what should be done when working with a prospect through these seven stages. Probably the most well known is Moves Management, which we talk about in this section. Other examples include:

- Terry Axelrod's system called Benevon, a four-step approach oriented toward "sustainable funding" and multiyear gifts through the use of events. (benevon.com)
- Advancement Resources has developed the "Donor Commitment Continuum," so far primarily delivered to the university sector. The objective is to help fundraisers focus on the emotional commitment of prospects to the mission or a project of the organization and move the prospects to the right on the continuum so they make larger and more meaningful gifts. (advancementresources.org)

The purpose here is not to recommend or endorse a particular approach or firm. In my consulting experience I have frequently observed organizations that are not able to articulate how they do major gifts fundraising, what they do at each stage (if they even use "stages"), or what terminology they use. The extent of their major gifts fundraising appears to be getting together with prospects and occasionally asking for a big gift. There seems to be little more structure to it than that. If your major gifts program is truly that simple, the basic tools previously discussed will suffice.

However, if you have, or wish to have, a more rigorous program, The Raiser's Edge cannot be set up to track what you cannot define. The purpose of mentioning these approaches is to recommend that you articulate your own, adopt one of these, or use another so that you can describe a process, *your* process, for how your organization raises major gifts. *Then* that process can be set up in The Raiser's Edge. The model that follows is just an example, not *the* way to do major gifts fundraising in The Raiser's Edge.

■ ■ ■

Moves Management is a disciplined approach to major gifts fundraising. It dates back years to G.T. "Buck" Smith and David Dunlop of Cornell University. I learned about Moves Management in the early 1990s from William "Bill" T. Sturtevant of the University of Illinois Foundation and the Institute for Charitable Giving at truly the best and most powerful fundraising training I have ever taken. I highly recommend his book *The Artful Journey: Cultivating and Soliciting the Major Gift* and his seminar, "Seize the Opportunity: Developing a Fail-Proof Major Gift Program," both available from the Institute at www.instituteforgiving.org.[1]

Summarized briefly, this approach to major gifts fundraising for individuals guides us to be strategic and purposeful in our major gifts work. Rather than cultivating prospects until they seem ready for solicitations, we should understand where prospects currently stand, develop strategies of "moves" that will prepare the prospects for the asks, implement those moves, and then make the asks. Each cultivation activity is planned, each with an objective to learn or communicate critical information, to motivate and move prospects toward acceptance of a gift request. We do not just meet with people because it has been a while since we last saw them; we meet with them as part of scheduled steps in strategies with objectives for those meetings.

Despite the term "move" and the planned, strategic nature of this approach, it is by no means intended to be manipulative. As Sturtevant states, "The successful fundraiser always makes paramount the interests of his or her donors" (p. 6). Moves Management simply recognizes that we are professionals with a responsibility to our institutions to be using our time productively. We should be spending time with prospects in the furtherance of that responsibility, but always in the most respectful, appropriate, and ethical ways.

Typically a strategy involves a number of moves, the last one being the solicitation. A move is equivalent to an action in The Raiser's Edge.

Particular attention is paid in Moves Management to the people involved. The key individuals participating in addition to the prospect include:

- *Natural Partners.* These are the people the prospect knows who can assist us in the cultivation and solicitation of the prospect. The assistance can be just providing information or active involvement in the process. They should be recorded in The Raiser's Edge as individual relationships.
- *Primary Player.* Although the term is uncomfortable, the concept is critical. This is the person who should be in the forefront of the prospect's cultivation and ideally the person who should ask for the gift. This should be the person the prospect can least say "no" to when asked for a gift. This person should be a peer of the prospect or a senior person at your organization. This person should be included in The Raiser's Edge as an assigned solicitor. Instead of "Primary Player," you might want to use "Primary Solicitor" or simply "Primary" as the solicitor type.
- *Secondary Players.* These are others who will be actively involved in the cultivation and solicitation but are not the primary solicitor.
- *Moves Manager.* Preferably the primary and secondary solicitors do not include the major gifts officer. Managing others to do the cultivation and solicitation of the prospect might take more work, but it usually produces better results. It is much harder for a prospect to say no to a gift request from a friend and

peer who has made her own gift than to a paid development officer from the organization. But the major gifts officer needs to work behind the scenes managing the activities, ensuring that the right moves are implemented at the right time, and the right players are involved. This role is the moves manager position. It, too, can be indicated in a constituent's record using assigned solicitor functionality with a solicitor type of "Moves Manager" or "Prospect Manager." In large organizations, the major gifts officer might be a secondary player and a prospect research staff member serves as the moves manager.

We will discuss Moves Management further as we build the model.

■ ■ ■

Let us now discuss how The Raiser's Edge could be used to support a major gifts program that is based on these two ways of thinking about major gifts fundraising.

Identification

FINDING PROSPECTS   The purpose of the Identification stage is to find prospects that you can begin working with toward a major gift.
    You can "mine" your copy of The Raiser's Edge to find prospects.

- There is a standard report (Reports, Analytical Reports) called the Top Donors Report, which can be used to make sure that your top donors—however you define the criteria—are part of your major gifts process.
- In the same location, there is a Consecutive Years Report. This might help as well, especially for identifying planned gift prospects.
- There are numerous other standard reports, some discussed in the next chapter, which you might also find informative for finding new prospects. Any criteria you can imagine can be used in a query to further identify constituents.

    Your current Raiser's Edge database can also be used with prospect research and modeling companies such as Blackbaud's Target Analytics, WealthEngine, and others. The Raiser's Edge is so pervasive in our industry that any of these companies are able to help you get your data out and back in for this purpose.
    Your best resources for finding new prospects are your board members, development officers, and prospect researchers.

NEW PROSPECTS   All new major gifts prospects should be entered into The Raiser's Edge. Even if someone is quickly rejected as a good prospect, the individual should be in The Raiser's Edge so this consideration can be recorded in case the name arises again.
    You do not need an address to enter the prospect into The Raiser's Edge. It is helpful, of course, but not a requirement, especially for a name that is going to be researched and has the potential for a major gift. Just have the prospect given a checkmark for **Has no valid addresses**.
    Please do not keep your prospect lists in Excel. The lists go in The Raiser's Edge.

The constituent code should not be "Prospect," "Major Gifts Prospect" or any other version referring to prospect. The constituent code should be Alumni, Grateful Patient, Corporation, Foundation, or even just Individual or Friend, whatever is appropriate. It should identify the *type of constituent*.

If you have the RE:Search module, and therefore, the constituent has a Prospect tab, use this tab to indicate that a constituent is a major gifts prospect. On that tab is a field named **Prospect Status**, and at this stage, the status to assign is "1-Identification."

This indicates the constituent is a potential major gifts prospect. Some people call these constituents "suspects." In our seven-stage example, this status merely flags the constituent as someone with whom more work needs to be done before the organization has committed to treat this constituent as a full-fledged major gifts prospect. We need a way to identify the constituents at this stage so they do not get forgotten.

If your organization does not have the RE:Search module, and therefore, your constituents do not have a **Prospect Status** field, you can mimic this functionality with a constituent attribute. The attribute category should be "Prospect Status," and the attribute description should be "1-Identification." An attribute also gives you the option of indicating the date this status was assigned and a **Comments** field to indicate a brief reference as to who made this determination and why.

Whether you use the Prospect tab or an attribute, a note should be added on the Notes tab explaining why the constituent was identified as a major gifts prospect and by whom. A simple note type of "Prospect" or "Prospect Strategy" is probably best.

PROSPECT CLASSIFICATION Another field on the Prospect tab that works closely with prospect status is **Prospect Classification**. The purpose of this field is to allow you to categorize your major gifts prospects beyond what stage they are in. This field can be left unused if it is not needed or you can assign the options that work best for your organization. It intentionally has a generic name because its specific use is up to you.

The field primarily has two purposes, like many fields we have seen thus far:

- A filter for lists and reports. When running lists and reports, you can easily say, based on this field, you only want prospects who are X and Y but not Z.
- An output field. When running those lists and reports you can easily include this field so you can see how the prospect has been classified.

There is no requirement that you use this field at all. Do not feel obligated to use it, and potentially make your major gifts process in The Raiser's Edge more complicated than it needs to be. Your prospects already have a number of fields filled out about them (e.g., constituent code, prospect status) and will have more fields filled out later (e.g., solicitor), so think hard about whether another way to classify and group your major gifts prospects is necessary.

Some examples of how organizations use the **Prospect Classification** field include:

- If you work for a large organization, you might want to break out the prospects by the team to which the prospect is assigned. For example:
  - Individual Major Gifts
  - Planned Gifts
  - Institutional Giving

- We will later use the assigned solicitor functionality to indicate the solicitors assigned to the prospect, including fundraisers. If all of a fundraiser's prospects are not of equal importance, this field could be used to make those distinctions. For example, if Gail is a full-time major gifts officer, she might be carrying a portfolio of 150 to 200 major gifts prospects. We might have in our database the following prospect classifications for her and values like them for the other major gifts officers:
  - "Gail's Top 25"—the best prospects most likely to make a major gift in the near future.
  - "Gail's Next 75"—those who will require some cultivation before their next gift but who need focused attention now to ensure they get there.
  - "Gail's Other Prospects"—those for whom she has primary responsibility to determine approach, begin cultivation, develop strategy, or drop from the institution's major gifts process.
- The priority could be done at an organizational rather than a solicitor level:
  - Tier 1: High priority
  - Tier 2: Medium priority
  - Tier 3: Low priority
- Bill Sturtevant provides another option from his book: long-term giving potential giving (p. 69), such as:
  - 1—$1 million or above
  - 2—$750,000 to $1 million
  - 3—$500,000 to $750,000
  - 4—$250,000 to $500,000
  - 5—$100,000 to $250,000
  - 6—$50,000 to $100,000
  - 7—$25,000 to $50,000

  Modify the ranges to what is appropriate to your organization. Keep in mind, however, that the lowest level should define the minimum amount to qualify as a major gift. This field is for major gifts purposes only, so the lowest range defines your smallest major gift, not all gifts.

As with prospect status, if you do not have the Prospect tab you can mimic prospect classification by using an attribute the same way.

Keep in mind that on the Prospect tab a constituent can only be assigned to one classification at a time. Your organization will have to allow only one major gifts process at a time for a constituent, will need to use this field for the most important of multiple classifications, or store this information in the Raiser's Edge proposal record (discussed later in the chapter) rather than using the **Prospect Classification** field.

If you use an attribute, however, it is up to you if you want to restrict a prospect to one classification at a time. The same attribute (i.e., Prospect Classification) can be assigned to a constituent more than one time if you choose to allow it.

PROSPECT STRATEGY MEETING   Both of the fundraising perspectives summarized as the basis for this major gifts approach are based on the expectation that prospect strategy meetings will be held. These are weekly, biweekly, or monthly meetings where everyone involved in the major gifts process gathers to review activity since the last meeting and make decisions about future major gifts activity.

Those involved usually include the head of major giving, the major gifts officers, prospect researchers, and other support personnel. Depending on size, all of these people can meet at once or they can meet in small groups. In smaller organizations, one person may wear several of these hats. Even in the smallest of organizations where one person wears all of these hats, it is expected that this person would take time to review the status of major gifts prospects.

Reference to these meetings will be made in several of the stages of the major gifts life cycle. This does not mean that every meeting must include a discussion of the prospects at all seven stages—such a meeting would simply be too long. Rather, it implies that, over the course of a few of these meetings, all seven stages need to be reviewed to keep the pipeline flowing.

For example, if several major gift solicitations are forthcoming in the next week, it is appropriate for the entire meeting to focus on preparation for those calls. But if every meeting is about upcoming solicitations, at some point there will be no one to solicit. Prospects at the other stages need to be monitored to ensure that the pipeline is kept flowing.

■ ■ ■

At the Identification stage, the prospect strategy meeting could be used. It is a fundraising management decision as to what should occur in your organization when someone has an idea for a new prospect. Below, I have shared one approach illustrating how The Raiser's Edge can be used at this stage in the major gifts process.

When a name is provided as a prospect, the first step is to enter the prospect as a constituent with the fields discussed previously. This can be done by the major gifts officer, prospect researcher, or support staff. However, until the prospect is reviewed at the prospect strategy meeting, no further activity should occur. This is based on the idea that there needs to be group consensus on the expenditure of effort on the prospect before anyone dives in. Others in the organization might have additional information or insight. The time required for the new prospect needs to be balanced with time for existing prospects, and so on.

To support this process, there should be a query in The Raiser's Edge that identifies anyone with a prospect status of 1-Identification. This query can be used in two ways:

1. A laptop can be attached to an LCD projector in the meeting room, and the constituents in this query can be reviewed one by one by the group.
2. A report in The Raiser's Edge called a "profile" can be run on each constituent and the hard copy profiles reviewed and discussed at the meeting. A profile report is just like the standard profiles we are used to in our profession: they are a report of the data about the constituent as recorded in our database. The difference is that they are composed primarily of lists of data rather than long, narrative paragraphs. You can specify what parts of a constituent record you want to see on a profile for this purpose and what tabs of data can be ignored.

Based on the information available from The Raiser's Edge thus far, the group discusses each potential prospect. The group:

- Shares what they know about the prospect for addition to the database.
- Determines whether the prospect merits the investment of further research time and, therefore, should move forward in the process. The alternative is that the prospect is not a viable candidate for a major gift and should be dropped from the process.

One could argue there are a number of other options available at this stage, such as immediately assigning the prospect a solicitor and beginning the cultivation process, altogether skipping the Research stage. Although a valid point, the effort here is to illustrate how The Raiser's Edge can be used to support the major gifts process. This is not an attempt to fully document the entire major gifts management process. I keep the discussion simple and straightforward to illustrate options and next steps. I enthusiastically invite you to further develop the process for your organization based on these simpler examples.

After the meeting the person with the assigned data entry responsibilities should:

- Add to the constituent record additional information revealed during the prospect strategy meeting, such as other relationships, wealth holdings, history with the institution, and potential for giving.
- Change the Prospect Status of the constituent to either "2-Research" or "9-Dropped."

Dropped

"Dropped" is a stage in the major gifts cycle to indicate that the constituent entered the cycle at some point in time but was determined not to be a good major gifts prospect. Although it is not the preferred situation after Identification, it is one of the possible outcomes of the Identification stage.

A prospect can be dropped at any stage when the constituent is deemed to be no longer worth the investment of major gifts activity. This would usually be due to a demonstrated lack of interest on the constituent's part or lack of capability to make a major gift. There should be a management policy about who can make the final determination that a prospect should be dropped. For example, is this a decision that a major gifts officer can make herself or should it require management approval?

Perhaps the issue is not that the person is not a good prospect for a major gift but that the focus or fundraiser needs to be changed. Any other fields for the constituent can be changed as well. Simply meeting a dead-end in one area or approach does not mean the prospect should be dropped.

It is better to assign "Dropped" than to delete the status and leave the **Status** field empty. Doing so makes it clear that the constituent had been considered previously. It also provides a way to measure activity, especially when reviewing the complete pipeline of major gifts activity, showing how many constituents were considered and rejected, a process that does take time and effort and should not be ignored.

Just because someone has a current prospect status of Dropped does not mean that the person can never be considered again. Situations change with both institutions and constituents. The value reflects their current status. Should someone be deemed of potential future interest, schedule an action in the constituent's record to remind a prospect researcher or fundraiser to reconsider the prospect.

It is important when dropping a constituent from the major gifts process that the reason for doing so be recorded and dated. It should be recorded in the same "Prospect" note on the Notes tab as used in earlier stages. This will be vital information in the future if the constituent is again considered for a major gift.

Finally, dropping a prospect does not mean the constituent cannot be asked for any other kind of gift. It is not a "Do Not Solicit" code. It simply means the constituent is not currently a major gifts prospect. The constituent could still be solicited for a direct mail gift or event registration. However, if even other approaches are no longer appropriate, solicit codes should be updated as well.

Research

The scale of "research" is vast. In smaller organizations, it might mean nothing more than the director of development doing web searches and perhaps talking to a few people who know the prospect. In a large organization, it might be a full-time, professional prospect researcher doing a complete biographical profile.

Of course, we can find out more information from a prospect during cultivation, but a premise of Moves Management is that cultivation should be personal and strategic. We should not just begin the cultivation; we should do some research and create a plan and a strategy to structure the cultivation for the greatest effect.

It is your decision how much research to do on a prospect. The amount and depth needed will also vary by prospect. The key points to be made with research and The Raiser's Edge are:

- The research findings should go in The Raiser's Edge. Doing so gives you much more flexibility and use of the information than if it is entered in a narrative format in a Microsoft Word document.
- The research findings should go into the appropriate fields in The Raiser's Edge, not into narrative entries or another format on the Notes tab. Reserve the Notes tab for data that truly has no other place in a constituent record.

For example:

- Family and friend information goes in individual relationships.
- Work history and community and religious involvement go in organization relationships.
- Education history goes in education relationships, even if your institution is not a school or university.
- Wealth and giving information to other organizations goes on the Prospect tab if you have the RE:Search module; only if not should it go into notes.
- Miscellaneous information, data without a designated tab and field, goes on the Notes tab. Use multiple note types rather than putting everything into one note. For example: "Personal and Family Background" for information that does not go in individual relationships; "Wealth History and Information" for narrative details beyond the amount and date data stored on the Prospect tab; and "Institutional

Affinity and Giving Interests" to get beyond the details of fields with only drop-down lists. Reserve the "Prospect" or "Prospect Strategy" note type for thoughts and plans to specifically cultivate and solicit the constituent for a gift. Be careful to limit the number of note types in your system, however; 5 to 10 should be the useful limit.

The primary exception to this recommendation is when you buy significant prospect research information from the for-profit companies that work in the prospect research field. One service these companies provide is called "wealth appending." Typically, there is so much information they return that it is too much to add in its entirety to The Raiser's Edge. Additionally, the information usually is not from firsthand or other direct sources. It is based on name and address matching, so sometimes its accuracy is questionable.

Key pieces of this information can be added to The Raiser's Edge on the Prospect tab in the Financial Information and Ratings sections. The other detailed data should be left in the database program the vendor provided for you to store and access it.

If the vendor provides scores from modeling, such as Target Analytics' Major Gift Likelihood, these scores should be added to The Raiser's Edge. You will find them helpful when pulling lists and profiles to identify your best prospects or to see a prospect's score. If you have the Prospect tab, the scores should be stored in ratings. If you do not have the RE:Search module, they should be stored in attributes.

Some organizations have their prospect researchers develop the initial internal scores for Capacity and Propensity (also called Inclination). Whether done by prospect researchers or by others, at this stage or later, these scores can also be stored in the ratings on the Prospect tab or in attributes.

Remember, in some jurisdictions people will be legally entitled to see their records. A good rule of thumb is not to record anything that would embarrass you or the prospect if they did ask to see their profile, whether legally required or not.

While the research is underway and when it is complete, staff members might wish to see the results. The best way for them to do so is to simply look at the constituent's record. The constituent record *is* the profile for the constituent. If a hard copy or PDF format of the information is needed, such as to summarize key elements for senior staff or volunteers, use a profile report in The Raiser's Edge to view the research findings, as shown in Figure 6.2.

Profile reports are a key reporting element to the major gifts process, at this stage and all others. An unlimited number of profiles can be set up, each containing the selection of tabs and data you wish to include. For your personal use, you might wish to have a profile that literally includes everything from the constituent record—all data from all tabs. You might need to be more restrictive with volunteer solicitors so you do not overwhelm them or share confidential data.

Profiles can be long, so it is usually not environmentally friendly or economical to print them. Profiles can be saved as PDFs for easy distribution to those who do not have direct access to The Raiser's Edge. Remember to be careful, however, about sensitive information contained on profiles, where they are saved, who receives them, and the discretion the recipients exercise in further distribution of the PDF or communication of the information. Profiles can be generated from within a constituent record for that constituent or from Reports for a group of constituents.

Dr. and Mrs. Robert C. Hernandez

Constituent Name

Robert C. Hernandez
410 17th Street
Denver, CO 80202-4402

Home: 303-555-3301
Cell Phone: 303-555-1211

Solicit Codes

No Phone Solicitation

Constituent Codes

Code Abbreviation	Code Description	Date From	Date To
BM	Board Member	1/1/2005	
VOL	Volunteer	3/2000	

Businesses

Organization Name	Industry	Position	Date From	Date To
Davis & Johnson Pharmaceuticals	Health care	CEO	7/1992	

Education/Schools

School Name	Degree	Major(s)	Date Graduated	Is Primary?
Princeton University	BS	Biology	5/1973	No

Education Attributes

Category	Attribute Description	Short Desc.	Date	Comments
Athletics	Wrestling		9/1/1970	
Athletics	Swim Team		6/1/1969	Scholarship awarded
Clubs	Student Union			

FIGURE 6.2   A Constituent Profile Report

Staff doing the research should query The Raiser's Edge for constituents with the "2-Research" prospect status. Once a constituent's research is complete, the status should be changed to "3-Strategy."

Strategy

The purpose of the Strategy stage is straightforward: develop and document the initial strategy that will be used to cultivate and solicit the prospect for a gift. It is in this stage at which the greatest influence of Moves Management will be evident.

We do not just begin cultivation. Rather, at a prospect strategy meeting, the group again convenes to:

- Review each prospect with a status of 3-Strategy (again, using an LCD projector or printed profiles).
- Allow the researcher to summarize the research findings.
- Determine whether the findings justify moving the prospect into Cultivation or the prospect should be dropped.
- If moving the prospect forward, assign the "moves manager"/prospect manager.

If the prospect is to be dropped, the procedures already discussed for dropping can be applied at this point.

If the prospect is to move on, either the group or the prospect manager should then determine the following strategy points:

- Natural partners
- Primary and secondary players, or solicitors
- Plan of the next five to seven moves, ideally the last one being the solicitation for the ask, including anticipated dates and activities
- Expected funding purpose to pursue
- Expected dollar amount of ask
- Anticipated ask date

It is certainly understood that, at any point in the forthcoming process, all of these initial determinations can, and likely will, change. The research might not have revealed a recent interest in a different funding area or increased resources to fund a larger gift. But a plan needs to be put together based on the knowledge obtained so far. The plan identifies the optimal approach for the largest gift in the least amount of time. This is one reason I like Moves Management: it assumes we fundraisers are professionals who are motivated by doing the right and best things, not merely friendly faces taking prospects out to eat. Prospect plans, like all plans, can change over time, but we are better having a plan than not.

These determinations should then be documented in The Raiser's Edge by the prospect manager or support staff. Additionally:

- The prospect status should be changed to "4-Cultivation."
- The natural partners should be entered as individual relationships.
- The prospect manager and primary and secondary players should be entered as assigned solicitors.
- The moves should be entered as actions.

Note: Action Tracks

There is a tool in The Raiser's Edge called "Action Tracks," which allows for the creation of a series of actions that can be saved. Later, they are applied to one or more constituents. Often, action tracks are mentioned in the context of Moves Management and major gifts fundraising by other trainers and consultants. I recommend action tracks for event and appeal checklists. Action tracks occasionally have a place with constituents in other situations. However, within the context of Moves Management, I do not recommend using action tracks for major gifts fundraising. As Bill Sturtevant says, Moves Management is "highly personalized."

"You must take each member of your highest level prospects one-at-a-time and develop strategies that are appropriate to the individual" (pp. 50–51).

For this reason, action tracks are usually not the best fit for major gifts fundraising.

RAISER'S EDGE "PROPOSALS"   The expected funding purpose, amount, and ask date should be entered into The Raiser's Edge as a "Proposal" on the Prospect tab. At this stage, do not think of a Raiser's Edge proposal on the Prospect tab as a literal proposal, a written document asking for a gift. Although that might come eventually, at this stage think of the proposal function in The Raiser's Edge as a *major gift opportunity*. For-profit sales software uses the term "opportunity," which is a good model for how to think about this function.

The proposal in The Raiser's Edge, as illustrated in Figure 6.3, allows us to track and tie together all the efforts being made to secure the major gift. We can record the purposes, dates, amounts, statuses, people, activities, and notes that all work together to close a major gift. There are a number of fields in a Raiser's Edge proposal, so this level of data entry maintenance is only justified by a major gift opportunity. The money to be raised and the importance of tracking and reporting on each opportunity justifies taking the time to fill out these fields.

There is no requirement that all proposal fields in The Raiser's Edge be used. Many organizations, for example, do not use the fields to be found on the right side of the proposal's main General tab. That you do not use all the fields, however, does

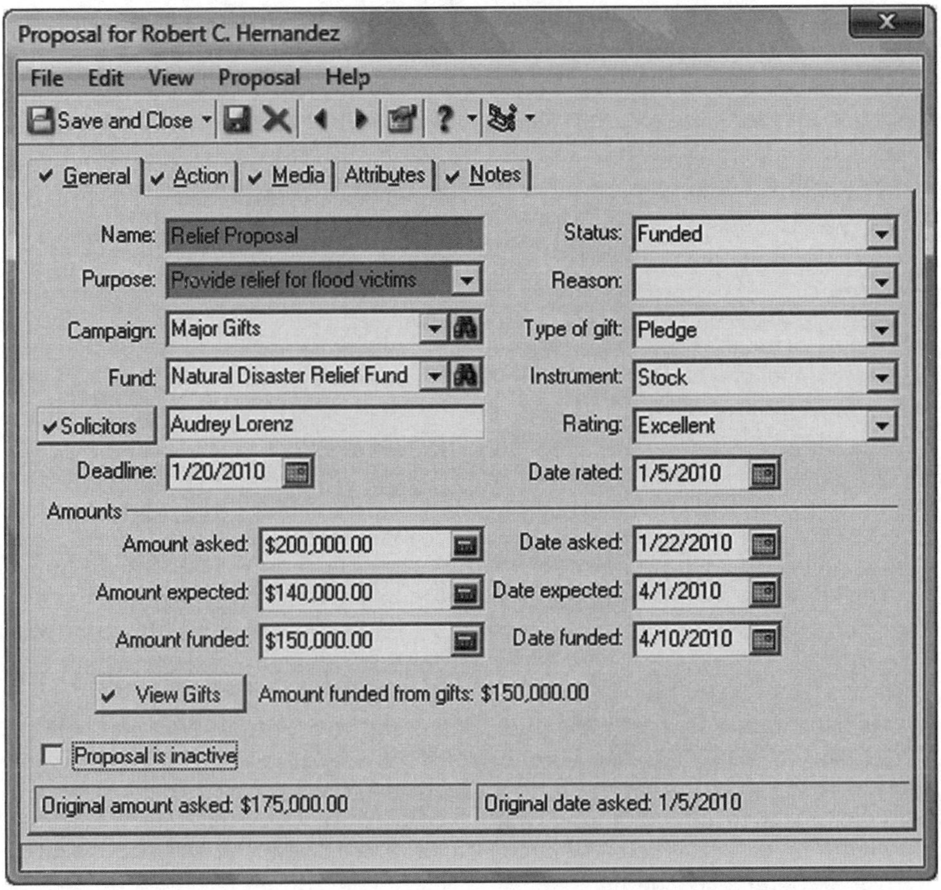

FIGURE 6.3   A Raiser's Edge Proposal

not mean that a number of them cannot provide value. In fact, if your organization has invested in the RE:Search module, you have four additional reports and five dashboards: all of the reports and two of the dashboards rely exclusively on proposal functionality and two of the remaining three dashboards rely heavily on it. These output tools are excellent—good enough, in fact, to replace your major gifts tracking Excel spreadsheet. But you need to use proposals, even in a simple fashion, to do that.

After the strategy development, a Raiser's Edge proposal should be created indicating:

- The funding purpose and goals
- The expected dollar amount and date of ask
- The solicitors involved
- The actions related to it. (The Actions tab in a proposal contains a *subset* of the actions on the constituent's Actions tab using the actions that have been linked to the proposal within the actions. A linked action is the same action appearing in both places, but it is one action record in the database.)

Determine and use the other fields and functions in the proposal in which your organization finds sufficient value. It is okay to draw the line and decide that some fields are simply too much data entry and will not be useful in tracking major gifts.

If you do not have the RE:Search module, the proposal function will be the hardest functionality to replicate. You might consider some of the data sufficiently important to track through attributes. You may decide you do not need specific fields to store other data, which can be recorded in the Prospect note on the Notes tab. You will still want to use relationships, assign solicitors, and create actions, however, just as those organizations with the RE:Search module do.

Cultivation

Cultivation is usually the longest stage. However, the work to be done in The Raiser's Edge is straightforward. In summary, this stage is about working the actions and updating the constituent record and the Raiser's Edge proposal based on the outcomes.

The Strategy stage included creating actions for personal, strategic cultivation of the prospect. The first step in Cultivation is to do the first cultivation action that was set up.

The best way to be reminded of what actions you need to take is to use the Action Reminders on the Home page of The Raiser's Edge as shown in Figure 6.4.

When you log in, go to the Home page first for two reasons:

1. You should check your action reminders on the Home page for the actions it is time to prepare for and do.
2. The Home page is *your* home page. This is not your organization's home page for The Raiser's Edge, but your personal Home page. You should see your user name at the top of the screen. Your Home page should contain links to those things you do most frequently in The Raiser's Edge. It should be set up to include the ability to open records so you do not need to go to the Records page. It should contain hyperlinks to each of your top major gifts prospects or a query so that you can quickly access and review your prospects.

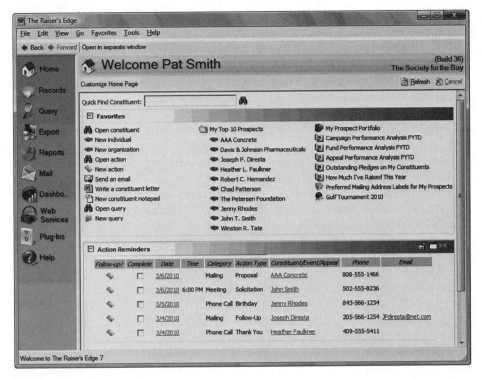

FIGURE 6.4   The Home Page

If you set the action reminders to also appear in Outlook when you create the actions, you will also be able to see them there. However, since not all actions are scheduled appointments, you might want reminders for some actions that do not appear as appointments on your Outlook calendar. Personally, I also find Outlook's reminders a little too easy to dismiss and for the item to do to get lost. It is usually best to rely on the Action Reminders on your Raiser's Edge Home page for a complete list of all reminders until you consciously mark each action completed.

Remember the major gifts process is ongoing, so your prospects are going to be at almost all the stages of the major gifts life cycle. Although in this discussion we are walking through the process for one prospect chronologically, all of your prospects are not going to enter the Cultivation cycle at the same time. You will have actions with many different purposes happening during the same week and month:

- Some constituents just starting Cultivation
- Some in the midst of Cultivation
- Some winding down Cultivation and preparing for Solicitation
- Some in Solicitation
- Some in Stewardship

If you schedule the actions needed for each person according to this process, each time you check your Home page, you will be reminded of the actions you need to take. You do not need to worry that someone will get missed.

If you need a hard copy of upcoming reminders, there is a report in The Raiser's Edge on the Reports page, in the Action Reports category, called the Tickler Report. Use this to print a list of your upcoming actions.

After you work an action, you or your support staff should:

- Update the constituent record with new information discovered during the action, such as more relationships, wealth data, and biographical background. For greatest benefit and flexibility with this information, the data should be entered on the tabs and fields in which it properly goes and not into one big note.
- Update the Raiser's Edge proposal record as necessary to change the planned funding objective, date, and amount.
- Update the action by marking it complete and adding notes about the action itself (as compared to broader findings about the constituent that go elsewhere in the record).
- Based on the interaction with the constituent, add and modify future actions in the constituent's record to refine your strategy.

Repeat this process throughout the Cultivation stage.

Solicitation

Although the Solicitation stage is usually short, the purpose of assigning it to a constituent is threefold:

1. To help you and your fundraising management understand the major gifts pipeline.
2. To help you and those who assist you, in both support and management capacities, get ready for the solicitation. Typically, we do not just see the solicitation action and do it. There is preparation and coordination involved to ensure the greatest success of the ask.
3. To code the record so it can be easily excluded from mass communications you do not want the prospect to receive at this sensitive stage. It can also be used to set up warnings inside The Raiser's Edge for anyone who might access the record and make other direct contact.

The major gifts officer should change the prospect status to "5-Solicitation" when the last cultivation action has been completed and the next action is the solicitation.

The solicitation action should be updated so it reflects the date and details needed to prepare for it.

The Raiser's Edge proposal record should be updated so it correctly reflects purpose, date, amount, and other fields you are using. The solicitation action might have its reminder set sufficiently in advance to give you time to create an actual written proposal to present to the prospect.

After you make the ask, one of the following three steps should be taken based on the outcome:

1. If you get an immediate "yes" (congratulations!):
   - Update the action as always.
   - Update the proposal.

- Notify the gift-processing staff so the gift and proposal can be linked.
- Move to the Stewardship stage.
2. If you get a "maybe" or any response less than a full "yes" or "no":
   - Update the solicitation action as always.
   - Update the proposal.
   - Move to the Negotiation stage.
3. If you get an immediate "no":
   - Update the solicitation action as always.
   - Update the proposal.
   - Determine the next steps with the constituent and update the status and other fields accordingly.

Regarding this last bullet for a "no," what the next steps will be depends on the kind of "no" you received. You might leave the constituent in the Solicitation stage, rework your request according to the feedback the prospect gave you, and plan another solicitation. By this stage, it is hoped that you know the prospect well enough that they should not go to the Dropped status, but that is a possibility. And every option between Dropped and resoliciting is possible, as well.

The key tasks in The Raiser's Edge are to:

- Update the prospect status so it reflects the prospect's current status.
- Add the actions necessary for next steps.
- Continue to update other fields such as the Raiser's Edge proposal and notes as necessary with new information as it develops.

Negotiation

"Negotiation" is not meant to imply anything adversarial about the process. Some organizations do not use this as a stage, others rename it, and yet others find it just fine as is. The intent is simply to indicate that many major gift asks are going to require consideration and discussions before the gift can finally be booked. For example:

- Spouses and partners might need to discuss it with each other.
- If the request is a "stretch ask," the prospect might legitimately need time to think about it, to ask you further questions, and to let the idea sink in.
- The prospect might need to speak with investment, financial, and legal advisors about the best way to structure and fund the gift.
- You and the prospect might need to discuss recognition opportunities and payment terms with which the prospect and your institution are comfortable.
- You might need time to discuss these same areas with your leadership and giving committees.

There are many legitimate reasons that the lack of an immediate "yes" is fine in the major gifts process. This stage recognizes this and helps you continue to protect the constituent during this sensitive time. You do not want the constituent to receive a minor telemarketing call and make it appear that your institution is disorganized. Further, fundraising management needs to know the status of prospects.

The key tasks in The Raiser's Edge for this stage are:

- Assign the "6-Negotation" prospect status value to the constituent.
- Continue to add and update actions, notes, the Raiser's Edge proposal, and other constituent fields as further information is revealed and activities are necessary.

Stewardship

Stewardship is the period of acknowledgement, recognition, and participation of donors for their major gifts, ensuring that the donors have a good giving experience and are pleased with their gifts' effects. It is important to do this for three reasons:

1. At least some of the acknowledgement is legally required (i.e., the receipting of the gift).
2. It is the right thing to do when someone has made a significant contribution to your organization, regardless of their ability to make another major gift.
3. It is the best cultivation and nurturing opportunity possible for another gift from the prospect at an appropriate time in the future.

We should be as strategic and mindful in our planning of stewardship as we were in the Strategy stage when planning cultivation. The tasks here are straightforward:

- Change the prospect status to "7-Stewardship."
- Create a plan for stewardship and schedule the activities in The Raiser's Edge as actions.

Because stewardship actions do not have a natural conclusion like cultivation actions do with a solicitation, there are two additional points:

1. As you complete each stewardship action, you need to ensure that another future action has been scheduled. Otherwise, in your busyness with other prospects, this donor might be forgotten.
2. As you complete stewardship actions for constituents and occasionally review your list of assigned constituents in the Stewardship stage, you need to decide when to move each prospect out of this stage.

For older donors who have made their final major gifts to your institution and already have you as a planned gift beneficiary, you might leave them in Stewardship indefinitely. Most of your previous major gifts prospects, however, are still candidates for a planned gift or another major gift. After appropriate stewardship has been completed, these constituents' prospect status should be changed to one of the earlier stages and the process reignited as discussed for that stage.

Keeping it Simple

Bill Sturtevant says about prospect tracking systems in general, "What I primarily recommend is that you keep your tracking system as simple as possible" (p. 224). I concur. Although I am a Raiser's Edge consultant, I was a fundraiser first. It is about results, not data.

The prospect life cycle we have discussed is actually fairly simple because it uses the same tools in The Raiser's Edge repeatedly at each stage. The specific purpose at each stage is different, but the tools and their methods of use are the same. The life cycle just discussed, which appears to be a more sophisticated application of The Raiser's Edge than the basic tools discussed at the beginning of the chapter, is really just the use of the same tools discussed in that section:

- Constituent records
- Relationships
- Solicitors
- Notes
- Actions

What the life cycle discussion adds is:

- A **Prospect Status** field
- An optional **Prospect Classification** field
- The Raiser's Edge proposal function, which is critical to reports and dashboards in The Raiser's Edge but can be used simply

The primary difference with the life cycle is the sophistication of the fundraising process, the methodology you are using. The level of complexity involved is up to you.

The key is to have a methodology and a documented use of it with The Raiser's Edge. This is important so that your management, fundraisers, and database and support staff can all use the system consistently and reliably.

Protecting Your Prospects

One of the primary reasons for coding the status and classification of prospects is to be able to protect prospects from processes that should not include them. For example:

- You might wish to remove major gifts prospects from your direct marketing programs at certain stages.
- You may not want the prospect to receive event invitations at those stages.
- You might wish to restrict the sending of newsletters and annual reports to major gifts prospects at sensitive stages such as Solicitation and Negotiation.
- You might even wish to restrict such mailings from constituents in the Cultivation stage so that you can send or hand deliver them personally as a further cultivation step.

It is important to develop a system for how your organization uses The Raiser's Edge for major gifts fundraising and how you code the prospects. Once you have developed a process that everyone can trust for data entry accuracy and integrity, you can coordinate with your database and direct marketing colleagues to include and exclude your major gifts prospects accordingly.

For example, in Chapter 4 we talked about the criteria for who receives a mailing. You might wish to go through each type of mass mailing your organization does and determine for each prospect status whether the status indicates

- Particular *inclusion* for the mailing
- Particular *exclusion* from the mailing

Without this criteria made explicit, the prospect may get the mailing based on other information in its record. Remember for each mailing to separate the thought process for include and exclude. *First* think of any prospect statuses that should explicitly get the mailing even if they meet no other criteria to get it (for example, a prospect with no giving history you wish to receive the newsletter). *Then* think about the statuses that should exclude a constituent from a mailing even if they meet the criteria (for example, all major gifts prospects in the Solicitation stage).

Tip: Opening Constituent Rules and Annotations

The Raiser's Edge has tools called "Opening Constituent Rules" and "Annotations" that immediately pop up messages when constituent records are opened. The record cannot be accessed until the message is closed by the user. These excellent tools support the major gifts process because they can say to a user opening the record: "Hey, be careful, this is a major gifts prospect! We are at a sensitive stage, so review any planned contact with the constituent with the prospect manager." This can be helpful to you if someone is opening the record to call the constituent or make an important change about which you wish to be notified.

- An "opening constituent rule" is set up by your database administrator based on criteria that is specified in a query. A message is added that appears any time a constituent record is opened that meets the criteria. This is the more useful approach when you want a consistent message for a group of prospects. It is also helpful because it is dynamic—as new prospects come and others go, displaying the message is updated automatically. For example, this approach is recommended if you want a message that warned users that the constituent was in the Solicitation stage.
- An "annotation" is a message that can appear when a record is opened that is specific to the constituent in whose record it is added. For example, if Marsha Atkinson had a bad experience with your organization recently and you are working to recover from it, you might wish all contact with her to go through her prospect manager Bob. Bob would open Marsha's record, add the annotation specifically to "See Bob before making any contact with Marsha!", and mark it to display automatically whenever Marsha's record is opened. When the issue is resolved, this annotation can simply be deleted from her record. Annotations can be used for any notes of any purpose that all users should see when opening a record. Annotations are easily added to a record by selecting **Edit**, **Annotate** from the menu bar or clicking the **Annotate** button on the toolbar. Be certain to add a checkmark to **Display annotation automatically** if you wish it to do so.

Major Gifts Process Reports

The value of putting the data into The Raiser's Edge is to get it back out to help us manage the process and be successful. Many of the reports useful for the major gifts process are used also for other processes, and are discussed more in Chapter 7.

Thus far we have discussed profile reports, which have particular significance to major gifts fundraising (in Chapter 2 and earlier in this chapter). We have also talked about the Action Reminders dashboard and Tickler report.

Reports that you wish to see about major gifts received are discussed in the next chapter. Also discussed in that chapter are reports about performance toward fundraising goals by:

- Campaign, fund, and appeal
- Solicitor/fundraiser

This section highlights what I believe to be the best of the major gifts-specific reporting tools in The Raiser's Edge. These are by no means all of the major gifts reports and dashboards, just those that I have found to be most useful to clients over the years.

The Classic Major Gifts Spreadsheet

Numerous times in my consulting work, I have been presented with a spreadsheet in landscape format that lists major gifts prospects and their:

- Goal amounts
- Funding objectives
- Solicitors
- Last activities
- Next activities
- Giving histories
- Notes

As with every other report in the fundraising industry, we have little standardization. Every version of this report that I have seen has different fields. There is, however, a common theme and structure to it.

There are two versions of this report available in The Raiser's Edge, but neither are a "report"—both are Dashboard panels. Dashboards and panels are explained more in Chapter 7, but briefly they are on-screen, interactive reports, meant to be used within the database rather than printed. The two panels for this major gifts spreadsheet are:

- Proposal Status
- Prospect List

The Proposal Status panel requires that a proposal exist for the prospect and lists the data in alphabetical order by proposal name. If you follow the process similar to the one I discussed earlier, however, you have a proposal for each major gifts prospect as early as needed for this panel to be useful. This is one example why I suggest you think of the Raiser's Edge proposal function as a major gift opportunity and not in its literal sense, creating it so early in the process.

The Prospect List provides similar data as the Proposal Status but is grouped by solicitor and alphabetized by prospect as shown in Figure 6.5. A proposal does not have to exist for the constituent to be on this panel. This data is slightly more oriented toward the assigned solicitor data on the prospect than the proposal. A major gifts officer with no management responsibilities could use this panel filtered to him- or herself. A manager of major gifts officers could use this tool effectively to monitor his or her own performance and that of those who report to the manager.

If you do not use proposals, or do not use them early enough in the process, use the Prospect List panel. If you use proposals, set up both panels, play with both, and leave whichever you like best. You will not harm the data by experimenting with the dashboard panels. It is even fine to use both if their nuanced differences are meaningful to you and you want to refer to both.

Dashboard panels are intended to be viewed within the software. They can be printed, but they are not optimized for printing. If you would like a hard copy of the Proposal Status panel, consider using the Outstanding Proposal Report on the Reports page in the Prospect Research Reports category.

Both of these panels are components of the RE:Search module. If your organization does not have that module, the best way to mimic the major gifts spreadsheet or these panels is to create an export to Excel that contains the data. If you take this approach, you should use the Excel export just as a reporting tool and treat the data as if it were unchangeable. All updates should be done in The Raiser's Edge and not on the spreadsheet.

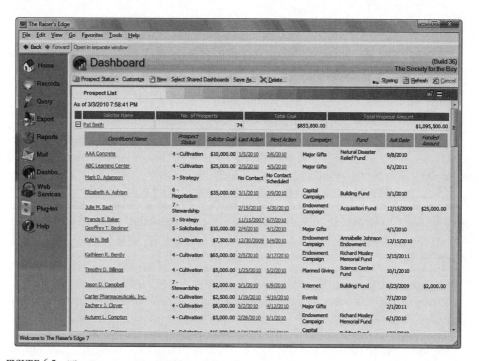

FIGURE 6.5   The Prospect List Dashboard Panel

Reporting on the Pipeline

There is a Dashboard panel called the Prospect Pipeline (shown in Figure 6.1) that will show you either:

- The number of prospects at each stage according to the **Prospect Status** field
- The number of proposals at each stage according to the proposal **Status** field

Both versions of the pipeline show the counts for each status for each solicitor.

To see who the prospects are at each stage, add a query with those details to the dashboard, your Home page, or on the Query page, based on how frequently you plan to access them. One nice approach would be to have a dashboard named "Prospect Pipeline" and, on it, include the Prospect Pipeline panel based on prospect status plus queries that show a list of constituents for each stage.

Major gifts officers can filter these to just the prospects with which they are working or to see other fundraisers' progress for comparison purposes. It is also possible to do a combination of both, such as the pipeline for everyone and queries limited to just the fundraiser's own prospects.

Fundraising managers, however, might want to see everyone's activity. One option would be to have one dashboard with all the staff's activity and a different dashboard for the manager's own portfolio.

If you follow the process described earlier, you will want to run the panel based on the prospect status. One approach to using the proposal **Status** field is discussed in more detail in the upcoming section for corporate and foundation fundraisers.

There is a report in the Prospect Research Reports category called the Proposal Pipeline Summary that will also display the pipeline based on proposal status. It is not available for prospect status.

Tracking Fundraiser Activity

Increasingly, I am asked by the heads of fundraising departments to help them track fundraiser activity. They often say, "I'm interested in taking a more sales management-oriented approach to how I manage my staff. I'd like to know what they are doing and how much of it." The intent is usually to quantify activity, to get metrics, to measure fundraisers' performance beyond just the amount of money raised.

In The Raiser's Edge, all fundraiser activity of any substance should be recorded as actions, so measuring the activity is not difficult. There is a report in The Raiser's Edge called the Action Summary Report. This report can easily provide summary numbers by fundraiser. Two keys to the success of this report:

1. *Determine what is worth measuring.* Establish standards, for example, as to what constitutes foreground and background actions and set up your data entry and reports accordingly. There needs to be differentiation among many easy e-mails and phone calls and significant face-to-face cultivation activity. Your organization needs to:
   - Define what you want to track and measure from a fundraising perspective.
   - Agree how to code The Raiser's Edge to measure them; focus on the use of the action **Category, Action type**, and perhaps action attribute fields.

- Ensure that those doing the action data entry, whether fundraiser or support staff, understand the definitions and policy.
- Occasionally run the Action Detail Report to ensure that the summary numbers you are reviewing represent the activity you expect to see. Run it with notes and based on the same criteria as the Summary Report.
- Run the report different ways, with different options selected. For example, sometimes you might wish to see all the fundraisers' activities. At other times you might want the report filtered to specific prospect stages to determine if major gifts officers are spending too much or too little time with constituents in those stages.

2. *Run the report for completed actions only.* Those actions scheduled but not completed should not count in these statistics.

If you wish to monitor fundraisers' activity in more detail to understand what they are doing and to support them in those efforts, there are several options available, including:

- The Action Detail Report and Tickler Report
- Several action panels in Dashboard

Other Reports

I have highlighted what my experience has shown are the most popular and beneficial major gifts reports. However, there are other reports that come with the RE:Search module, and you might wish to experiment with them on your own or with your database administrator.

In Reports, the category is called Prospect Research Reports. All of the reports in this category are specifically reports on proposals. They are called "Prospect Research" Reports to be consistent with the Prospect tab nomenclature on which the proposal function can be found. Also, prospect tracking is typically one of the roles of the prospect research team. Profiles, which show the results of research on the prospect, are their own report category. The reports in the Prospect Research Reports category not discussed earlier include:

- *Proposal Analysis Report.* The primary value of this report is occasional analysis on your major gifts process. This report's distinguishing feature is that it shows the difference between how much was asked and how much was actually given, and the number of days between the date of the ask and the date the gift was funded (or today's date if it has not yet been funded). This report can provide two benefits to you:
    1. For management, estimating probable cash flow based on the history of previous asks applied to future asks.
    2. Identifying open proposals in which asks have been made but too much time has passed without a reply.
- *Proposal Follow-up Report.* This is another actions report, but the actions are grouped by proposal.

In Dashboard, an additional panel type is available in the Proposal category. The Expected Proposals Summary shows expected cash flow based on the **Amount expected** and **Date expected** fields in proposals.

A Word to Corporate and Foundation Fundraisers

I assure you that most of the material in this chapter is equally applicable to the work of institutional fundraisers. I have primarily used the terminology and examples of individuals to avoid overcomplicating the discussion by repeatedly referring to both types of prospects.

- Institutional prospects are constituents, and those records fully participate in the database just like individual prospects.
- Relationships are important to your work. You probably have at least a program officer contact if not other staff and board contacts. I recognize it is not always possible to establish personal relationships and personally cultivate a foundation the way we have discussed working with individuals. However, I do know from my Junior Achievement experience that relationship-building can be critical for corporate fundraising and we should at least try to open those doors with foundations.
- Solicitor functionality can be used, especially if there is more than one fundraiser working with institutional prospects. This is still the correct way to indicate the prospect is "yours" with all the implications of that role as discussed throughout this chapter. There might be others also involved, especially for corporations and even for foundations.
- Notes are just as critical to your work. Thanks to the Foundation Center, Form 990s, and other resources, even more information is available publicly about organization prospects than individual prospects. Notes and the other tabs, used in the same way as discussed earlier, should be critical tools for recording giving guidelines, areas of interest, conversations with internal parties in preparation for a proposal, other ask strategies and notes, and so forth.
- Actions are key to your use of The Raiser's Edge. Use actions to schedule phone calls with program officers, the deadline for grant applications and proposals, and follow-up reports. Use them for interactions with the prospect and other parties to maintain a full history on the prospect and your proposal.
- Prospect status can be used with organization prospects. Although you should certainly adapt the stages, the meanings, and their activities as they apply to organizations, the concepts apply well here, too. This is certainly true for many corporate gifts, but even foundations can go through a cycle of:
  - Identification
  - Research to identify appropriate fit
  - Perhaps a Strategy stage if more work than just a proposal submission is necessary
  - Cultivation if the opportunity arises (meetings with program officers are terrific even if you do not have any significant questions)
  - Solicitation when you submit the proposal
  - Negotiation if the institution wishes to discuss the terms of the gift
  - Stewardship as you recognize, thank, and report to the organization
  - Even Dropped is still necessary to indicate organizations you have determined to not be a fit
- Prospect classification can be helpful to distinguish your prospects from the individuals or to further classify your institutional prospects.

- Finally, the Raiser's Edge proposal function was meant for you given the literal meaning of the tool's name. Individual major gifts prospects usually do not receive a proposal requiring as much work as proposals for institutions do. You can use the Raiser's Edge proposal tool to manage the multiple proposals that your organization may have in process to ensure that each gets written and delivered on time while keeping management informed.

In fact, there is one field in particular in the Raiser's Edge proposal that you might wish to use: **Status**. The proposal **Status** is a different field than the **Prospect Status**. The prospect status is the status of the *prospect*, the stages discussed earlier. The proposal status can be used to track the status of an actual *proposal*, such as:

- Open
- Proposal Preparation
- Submitted
- Accepted
- Declined

You can define the proposal statuses you wish to use.

Making It Happen

The Raiser's Edge can be an effective tool for managing the major gifts fundraising process. It certainly has the tools necessary to record the core major gifts data. The key to your success with it is to:

- Understand your major gifts fundraising methodology, your fundraising process outside The Raiser's Edge.
- Determine which tools in The Raiser's Edge you wish to use to support that process.
- Define the lookup fields and choices for those tools.
- Document this process.
- Train your staff.

For this process to work, however, a few other requirements need to be met:

- Management leadership is required. If the head of fundraising for your institution, or at least the head of major gifts fundraising, has not bought in, it will be hard to make this happen. Fundraising management has some of the greatest benefits to receive from managing a process like this in The Raiser's Edge, with data consistently coded, widely accessible, and reportable.
  - Leadership needs to be willing to use and participate in the process themselves. Although management might have more support staff available to help, at each step their activities should mesh with the procedure. They need to lead by example.
  - Management needs to manage by the process. Reports should be run from The Raiser's Edge when management needs information. They should speak The Raiser's Edge terminology. If necessary, they should take a stance that says, "If it's not in The Raiser's Edge, you didn't do it."

- The previous bullet by no means implies that I recommend pushing the process for managing major gifts in The Raiser's Edge from the top down. Work with the fundraisers to find the right balance of data entry and maintenance with value in reporting. Jettison ideas that require more effort to enter and maintain than provide value in output. Most fields in The Raiser's Edge can be hidden or just ignored and the system will work fine.
- This process requires decision making. The Raiser's Edge should not dictate how your organization raises money. It should support the practices you have found most successful for your institution, your constituencies, your leadership, and staff. Someone is going to have to make decisions about what tools in The Raiser's Edge to use and how to use them. Although the database administrator should unquestionably participate in these discussions, they should be following the fundraising lead. Fundraiser participation is required.
- Finally, this process requires follow-through. The lists and reports will be meaningless if the data is not entered or entered correctly. Monitor the process and revise it as necessary to track more or less detail to ensure that the process is responding to the fundraisers' needs. Help the fundraisers grow into the system and have success with it.

Summary

The Raiser's Edge has many powerful tools for direct marketing fundraising, and it also has a number of excellent tools for major gifts and grants fundraising. But The Raiser's Edge does not tell you how you should be conducting your major gifts and grants work any more than it dictates to the annual fund manager who should be solicited in the direct mail program.

In this chapter we discussed the functions in a constituent record and the reports and dashboards that support major gifts and grants fundraising. We have also walked through an example of how The Raiser's Edge can be used when applying the traditional seven stages of a major gifts prospect with the particular methodology of Moves Management.

Now it is up to you to articulate your major gifts and grants fundraising processes and decide which tools in The Raiser's Edge will be used to support those efforts.

■ ■ ■

Even major gifts officers who are exclusively devoted to the work of major gifts fundraising are users of the larger database. Although this chapter addressed some reports specifically for the major gifts process, let us now turn our attention to the full spectrum of reports that organizations and fundraisers should be using in The Raiser's Edge.

Note

1. Sturtevant, William T. *The Artful Journey: Cultivating and Soliciting the Major Gift.* (Chicago: Institutions Press, 2004). Available from www.instituteforgiving.org.

CHAPTER 7

Reporting, Lists, and Other Output

One feature of The Raiser's Edge that repeatedly sets it apart from the competition, especially at the high end of the market, is the multiple ways it provides output options accessible to the average user. Many other databases require a programmer to be on staff to generate output. Not The Raiser's Edge.

There are so many options available we need to provide some guidance about which are best for you and your staff. Many of these options were intended for you, as a fundraiser, to use yourself. Resources include:

- Tools intended for fundraisers to select, set up, and use by themselves.
- Tools to be set up by others for you to easily run on your own when needed later.
- Output options intended to be run by the database staff for you.
- Output options for the database staff's processes that you will want to ensure are getting done.

The purpose of this chapter is not to teach you how to set up and run the output yourself. The objectives are to:

- Recommend to you the best and most widely used output tools you and your organization should be using.
- Help you understand the terminology and concepts necessary to communicate effectively with your staff so you get the output you want.
- Give you clues to watch for in case your staff seems to be struggling to give you the results you want.

Output Tools

There are a number of output tools in The Raiser's Edge. Briefly, they include:

- *Query:* Query is the tool for making lists. These lists can be viewed and printed on their own. They can also work with the other functions in The Raiser's Edge to limit the results to those in the lists.
- *Mail:* Mail is the tool for producing mailings, both of specific purpose (e.g., donor acknowledgement letters) and of wide application (e.g., envelopes and labels).

- *Export:* Export is the tool to bring data out of The Raiser's Edge, such as into Microsoft Excel spreadsheets.
- *Reports:* This is the tool to create on-screen, hard copy, and PDF versions of what are traditionally thought of as reports.
- *Summaries:* Summaries are screens for viewing within the software the gift activity to date of constituents, solicitors, campaigns, funds, appeals, and events.
- *Dashboard:* Dashboard is the tool to present lists and report-type data on screen for viewing and use within The Raiser's Edge.

Why should you care about these tools? How do they affect you as a fundraiser? What can they do for you? They illustrate the capabilities you and your staff have available to accomplish and analyze your fundraising. If you do not know what the system can do for you, you will not know how to take advantage of the capabilities of The Raiser's Edge. In the discussion that follows, do not worry about these tools per se. Instead, think about your output needs from the system.

Query

Query is the list-making tool in The Raiser's Edge. If you need what I call a "quick and dirty list" of constituents, gifts, actions, appeals, or other data, a query might be your answer.

Queries can sort the data, but not much more. There is no grouping, subtotaling, or grand totaling. The formatting options are quite limited and not intended to produce a professional-looking result for board viewing. A query is just a "data dump," the raw data from the database displayed in a grid.

Query is a powerful tool when used for mailing, as discussed in Chapter 4, but you and your staff should be careful with this tool. Far too many organizations and users make this their primary output tool. It was not designed or intended for that. If your staff members are constantly talking about creating queries and rarely any other output formats, there is a good chance they are using the system incorrectly.

Queries should be used for giving you simple lists. If you need more than that, this is not the format or process you and your staff should use.

Technical Note: Duplicates in Queries

If you are getting duplicates in your query results, this is one reason you and your staff should not be using it as the final output tool. Like any other relational database's query tool, The Raiser's Edge can create duplicates in queries when:

- A constituent meets the query criteria more than one time.
- A query output field has been selected that the constituent has more than one of (e.g., phone number, gift amount).

When queries are used with the other output functions of The Raiser's Edge, which is the design intent, the duplicates will go away.

Mail

Mail is also a powerful tool. Most organizations know to use it to generate their donor acknowledgement letters. Unfortunately, many organizations often do not use it for anything else. Whereas Query is quite frequently overused, Mail is as frequently underused.

This module and its functions are discussed in detail in Chapter 4. If you want to ensure that your organization is getting its full return on the investment in The Raiser's Edge, talk with your database and support staff to ensure that they are using it for more than just donor thank-you letters.

Export

Export allows you and your staff to bring data out of The Raiser's Edge into another electronic file format, most commonly Microsoft Excel.

Like Query, this is a tool that is often overused because staff members do not understand the other output tools in The Raiser's Edge. Export should only be used if there is no other way to obtain the data and analysis. If every time you ask for a report, list, or analysis from The Raiser's Edge you get an Excel spreadsheet, something is probably amiss.

It is good for you to know that The Raiser's Edge can export. There are times when you should get spreadsheets or other file formats from The Raiser's Edge:

- To review data for a mailing
- To send a file of data to a mail house
- To do analysis that none of the other tools in The Raiser's Edge will provide

This last point is the key. Export is the "fall back" tool, the function that should be used to get data out of The Raiser's Edge for lists, graphs, and analysis that just cannot be done within the software. My experience is that when staff really know The Raiser's Edge well, this is rarely necessary. I recommend that when you are presented data in Excel or another export format from your staff, you tactfully ask them, "Why is this in Excel? Have you checked all the other output functions in The Raiser's Edge to ensure there is no other tool that will deliver what I need? Did you talk to Blackbaud customer support to be sure?"

Export is a good tool, it does have a place, and exports will occasionally be necessary. You just want to ensure that it is not being overused in your organization when better tools are available for quicker, easier, and perhaps more accurate results right in the system.

Reports

Reporting, the main topic of this chapter, is certainly a concept you are familiar with. Reports in The Raiser's Edge provide the type of reporting one would expect: data filtered, analyzed, and presented in a meaningful, accessible, professional format that can be printed on paper.

When setting up a report in The Raiser's Edge, there are a number of questions that you or your database staff will have to answer. The reports in The Raiser's Edge are templates, in predesigned formats with built-in layouts and analysis of the data. You and your database staff have to answer two types of questions to complete these templates. These questions and their answers are called the report "parameters."

1. *Exactly what kind of data do you want on the report considering all the data in the database?* When a report contains gift data, it needs to be filtered by dates, campaigns, funds, appeals, gift types, soft credits, and so forth.

   As another example, everyone who runs a report in The Raiser's Edge needs to specify whether to include constituents who are inactive, deceased, and lost (have no valid addresses). The answers to these questions will vary based on the purpose of the report:
   - If the report is for historical understanding and analysis, yes, we would include any constituent currently marked in one of those ways. If someone made a donation during our report period and has since passed away, we still want to see their giving for a complete picture of what happened historically.
   - If, however, we are running reports looking for prospects for our next fundraising effort, anyone who is now inactive, deceased, or lost will be of no help. We should exclude these constituents.

2. *How do you want the report formatted?* Most reports are standard reports with built-in structures. But you do have some formatting options available to you depending on the report. Examples include fields to group by, sort order, the level of detail on the report, the format for constituent names, whether addresses and/or phone numbers are included, and the display of the report's name, date, page numbers, and page and report headers and footers.

Similar to the mailings discussed in Chapter 4, setting up a report is a team effort. Your database administrator needs to ask you a series of questions and to present you with some options in order to give you the best result possible. This is one reason that reports are better than queries in The Raiser's Edge: you and the person setting up the report will be prompted to think about many things that Query will expect you to have already thought through on your own. Some users look at all the questions in a report in The Raiser's Edge and think, "Oh no, I have to understand and fill out all *that*?" Actually, these questions are a good thing, making us think about issues for the report we should be thinking about anyway. If we bypass the report and run a query without thinking about these things, we have not outsmarted the system—we are just unaware of the potential pitfalls and mistakes in the data we are viewing.

The options for each report vary. There are quite a few options, as many as eight or more tabs of parameters for each report. Work with your database staff to understand their questions and provide the answers they need to give you the right results. Neither they nor The Raiser's Edge are being overly detailed; these are the options needed to give you the report that you want. Several times I have heard from fundraisers, "Why are there all of these questions?! All I want is X." The challenge is that two fundraisers' wants are rarely the same. The multiple parameters provide the ability to give you what you want while giving other fundraisers what they want.

Another nice feature of reports in The Raiser's Edge is that they do not have to be printed on paper. Although printing is still occasionally necessary, quite often it is not. If the report is for fundraisers to review, it can be previewed and examined on the screen. If the report needs to be viewed by others who have no access to The Raiser's Edge, such as the executive director or board members, they can be saved as PDF documents and e-mailed directly from the database.

One approach we have used successfully at the Greater Bay Area Make-A-Wish Foundation is to copy and paste screenshots of high-level summary reports into the body of e-mails to distribute the information (instead of attaching a report as a PDF). We do this weekly with the status of campaigns and funds.

The potentially difficult work with a report is setting it up. But once set up, it can be saved and used repeatedly. Even date ranges in reports can be saved as "Today," "Last week," "This month," "Last fiscal year," "This calendar year," and so forth. This way the report's date range is always accurate and does not have to be manually updated. Fundraisers can save links to these reports as favorites on their Home pages so that running these reports requires literally only one click.

Fundraisers running reports this way provides a number of benefits:

- Paper is conserved.
- Each fundraiser has immediate access without having to wait for the report to be run and for the copy to get to them. This includes access at home, in the evenings, and weekends—fundraisers are not dependent on anyone to get the information they want when they want it.
- The information is as up-to-date as possible, always reflecting what is in the database at that very moment.
- Support staff can be doing other, more productive activities than responding to these requests. In fact, running a report set up as a favorite on the Home page takes less time than it would take to ask someone for the report!

I realize this is impossible sometimes and we need to "push" the data in front of people. Usually, the way I decide the distribution method is based on who wants the data. If fundraisers are asking for it and need it, they can access it directly for the reasons listed above. If there is something the database staff needs fundraisers to review that the fundraisers are less likely to take the initiative on, I advocate sending it to the fundraisers if the database staff cannot get them to buy in to do what is needed on their own.

Another reason for pushing the information from The Raiser's Edge out to fundraisers and others is to communicate that The Raiser's Edge is *the* database, the central repository of information. If it is not right in The Raiser's Edge, it is not right. The weekly e-mail on campaign and fund performance sent at the Greater Bay Area Make-A-Wish Foundation now makes it easy for fundraisers and *all* staff to understand how the organization is doing toward its fundraising goals. However, I initially started the process to communicate to the staff that fundraising reporting should be coming from The Raiser's Edge, not financial reports. Because the weekly e-mail was going to everyone showing each fundraiser's results, this provided motivation for them to work with us to give the database the central role it should play in storing and reporting fundraising information.

We talk much more later in this chapter about which of the many reports in The Raiser's Edge your organization should consider running.

Summaries

Summaries are on-screen, interactive tools used to analyze and total activity in The Raiser's Edge. We have already discussed one type extensively in this book, the constituent Gift Summary explained in Chapter 3.

The most useful summaries also available are for:

- Campaigns
- Funds
- Appeals
- Events if your organization has the RE:Event optional module

The Campaign, Fund, and Appeal Summaries are fondly nicknamed the "thermometer screens" for their use of the traditional thermometer illustration to show progress toward goal. See Figure 7.1.

If you need to focus on the results of *one* of these records, such as a single appeal, the summary is going to be the best tool for you, better than any of the standard reports. It is easily accessed from the record using the **View** menu on the menu bar.

As with the constituent Gift Summary, a summary is interactive, letting you modify the filters and the display of information so you can fully analyze the record. It can also be printed, but this is not its primary purpose.

Summaries are tools designed for the fundraiser to use. They are intended to be used interactively, a feature that fundraisers will benefit from, not database support staff. Do not forget that they are available.

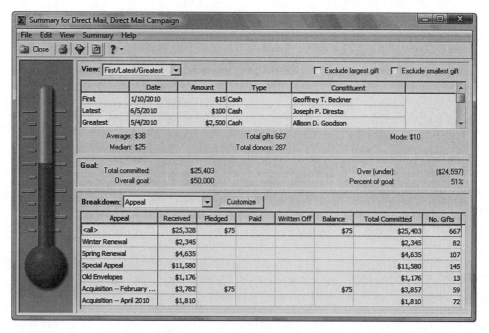

FIGURE 7.1   A Campaign Summary

Note: Additional Summaries

Constituent Gift, Campaign, Fund, Appeal, and Event Summaries are those that should be most used. If you find these particularly useful and want to explore others, additional summaries are available for solicitor performance for all copies of The Raiser's Edge; for gift accountability for those organizations also using The Financial Edge; and for the following optional modules' tabs: Honor/Memorial, Volunteer, Membership, and Prospect (called Chronology).

Dashboard

Dashboard is one of my favorite output tools in The Raiser's Edge. It was designed for fundraisers to use.

A dashboard is an on-screen presentation of list and reporting data that is most relevant to fundraisers (as compared to reports, many of which are for gift processing and other back-office activities). Dashboard is a concept that arose a few years ago in fundraising software after their development in for-profit databases. Dashboards help managers understand the performance of the "engine" of their organization. An example is shown in Figure 7.2.

A dashboard in a car has a number of gauges: speedometer, odometer, engine temperature, fuel level, and so forth. These gauges help us understand how well the

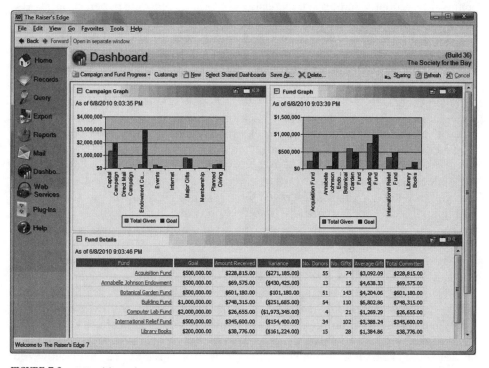

FIGURE 7.2   A Dashboard

car is operating, assuring us that all is well or providing warning signs that we can act on before the situation gets worse.

A dashboard in The Raiser's Edge also has gauges, called "panels," that help us understand how well our fundraising operation is performing, assuring us that we are on our way to meeting our goals or warning us when areas are failing behind. These panels also inform us when other efforts need to be made. For example, the most popular dashboards contain charts about campaign, fund, and appeal performance toward goals. One of the most popular panels is the Recent Gifts List, which shows large gifts (or others we identify). It is used to notify fundraisers as soon as possible about these gifts so they can contact the donors by phone to thank them.

Dashboard in The Raiser's Edge can be more like a dashboard in an airplane cockpit than a dashboard in a car. You can have multiple dashboards in The Raiser's Edge, not just one. Furthermore, you can define how many and which gauges—panels—go on each dashboard. Once set up, these dashboards can provide a nice visual presentation of the exact lists and metrics you as a fundraiser want to know on a regular basis. There is no more dependency on support staff to deliver these numbers.

To summarize the concepts and terminology thus far, there is a Dashboard page among the options on the left side of the main screen of The Raiser's Edge. On the Dashboard page, you can create as many dashboards as you want, each named and defined to show you the panels you want to see. On each dashboard are the panels, the gauges that calculate and show the statistics and lists you have selected. Each dashboard on the Dashboard page is selected from a drop-down list on the screen.

Dashboards look better on the screen than reports. Reports, after all, are based on the older model of static black text data to be printed on white paper. Dashboards, intended to be viewed on screen, have a nicer presentation and can use color in charts to illustrate the results—even 3-D charts and graphs, if you wish.

Another benefit of dashboard's intended use on the screen is that they allow for "drill-through" capability. That means that any data presented as a hyperlink on the screen can be clicked on and the record behind it will open. For example, on the popular Recent Gifts List panel the gift date and donor name are hyperlinks. Want to know more details about the gift? Just click on the date to see all the gift data. Want to know more about the donor? Just click on the name. Reports cannot do this.

Another benefit of note about dashboards is that setting them up is easier than reports. Again, they were intended to be used by fundraisers, not database staff. So the options have been focused on those you are most likely to want. If you have read Chapter 3 about gifts and followed the book thus far, you will probably be fine setting up the dashboards yourself. If you do not want to do that, however, do not worry. Your database staff can help you get them set up quickly and the dashboard will then be available for you to use.

There is one important thing to remember about dashboards: they only update the data when you tell them to. Because dashboards can contain so much data, they do not automatically and constantly update. All you have to do is click the **Refresh** button on the screen and the selected dashboard will update in a few moments.

When you think "reporting," do not just think of the traditional black-and-white report. Dashboard is a tool that all fundraisers should be using—it was programmed just for you. Furthermore, when you ask your staff for "a report," let them know you would be happy with a dashboard as the result. We talk more about which are the best to use later in the chapter.

Summary of Output Options

Let us summarize how to use the tools most properly to get the data you need out of The Raiser's Edge.

If you are doing a mailing:

Use Mail if it will give you what you need.

↓

If not, use Export.

If you need a list or "report" for data analysis:

Use a Summary if that will meet your needs.

↓

Use Dashboard if that will meet your needs.

↓

Use Reports if that will meet your needs.

↓

Use Export.

In each of these cases a query may be necessary to filter to the exact group of records needed. However, the query should usually play a supporting role in the process and not be the primary tool.

The point of this for you as a fundraiser is that you need to participate in the process for the best result. You need to provide the direction to your database staff about exactly what you need and its purpose so they can identify the best tool. If your staff members seem to be struggling to do that, you now know what tools you can suggest to them to help them get the job done for you.

Dashboards and Reports to Run

Let us now discuss the best and most commonly used dashboards and reports that each organization should be running.

The primary focus of this section is the dashboards and reports that you care about and use as a fundraiser. However, some mention is made of the reports that others on your staff need to be using as well. This is so that you can understand what is happening in your department, manage it, and suggest potential solutions when none seem evident to your staff.

Daily Reports

One way to emphasize the role and importance of certain reports is to discuss them in the frequency with which they should be run. We will start with the reports that should be run just about every day.

DAILY GIFT REPORTS FOR ACCOUNTING   As discussed in Chapter 3, each time a batch is committed two reports should be generated:

1. *The Batch Commit Control Report.* This report is generated during the process of committing the batch. It provides proof of the gift entry for audit and control purposes.

2. *Gift Detail and Summary Report by Fund.* This report provides accounting the data that staff need to quickly make the required entries into the accounting software in summary by fund. It also provides the backup to those numbers.

If your staff is running other reports for gifts, such as the Batch Validation Report, you might wish to check with them on the need for the other reports. I have frequently observed gift staff running other reports for each batch and, upon further discussion, thought it unnecessary to do this. Certainly data entry accuracy is critically important, but that can be done right in the software. A full printout of all gift entry for every batch is unnecessary as well.

To reduce the use of paper, you might want to instruct your staff to save the Batch Control Report as a PDF to a designated network location instead of printing it.

Your accounting staff might prefer a report or format other than the Gift Detail and Summary Report by Fund, but this is usually the best format. If they say they do not need it because they enter every gift again, it is time to talk to the head of accounting. Double-entry of every gift is a poor use of resources for the organization.

TODAY'S GIFT ACTIVITY   The reports just discussed for each batch are more detail than fundraisers want. Understandably, however, fundraisers do want to know what gifts come in each day. Good audit controls keep them from opening the mail and handling the checks, but they are obviously interested in seeing the results of their hard work. For big gifts, they want to immediately begin the acknowledgement process, perhaps calling some donors and thanking them for their gifts.

The best approach for this reporting is no report at all: Dashboard provides the best tools.

For fundraisers interested in particular gifts or donors, the Recent Gifts List panel is ideal. Among other options, it can be filtered by gift amount to only show gifts larger than a specified amount. This allows you to focus on the big gifts of the day, however you define "big." This panel also allows for filtering by all the standard gift filters we have discussed previously and through a query. For example, users like major gifts officers might just want to see the gifts given by their prospects.

One useful strategy is to place two copies of the Recent Gifts List panel on one dashboard as shown in Figure 7.3. The panel on the top can show gifts This Week and the one on the bottom the gifts from Last Week. This approach ensures that, if you forget to check the dashboard one day, or are out or otherwise busy, you do not miss any gifts.

Fundraisers who do direct marketing fundraising may not be interested in a list of specific gifts. Typically, these fundraisers are going to be more interested in the total activity for the day and to date, and how close the day's gifts have brought them to goal. For these purposes, use the Appeal Summary, Fund Summary, or Campaign Summary dashboard panels, depending on the level of detail the fundraiser is interested in tracking.

These dashboard summaries show multiple campaigns, funds, and appeals in one panel. A graph can be included that visually shows progress against goal. And a table can be included that shows the specific dollar and other statistics about performance and progress toward goal.

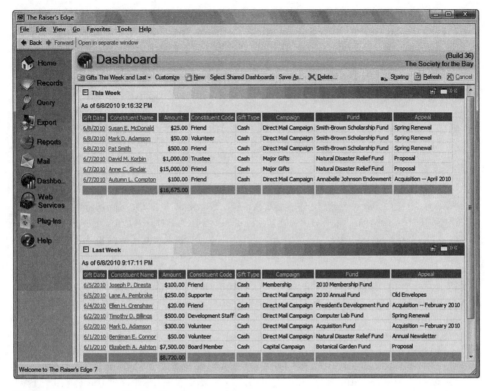

FIGURE 7.3   Recent Gifts List Panels

TODAY'S ACTIONS TO DO   The best way for each person to know what they need to do every day for constituent interactions is to use the Action Reminders dashboard panel. Dashboard panels can be placed on the Home page in addition to the Dashboard page, though it is my preference that the Action Reminders be the only panel on the Home page (this is the default).

This panel allows you to see what needs to be done as well as click on the action to open it. The action details can be seen, the activity performed, and the action updated and marked completed.

Use the Tickler Report in the Action Reports category for reminders for those without access to The Raiser's Edge, such as the organization's senior management, board members, and other fundraising volunteers. Establish a schedule, such as weekly, to generate and e-mail these reports. The reports can be easily set up for one report per person. As each is generated it can be e-mailed directly to the person as a PDF.

Weekly Reports

Managing each day's gifts and actions needs to be attended to daily. Every week is a good timeframe in which to check on the progress of the overall fundraising activity, however.

FUNDRAISING PERFORMANCE Certainly, directors of development and other fundraising managers are going to want to know on a regular basis how the fundraising efforts are progressing toward goal. It is probably a good idea to let everyone in development know about the progress.

For those who want to follow these metrics themselves, the best tools to use are the Campaign, Fund, and Appeal Summaries in Dashboard as discussed earlier.

If you need to push out the statistics, however, or you need them in hard copy, I highly recommend the Campaign, Fund, and Appeal Performance Analysis Reports. These reports can be found in Reports in the Campaigns, Funds, and Appeals Reports category. These reports contain statistics like number of donors, average per donor, total given, the amount over and under goal, and the percent toward goal. The appeal version also includes statistics such as percent response and cost per gift.

At the Greater Bay Area Make-A-Wish Foundation, it is the campaign and fund versions of this report that we use for the screenshots. The database administrator pastes the screenshots directly into an e-mail to all staff each week to proactively keep them informed of the organization's fundraising progress.

If you would like to see the statistics for this year to date as compared to last year to date (or even compared to the last two, three, or four years), use the Comparisons and Summaries Report. This is found in Reports in the Demographic and Statistical Reports category.

TOP GIFT VERIFICATION If the fundraisers are not actively monitoring each day's gifts, you might want to e-mail a report of the week's top donors and their gift information to ensure that the constituent and gift data is correct. We do this at the Greater Bay Area Make-A-Wish Foundation.

- Use the Gift Detail and Summary Report.
- Base it on a gift query that identifies the top 25 gifts from last week sorted in descending order by gift amount.
- Include in the report the constituent's full name and address information as well as the most important gift fields such as campaign, fund, and appeal.
- E-mail it to fundraisers, asking them to ensure that the constituent and gift data are correct and to notify the database staff if not.

Monthly Reports

These reports are typically run once a month. That does not mean they need to all be run on the first or beginning of the month. Because the purpose of these reports is to prompt activity, they should be scheduled throughout each month to pace the work.

Also, several of these reports are part of larger processes and not just stand-alone reports. The reports are listed here to help you learn about them, but be sure your database staff incorporate them into the larger processes in which they belong. For example, this applies to the Recurring Gift Missed Payment, Action Summary, and Solicitor Performance Analysis Reports.

PAST DUE PLEDGES Pledges are not worth anything if they are not paid. Unfortunately, sending a reminder does not automatically result in payment. Therefore, each month your database staff should generate the Past Due Report in the Pledge and

Recurring Gift Reports category. The report should be distributed as a PDF through e-mail to the fundraisers with responsibility for the pledges past due and fundraising management. I once ran this for a client who had not been doing so, and we discovered a $100,000 past due pledge that had been forgotten! Needless to say, they followed up immediately. It is better to run the report every month so this does not happen.

INCOMPLETE ACTIONS We have stressed the importance of recording actions. For database cleanliness, but even more importantly for good fundraising practice, the actions should be done and marked as completed. Your database staff should run a report every month of actions older than four weeks that are still showing as incomplete so they can follow up with whoever was supposed to do the action. As the primary purpose of this is not database maintenance but helping staff avoid forgetting things they should have done, you might want this run for more recent incomplete actions.

This report is the Action Detail Report in the Action Reports category filtered to include incomplete actions prior to a specified date.

MISSED RECURRING GIFT PAYMENTS If you have a monthly donor program, someone needs to follow up with those whose monthly gifts were not received. The Recurring Gift Missed Payment Report in the Pledge and Recurring Gift Reports category will help you easily identify those constituents.

FUNDRAISER AND STAFF ACTIVITY The Action Summary Report was discussed in Chapter 6 in the context of major gifts officers. Because staff should be interacting with constituents for many more reasons than only major gifts fundraising, this report can also be used for tracking other fundraiser and staff activity.

SOLICITOR PERFORMANCE It is entirely reasonable for fundraising management to want to know how staff and volunteer fundraisers are performing, how much money they have raised. For certain fundraisers, such as the annual fund manager, this can be most easily done by reports at the appeal level.

For other fundraisers, however, such as major gifts officers or board members, their work is part of a group effort as reflected at the campaign, fund and appeal levels. To track their performance you need a report that shows their names individually with the prospects they have been assigned, the gifts they have raised, and their performance toward their individual goals. This can be done by:

- Assigning the solicitors to their prospects on the prospects' Relationships tab
- Assigning the solicitors on the gifts they raise
- Assigning the goals on the solicitor **Details** button on the Bio 1 tab of the solicitor if you want to see performance toward individual goal
- Using the Solicitor Performance Analysis report in the Analytical Reports category

This is an excellent report that I highly recommend. It can be used not only for tracking staff fundraising but also for board fundraising. There is no single "Board Give or Get" report. Use a Gift Detail and Summary Report filtered to the constituent

6/8/2010   **Solicitor Performance Analysis**

Constituent	Gift Date	Fund	Amount	Pledge Balance	Reference
Robert C. Hernandez					
Julie M. Bach	2/1/2010	Acquisition Fund	$1,000.00	$0.00	
Allision D. Goodson	5/4/2010	Richard Mosley	$2,500.00	$0.00	
Inman's Industrial Supply	2/1/2010	Smith-Brown	$1,000.00	$0.00	
RCS Corporation	9/13/2009	Annabelle Johnson	$25,000.00	$0.00	
Ginger Rosenberg	8/23/2009	Richard Mosley	$7,500.00	$0.00	
Anne C. Sinclair	6/7/2010	Acquisition Fund	$15,000.00	$0.00	
Nicholas Vincent	5/16/2010	Annabelle Johnson	$7,500.00	$0.00	
			$59,500.00	**$0.00**	

8.75% (7 out of 80) gave/pledged
Endowment Campaign Goal:	$50,000.00
Total Raised:	$59,500.00
Over (Under):	$9,500.00

FIGURE 7.4   The Solicitor Performance Analysis Report

code of Board to see their "give" data. You can use the Solicitor Performance Analysis, shown in Figure 7.4, filtered to the board as solicitors for the "get" tracking.

With the Solicitor Performance Analysis Report, be sure that the solicitor is assigned to both the constituent and the gift. This report will not show gifts given by the solicitor's constituents for which the solicitor is not also assigned to the gift.

If seeing the solicitor's activity in summary is sufficient, without the prospects' names, there is a Dashboard panel for Solicitor Status you should consider.

RECONCILING WITH ACCOUNTING   Each month someone on the fundraising staff should reconcile The Raiser's Edge with the accounting software. There are a number of reports that your staff have available to ensure that the data in The Raiser's Edge can be reconciled.

To reconcile fund balances:

- A pivot report based on fund and batch
- Gift Detail and Summary Report summarized by fund
- Adjusted Gift Report
- Stock Gain/Loss Report for sale of stock transactions
- General Ledger Audit Report for deleted posted gifts, if any

Pivot reports can be created in the Reports category of that name. The other four reports are in the Financial Reports category.

To reconcile pledge activity and balances:

- Pledge Status Report, selecting Format 2 on the Format tab
- Written-Off Report for details on write-offs
- If necessary, new pledges and pledge payments can be listed using the Gift Detail and Summary Report

The first two pledge reports can be found in the Pledge and Recurring Gift Reports category.

Annual Report and Other Recognition Needs

Creating the lists needed for the annual report is an area in which The Raiser's Edge excels. It was designed for such a purpose. However, many users struggle because they try to do everything with queries. The key reports that will help your staff create your annual report for you as easily as possible are listed here.

These same processes can be used for other times when recognition lists are needed. For example, these reports work for the same kinds of lists in newsletters and magazines. They also supply the data necessary for donor walls.

DONORS BY GIVING LEVEL   The standard listing format in an annual report groups donors together by cumulative giving ranges, with the highest range listed first. Often these ranges are named, such as the "Platinum Society," "Gold Society," and "Silver Society." The names might instead use person or place names of significance to the organization, such as founders of the organization. The Raiser's Edge has a standard report that creates this list for you. It provides you the option to both identify your unique giving ranges by amounts and to name the ranges if you wish. You can also store multiple sets of ranges to support multiple lists by giving level, such as

- Fiscal year cumulative giving by individuals
- Fiscal year cumulative giving by organizations
- Lifetime giving
- Campaign giving, such as capital and endowment campaigns

You, as the fundraiser, define the ranges and name them. Provide those ranges to your database administrator who will enter them into the database's Configuration page. The report that can be run based on these ranges is called the Donor Category Report and it is located in the Analytical Reports category. A few key notes:

- Using the criteria discussed in Chapter 3, be clear about what gifts do and do not count toward the calculation of cumulative giving.
- Use the Donor Recognition addressee if present, otherwise use the primary addressee to get the right name on the report.
- Be certain that the User Options are set properly to display anonymous gifts as discussed in Chapter 3. In the draft version of this report, it is entirely appropriate to see the anonymous donors' names. However, you must be certain that the final version of the report given to the printer reflects those gifts as "Anonymous."

PIE CHART BY DONOR TYPE   A primary intent of the **Constituent Code** field is to produce a pie chart for your annual report showing the percentage of support by donor type (e.g., board, foundation, and corporation). Your report designer probably prefers to be given the categories and their percentages rather than a completed pie chart. This information can be most easily obtained from The Raiser's Edge by using the Statistical Reports in the Demographic and Statistical Reports category. Of note:

- Talk to your database administrator to think through the option for the nuance between *constituent* Constituency code and *gift* Constituent code.
- The column you want to use for the pie chart is the **Percent of total given**.

TRIBUTE LISTINGS Many annual reports contain lists of "gifts received in memory of the following people this year" and "gifts received in honor of the following this year." If your organization has the RE:Tribute module, the report that most easily gives you the data for those lists is the Honor/Memorial Contributors List in the Tribute Reports category.

Some organizations just show the names of the people honored and remembered, while others show the donor names for each. You can select from this report the level of detail you wish. For "in honor of" gifts you can also select whether to use just the constituent's name or the full description of the honor (e.g., "in honor of the retirement of Robert Hernandez"). This report can be easily filtered and run twice so "in honor of" and "in memory of" lists are separate.

If your organization does not have the RE:Tribute module, use a gift query to find the names used in the gift attribute for this purpose.

GIVING BY CLASS YEAR If your organization is an educational institution and has the RE:Alum additional module, use the Alumni Class Analysis report in the Analytical Reports category to show giving by class.

Other Yearly Reports

In addition to the reports needed for the annual report, there are other reports you should consider running once a year, though at different times of the year for each.

IDENTIFYING GOOD PROSPECTS The best prospects are those who have previously given. If you are getting near the end of the fiscal year and you want to identify the best prospects to contact for gifts, consider the LYBUNT and SYBUNT Reports. The acronyms stand for those that have given Last/Some Year But Unfortunately Not This year. Run the LYBUNT report, work those constituents, and then run the SYBUNT report and work those prospects. These reports can be found in the Analytical Reports category.

DONORS WHO HAVE GIVEN MORE AND LESS The Raiser's Edge has a report called the Comparative Report in the Analytical Reports category that shows you donors who have given more or less than last year. It is easiest if the report is filtered to show only one of these two groups. Because reports have the ability to create queries for you of those included on the report, you can use this report to:

- Send a tactfully worded appeal to those donors who have given less asking them to make up the difference. The Export page in The Raiser's Edge lets your staff export the amounts from the two years. Word, Excel, or your mail house can calculate the difference so that you can request a gift of that amount if you feel that is an appropriate ask.
- Send a special thank-you letter to the donors who have given more than previously, acknowledging this added support and the good it has helped your organization do. Use this as a cultivation opportunity to renew the donor at the higher level of giving the next time you do a solicitation.

ANNUAL GIVING STATEMENT   Each January, you might wish to send statements to some donors summarizing their giving from the past calendar year. These statements will help donors with their tax preparation. Donors who have not received acknowledgement letters for each gift, such as monthly donors and staff employee giving donors, should also be provided with such a statement along with a thank you.

The report intended for this purpose in The Raiser's Edge is the Annual Statement Report in the Financial Reports category. Of note:

- This report, unlike most others, starts each constituent on a new page so the report can be easily mailed to the donor.
- Adjust the columns you put on the report and their headings to make the report as clear as possible from a donor perspective.
- Focus on the gift Receipt amount that should have been entered into The Raiser's Edge as the portion of the gift that is tax deductible.
- The report will need to be accompanied by a cover letter generated from Mail explaining the report's contents when sent to the donors. The report is not meant to stand alone meaningfully to a donor.
- You might want to add in the report footer and in the cover letter a reminder that this report could contain gifts for which acknowledgement letters were previously sent. The donor should be careful to not duplicate the gift in their tax deductions.

VSE SURVEY REPORT   The VSE Survey Report is for educational institutions that participate in the Voluntary Support of Education survey from the Council for Aid to Education. This report is in the Analytical Reports category and will help your staff fill out certain sections of the VSE survey.

Ad Hoc Reports

These are reports to run on an as-needed basis. Typical needs for these reports are frequent enough to have identified them for your consideration.

PRINTOUTS OF A RECORD   If you need a hard copy version of a constituent's data, a Profile can provide that. We have discussed Profiles in Chapters 2 and 6. Profiles are available for constituents, events, campaigns, funds, and appeals.

A profile need not be a complete printout of the entire record. You can set up a variety of profile formats that include only the types of data you wish to see, even as simple as a "Name and Address" profile.

Profiles are set up in Reports in the Profiles, Lists, and Directories category. They can be printed from there as well, either for one record or for all the records in a query. However, profiles also have the special property that they can be printed directly from the record using the **Print** and **Preview** options.

ANALYSIS OVER TIME   If you like to examine trends and see the change in activity over time in your fundraising, The Raiser's Edge can accommodate this. It supports a comparison of two time periods, such as this fiscal year to date and last fiscal year to date. When two time periods are chosen, it shows a variance in terms of dollars or percent. It also supports comparing three, four, and five time periods side-by-side.

You define the time periods: fiscal or calendar years, quarters, months; it is up to you. You also have a number of options for the breakdown of the giving, including campaign, fund, and appeal; address fields (e.g., State/Province and ZIP/Postal Code); and days in the month.

The report is the Comparisons and Summaries report in the Demographic and Statistical Reports category. In the option for **Report Type,** a "Comparison" is two time periods with a variance while a "Summary" is three to five time periods. You can always run any report in The Raiser's Edge twice or more, each with a different time period, and place them side-by-side on the table. This report allows that option on one report.

OTHER LISTS OF DONORS AND GIFTS   There are many times and many reasons over the course of a year in which you are going to simply need a list of donors or a list of gifts that meet a specific set of criteria for that moment: within a date range; to a particular campaign, fund, or appeal; by one or more constituencies; for an event; and many other reasons. Most users of The Raiser's Edge are likely to create a query for this purpose, but I highly recommend the Gift Detail and Summary Report instead shown in Figure 7.5 in the Detail format. This report is found in the Financial Reports category.

The Gift Detail and Summary Report is your workhorse report. It is by far the most widely used report among organizations that use The Raiser's Edge. It is probably the most flexible report, also. Whenever you just need a listing of donors and gifts without any sophisticated analysis, use this report.

Tip: Constituent Giving History Report

If gift type is important to you but you do not want the gift amounts in different columns by gift type (as the Gift Detail and Summary Report does), use the Constituent Giving History Report instead, found in the Financial Reports category.

		Gift Detail and Summary Report		
6/8/2010				Page 1

Constituent Name	Date	Campaign Description	Fund Description	Amount
Mark D. Adamson	6/2/2010	Direct Mail Campaign	Acquisition Fund	$300.000
	6/8/2010	Direct Mail Campaign	Smith-Brown Scholarsh	$50.00
Elizabeth A. Ashton	6/1/2010	Capital Campaign	Botanical Garden Fund	$7,500.00
Julie M. Bach	2/1/2010	Endowment Campaign	Acquisition Fund	$1,000.00
	4/8/2010	Capital Campaign	President's Development I	$7,500.00
Francis E. Baker	3/11/2010	Events	Smith-Brown Scholarsh	$250.00
Baldwin Entertainment Corporation	3/8/2010	Internet	Computer Lab Fund	$5,000.00
Geoffrey T. Beckner	1/10/2010	Direct Mail Campaign	2010 Annual Fund	$15.00
Timothy D. Billings	5/1/2010	Capital Campaign	Botanical Garden Fund	$,500.00
	6/2/2010	Direct Mail Campaign	Computer Lab Fund	$500.00
City Insurance Company	1/31/2010	Direct Mail Campaign	2010 Annual Fund	$10.00
Autumn L. Compton	6/7/2010	Direct Mail Campaign	Annabelle Johnson Endo	$100.00
Agnes M. Cone	2/4/2010	Planned Giving	Building Fund	$25,000.00
Benjiman E. Connor	6/1/2010	Direct Mail Campaign	Natural Disaster Relief F	$50.00
Ellen H. Crenshaw	6/4/2010	Direct Mail Campaign	President's Development I	$20.00
Joseph P. Diresta	6/5/2010	Membership	2010 Membership Fund	$100.00
Allison D. Goodson	5/4/2010	Endowment Campaign	Richard Mosley Memoria	$2,500.00
Robert C. Hernandez	3/3/2010	Major Gifts	Natural Disaster Relief F	$10,000.00
Inman's Industrial Supply	2/1/2010	Endowment Campaign	Smith-Brown Scholarsh	$1,000.00
David M. Korbin	6/7/2010	Major Gifts	Natural Disaster Relief F	$1,000.00
Susan E. McDonald	6/8/2010	Direct Mail Campaign	Smith-Brown Scholarsh	$25.00
Lane A. Pembroke	6/5/2010	Direct Mail Campaign	2010 Annual Fund	$250.00
Anne C. Sinclair	6/7/2010	Endowment Campaign	Acquisition Fund	$15,000.00
Pat Smith	6/8/2010	Direct Mail Campaign	Smith-Brown Scholarsh	$500.00
Tenli Smyth	1/22/2010	Internet	Building Fund	$50.00
Emma V. Terrell	1/23/2010	Direct Mail Campaign	2010 Annual Fund	$100.00
Nicholas Vincent	5/16/2010	Endowment Campaign	Annabelle Johnson Endo	$7,500.00

			Grand Totals:	**$88,820.00**

27 Gifts(s) listed
24 Donor(s) listed

FIGURE 7.5   The Gift Detail and Summary Report

Event, Membership, and Volunteer Reports

If your organization has one or more of the optional modules RE:Event, RE:Member, or RE:Volunteer, each has its own category on the Reports page. Below is a list of the most valuable and used reports from those categories.

- Event Management Reports
  - Event Lists
  - Seating Arrangements
  - Seating Validation Report
- Membership Reports
  - Comparative Membership Statistics
  - Membership Statistics by Category

- Volunteer Reports
  - Volunteer Job Assignments
  - Volunteer Match List

Custom Reports

All of the reports discussed so far are standard reports, templates built in the software for which you only need to provide the parameters (e.g., which constituents, which gifts, what formatting). The Raiser's Edge supports custom reporting through a tool that Blackbaud includes with the system called Crystal Reports. This tool allows your staff to create a report from scratch according to the exact specifications you define.

The challenge is that doing such a thing is not easy. This is not a reflection on The Raiser's Edge or Crystal Reports, it is the nature of report writing. Even if you have someone on your staff who has this interest and capability, you should think long and hard about taking this approach. How long will this person be with you, to trouble-shoot problems with the report and update it as your needs and The Raiser's Edge change? Are you willing to pay the salary necessary to keep this person or to hire a replacement? It is difficult to find new staff people who already know The Raiser's Edge. It is much more difficult to find someone who also knows Crystal Reports.

Finally, you should know that Crystal Reports will no longer be the included and supported report-writing tool in The Raiser's Edge version 8. Blackbaud is moving to Microsoft SQL Server Reporting Services. The technology itself is not important in this context. What is important is that your organization not make an exorbitant investment in Crystal Reports training and development without knowing that these reports probably have a limited shelf life. (Crystal Reports is a tool currently included with The Raiser's Edge, but it is not a Blackbaud product. Your organization could choose to use Crystal Reports outside of The Raiser's Edge version 8 by exporting data from the system.)

If you do have the resources in your organization to support such an undertaking, your role as the fundraiser in the process is to:

- Help define the query criteria to select the records that should be on the report.
- Help define the data fields necessary to display, group, and calculate the information on the report.
- Explain the needed layout and display of the information on the report.

Once a custom report is written in Crystal Reports, the report file can be added into The Raiser's Edge on the Reports page in the Custom Reports category. This allows you to:

- Access the report yourself to run it inside The Raiser's Edge with no technical knowledge required for you.
- Save the report as a favorite to your Home page for even quicker access to it.
- Share the report with all other users who may benefit from it.
- Work with the person writing the report to base it on an "Ask" query. This prompts for criteria about whom and what to include on the report like you can with standard reports. For example, each time you run the report, it can ask you for the date range for gifts that should be on the report.

Most organizations do not have the resource to support custom reports through Crystal Reports. What options do you have if that is true of your organization?

- Use the standard reports. We have only discussed a small selection of the many reports available in The Raiser's Edge. Use the many resources available to you to find a standard report that will meet your needs.
- Be flexible. Frequently, I see reports that have many columns and numbers on them. When I ask the fundraiser what they do with the report, they often tell me they focus on one or two numbers. Seriously think about what you *really* need from the report and there is more likely to be a standard tool in The Raiser's Edge to give you that data.
- Run multiple Raiser's Edge reports. Although I can certainly appreciate the preference for one report that has everything you want to see, we have no report standardization in our industry. Unlike our accounting colleagues who have standardized Balance Sheet and Income Statement formats, we have nothing comparable. Blackbaud has used its experience of over a quarter of a century in this business to deliver a large choice of reports that provide a great diversity of statistics. If one report does not tell you everything you need, run the ones that do and use them.
- If you need the data combined for presentation to senior management and the board, the best approach to accomplish this is to design the template in Word or Excel, have your staff run Raiser's Edge reports that provide the needed numbers, and enter the numbers into the Word or Excel template. Although this is not as fast a process as running a customized report, it is one that is easy to do, support, and change, especially as your staff changes over time.
- Explore the pivot report functionality in Reports. A pivot report is a tool from Excel in which you specify fields for columns and rows. Where the columns and rows meet are data points such as amounts and numbers. For example, if you wanted a simple report of amount in each fund by campaign:
  - Fund would be the rows.
  - Campaign would be the columns.
  - Gift amount would be totaled where the rows and columns intersect.
  A pivot report is based on a query and uses The Raiser's Edge integration with Microsoft Excel. This is a much easier process than a custom report in Crystal Reports and can often meet custom needs more efficiently.
- Consider a query. Can a simple query of the raw data suffice?
- Use Export. If all else fails and you simply cannot get the report you want within The Raiser's Edge, export the data to Excel and use the full set of tools Excel provides to manipulate the data. Only remember that each time you run the export you need to manipulate the file to get the final result you want.

Except for the largest organizations using The Raiser's Edge, most institutions get by just fine without any custom reports. This is a resource for you should you need it, but embark on this path carefully if at all.

Summary

There are many, many other reports and dashboard panels in The Raiser's Edge. If you have just the core components of The Raiser's Edge with no optional modules, you have more than 70 report templates and 25 dashboard panels available. If you have all the modules, you have more than 125 report templates and 45 dashboard panels. I say "more than" because many of these templates and panels have detail and summary versions, which produce different reports, some have different "Format" options, and they all have infinite variations based on the filters, fields, and formatting options you select.

Begin with those recommended here. Encourage your database staff to slowly explore more and run ideas by you. There is a *Sample Reports* user guide that shows a picture of at least one version of every report. The Dashboard guide shows an illustration of each as well. Take a look at them. Consider having your database or support staff make your own sample reports and dashboard manual by running one-page samples of each. The data will be more meaningful and "speak" to you better when you look at the report to consider using it for your organization.

Experiment by looking at the reports and dashboards in The Raiser's Edge. As you select each report, there are two hyperlinks at the bottom of the page, one that gives you a detailed description of the report and the other that gives you a picture of one version of it. When you select panels in Dashboard, descriptions are provided as well. When you run a report or dashboard, you spend a little time and the system has to process it, but on most systems this happens quickly. There is nothing you can do purposely or accidentally in Reports or Dashboard to harm the data in your system. Do not be shy to try something that looks promising.

Also, do not hesitate to contact Blackbaud customer support to ask them what report or dashboard will best meet your specific needs. This is an appropriate request for their help.

By no means should one organization use all the reports and dashboard panels or even most of them. There is a wide variety of organizations using The Raiser's Edge, and the report and dashboard options reflect that. Use the reports and dashboards that meet your needs, and you will be getting return on your investment.

■ ■ ■

In this chapter and throughout the book, we have talked about the roles your database administrator and database support staff should play in helping you directly with your use of The Raiser's Edge. We now turn our final attention to your role in the hiring and management of these important people.

CHAPTER 8

Database Oversight

The database administrator and database support staff play important roles in the success of The Raiser's Edge at an organization. Many times in this book, we note how you should work with the people in these positions. In addition, there are numerous things they do to support fundraising and maintain the database that most fundraisers do not need to know about.

Except in the smallest of organizations where the director of development is also responsible for the database, the database administrator usually reports to a fundraiser. If you are that fundraiser, this chapter is for you. The chapter is also for directors of development and other managers who want to understand this important management role within a fundraising operation. It is also for those who aspire to be in fundraising management.

The discussion is for the database administrators' *managers*, however, not the administrators themselves. Even here we keep to our non-technical approach and discuss the concepts in a non-technical way. This chapter covers:

- The regular tasks you should make sure that your database administrator is completing and how to assist in those processes.
- How to hire and retain a good database administrator for The Raiser's Edge.

Although database administrators have to be hired before they can be managed, it is assumed here that you already have one. It takes much more time to manage than hire, and the hiring discussion will make more sense if it is understood within the context of the position's role and responsibilities. Therefore we begin with the database administrator's roles and responsibilities before moving to hiring and retention, concluding with a short discussion of the forthcoming version 8 of The Raiser's Edge.

Development or IT?

The position for database administrator for The Raiser's Edge is a development department role. It does not belong in the Information Technology (IT) department. I have the greatest respect for our colleagues in IT. Certainly, everything we need to do with The Raiser's Edge could not be done if IT were not there to provide the hardware and software support behind it. (In fact, I would suggest that you send them an e-mail right now letting them know everything is working fine and you just wanted to say thank you.)

The role of the database administrator for The Raiser's Edge is not a programming or technical role in the true sense of those terms. It absolutely requires technical interest and aptitude, but the role is primarily about development. For example, support staff does not work for IT because they do mail merges in Word or create charts and graphs in Excel. They certainly use and must know the technology to accomplish those tasks, but their knowledge of the work of your department is more important.

The same is true of the database administrator for The Raiser's Edge. This person needs to know and use The Raiser's Edge well, but their understanding of fundraising, their ability to communicate with fundraisers, and their responsibility to translate the fundraisers' needs into The Raiser's Edge are the primary responsibilities of the position. They need to "speak fundraising," making judgment calls more about what is the best fundraising option than the right technical tool.

For this reason, many IT professionals do not like us to use the term "database administrator" for The Raiser's Edge. They would prefer instead "application administrator," "database manager," or "database coordinator." Typically, in IT the term "database administrator" is a highly technical, specialized, and compensated position working with Microsoft and Oracle databases. However, in the fundraising industry "database administrator"—DBA for short—has stuck.

Your DBA for The Raiser's Edge should have a good relationship with IT. As we will shortly discuss, there are some important IT liaison roles they must fill. You and your DBA should use your fundraising stewardship skills to acknowledge and thank your IT staff for the work they do. Please remember to *publicly* acknowledge and thank them. It is not only the right thing to do, it will pay you many dividends in the years to come. But The Raiser's Edge database administrator should report to a fundraiser in development, not IT.

Database Administrator Roles and Responsibilities

There are several roles with The Raiser's Edge that often get interwoven:

- The database administrator, the role responsible for the setup, maintenance, and proper use of The Raiser's Edge.
- The power user who generates the most complicated mailings, reports, lists, and exports.
- The manager of constituent and gift data entry.
- Constituent and gift data entry staff.

In smaller organizations, one person may wear all or several of these hats. In the largest organizations, multiple people may share the same hat. But these are different roles. This chapter primarily addresses the first role in the preceding list, that of the database administrator.

Appendix B includes a specific list of the tasks and responsibilities for your database administrator. Even in the largest organization, it is not a full-time job. Adding the other roles listed above to the DBA's responsibilities can easily make the position a full-time position. However, once the database has been set up and cleaned up, the DBA role should take no more than four to eight hours in an average week.

Let me be clear, however, that getting a database properly set up and cleaned up in the midst of the other daily demands that usually exist can be a time-consuming task. If you have had many hands in your database over the years and no one has created any documentation, getting to the point of being set up and cleaned up could be a full-time job for a year.

If you are about to embark on an implementation or have recently done so, please heed this warning. Your organization will benefit tremendously for years to come if you get a handle on this role and its tasks now.

If your organization already has a difficult database, it is never too late to stop the situation from getting worse. First, get the current procedures under control. Then, gradually clean up by setting time aside a few hours a week for the DBA no matter what else is going on.

Appendix B is fairly technical and is intended for you to share with your database administrator. I recommend:

- Providing a copy of Appendix B to your DBA (if not the whole book).
- Asking your DBA to review it.
- Getting together to discuss it to determine what work needs to be done to implement its recommendations.
- Working together to prioritize the tasks that will take a while to complete.
- Adding responsibilities for these tasks to the DBA's annual accountabilities.
- Measuring the performance of these tasks in the DBA's annual performance review.

The sections that follow highlight, in a nontechnical discussion, what you as a fundraiser should know about these tasks.

Tip: Database Maintenance Checklist

At the Greater Bay Area Make-A-Wish Foundation, we took the tasks from Appendix B, plus others unique to us, and listed them in a spreadsheet. The spreadsheet is used to track the accomplishment of each task. It is set up as follows:

- The rows are divided into five sections, one for each week of the month. Five weeks allows for long months. Start the first week on at least the second row.
- The first column lists the day of the week for each week, Monday through Friday.
- The second column is for the task description, along with short notes about how to do the task, such as the name of the query or report and its location in The Raiser's Edge.
- Each of the weekly tasks is assigned to a day of the week in each week's section.
- The monthly tasks are spaced appropriately across the weeks so that all the activity does not need to be done in the same week.

(continued)

(Continued)

- A separate worksheet is created in the workbook for yearly tasks.
- On the main worksheet, the first task on Monday of the first week of each month is a reminder to check the yearly tab.
- The third and subsequent columns are each assigned a month and year.

As each task is accomplished, the user who did the task should enter his or her initials and the actual date completed in the cell where the task and month intersect.

Let us conclude this section with one final, important point: *your organization should have one, and only one, database administrator for The Raiser's Edge.* This should not be a shared position. Several departments can use The Raiser's Edge and may work quite independently, but one person in the entire organization should have final *authority and responsibility* for the database.

You need someone who is going to say, "This is my database. This is my responsibility. I take ownership of this and will work with all users and management to ensure it is used as accurately and consistently as possible. I take responsibility for the whole thing."

I have found the second most common cause of malfunctioning databases to be the lack of someone in this role. (The most common cause, security, is related and discussed later in this chapter.) The person should be the database administrator, not "database dictator." There should certainly be a backup administrator in case this person is sick, on vacation, at training, or otherwise not available to handle a situation requiring that level of access. This person must work closely with the users and management. But ultimately, as we say in the United States, the "buck must stop" with the database administrator. I cannot stress this strongly enough.

Let us now talk about what this person should be doing.

Technical Oversight

Blackbaud has done an extraordinary job making the technology of The Raiser's Edge easy to implement and support. When I consult on brand new implementations, I normally spend no more than 30 minutes acquainting IT staff with their role in supporting the database. What they are responsible for, however, is critically important. And it is the database administrator's job to ensure that on behalf of development these tasks are being done.

This does not mean that the DBA is to do these tasks. They might not have the server and network security rights to do so, and that is fine. They should work with your IT staff, however, to help ensure that these tasks are getting done. For example, if a backup of The Raiser's Edge is not working properly and you need it, your organization might fire or otherwise discipline the IT person responsible. But *you* are going to suffer the consequences of lost donor records, inaccurate mailings, and upset donors and board members.

This is why technical oversight is listed first. If these few but most important things are not done, everything else is a house of cards waiting to collapse on you.

Appendix B includes the details for your database administrator, but in summary they include:

- *Ensuring that backups are done daily and correctly.* "Correctly" is as key as "daily." In order for your database to be available to you 24 hours a day, seven days a week, there are some special steps that need to be done for the backup to be handled correctly. Because many IT staff do not like to read user guides (I am guilty of this as well), I have frequently seen backups of The Raiser's Edge not being done correctly. Also:
  - Backups need to be stored off-site, but it is no longer wise for someone to take backups home. You need a *secure* off-site backup strategy.
  - Backups must be *tested*. Just because the backup software says everything is okay does not mean that it is. There are plenty of horror stories in this regard; do not become one.
  - You must have a *disaster recovery plan*. You have a backup, but what software and hardware are necessary to restore that backup? How would you get it? A full disaster recovery plan is much more extensive than this, and your organization should have one.
- *Making sure that technical maintenance tasks are run.* These should run weekly by themselves to keep the database files healthy, but need to be occasionally monitored.
- *Ensuring that technical staff members do not change any data in the database through technical tools that Blackbaud does not support.* Doing so could ruin your database and invalidate your maintenance agreement with Blackbaud.
- *Ensuring that software that affects The Raiser's Edge is the version that Blackbaud supports.* You can help your DBA with this task by reminding development staff that they should never upgrade Microsoft Windows, Microsoft Office, Crystal Reports (if used with The Raiser's Edge) or even Internet Explorer until your DBA says it is okay. The Raiser's Edge interacts with these programs. Although Blackbaud is quick to update The Raiser's Edge when these programs change, they should not be updated until Blackbaud has announced they are compatible with The Raiser's Edge and supported by Blackbaud.
- *Keeping The Raiser's Edge on the latest version.* It is understandable to typically wait a month or two before installing each update. However, your organization should stay on the latest version of The Raiser's Edge. Even if the new features do not appear to be of interest, there are always fixes to the software that you should have. If a major issue does arise, Blackbaud will only support you on the latest version. The upgrades are already paid for in your annual maintenance, are easily downloaded from the Blackbaud web site, and are straightforward to install.

If your data is hosted by Blackbaud, Blackbaud is responsible for doing most of these tasks, not your IT staff.

User Oversight

Another role of the database administrator for The Raiser's Edge is to manage and assist users with the software. This should be a proactive responsibility, identifying opportunities to be of help. This area contains several important responsibilities.

SECURITY   Security is incredibly important in The Raiser's Edge for two reasons:

1. It keeps sensitive information away from those who should not see it.
2. It keeps authorized users of The Raiser's Edge from doing things they should not be doing.

Security for The Raiser's Edge is a responsibility of the DBA, not IT. Your DBA is going to best understand the security options in The Raiser's Edge and how they should be applied to each user.

Today security cannot be emphasized enough. Although this book cannot address all of the steps your organization should take to protect your constituent data, we note some of the most important. As the fundraising manager the database administrator reports to, you need to take this seriously and assist the DBA with other staff.

- *Each person should log into The Raiser's Edge with his or her own personal name.* Very, very rarely are there exceptions to this statement. No one should log in under a shared name or generic volunteer, temp, or intern names. Every single person who accesses this sensitive information should have a user account set up with a name, password, and appropriate security rights. You can legally set up as many user accounts in security as you wish regardless of how many user licenses you have purchased. The purchased licenses only affect the number of users that can be logged in *at the same time* and is monitored automatically by the system.
- *Proper setup and use of passwords is paramount.* Help emphasize this to the staff. No easily guessed organization or family names and words. No sticky notes with the password on the monitor or inside desk drawers. No shouting them across the office or sharing them with other users—no matter what. (Yes, I have seen all of this.) Additionally, user passwords should not be stored in writing or electronically by the DBA. If users forget their passwords, the DBA can easily reset them.
- *Work with your database administrator to ensure that the rights of users are set up properly based on their job positions and database abilities.* Some of the security options that are available are shown in Figure 8.1. As noted in the last section, the single biggest reason for bad databases is poor security that has allowed users to do too many things. Here are my rules of thumb: Users should only be allowed to add, edit, or delete data they specifically need to modify *and* have been trained to modify properly. Viewing rights, however, should be as broad as possible unless there is a specific need to prohibit access. Of particular note:
  - No one should have complete access (called "Supervisor-level access" in The Raiser's Edge) except for the database administrator. The backup DBA should have a second login name and password with those rights that he or she only exercises when the primary DBA is absent and the change must be made before the DBA returns. This rule includes the head of the department, the DBA's manager, and others with extensive knowledge and experience with The Raiser's Edge—they should *not* have Supervisor-level rights.
  - Usually no one should have access to delete constituents except for the DBA. Deleting a constituent deletes the entire gift, action, membership, event, and all other history from the database.

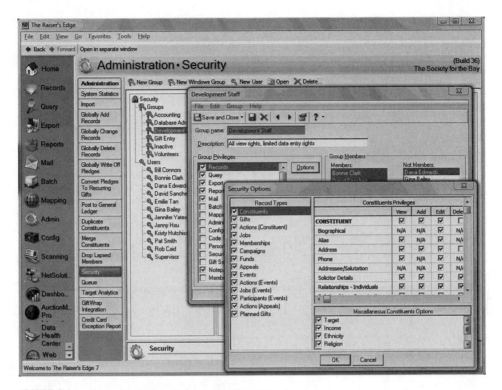

FIGURE 8.1   A Security Group and Security Option

- Only gift-processing staff should have any rights to add, edit, or delete gifts. All fundraisers should have only View rights to gifts.
- With very limited exceptions, no one but the DBA should have access to Configuration and Administration.

Note: Supervisor and the Master Password

With every copy of The Raiser's Edge, there is a built-in user named "Supervisor." This is the master user of the database that has all rights. This user cannot be deleted. Its password serves as the "master password" for The Raiser's Edge.

- Ensure that the default password that came with the software has been changed. The new password should follow the good password protocol of being more than eight characters and include numbers and upper and lower case letters. (The Raiser's Edge requires at least one character to be an upper case letter.) None of the numbers or letters should include anything associated with your organization, such as the street address or acronym.
- Neither the database administrator nor other users should be logging in as Supervisor. All users, *including the DBA,* should be logging in under their own personal names.

(continued)

(Continued)

- The head of the department and the DBA's manager should not be logging in as Supervisor or with Supervisor-level access rights. The only position that warrants Supervisor access is the DBA.
- Even those with extensive knowledge and experience with The Raiser's Edge should not log in as Supervisor or be given Supervisor-level access if they are not the DBA. This is about responsibilities and proper controls, not just training and abilities.
- The Supervisor password should be written down on a piece of paper, sealed in an envelope, and locked in a secure location (perhaps ask accounting if you can borrow space in their safe). If the DBA needs to be let go or something unfortunate happens and supervisor-level access is not available (such as from a backup DBA), you can then retrieve this password for the access you need. (If this recommendation is not followed and you do not know the Supervisor password, contact Blackbaud customer support for assistance.)

- *Work with human resources and managers to involve the DBA if an employee is to be disciplined or let go.* You should review the employee's access rights and modify them before the employee has potential reason to cause harm to the data.
- *When users leave, their security access should be removed.* Leaving old users unmodified in the system creates more opportunities for unauthorized access. The Raiser's Edge will leave deleted user's names on the records and other items they created and changed in the database.

TRAINING   It is the database administrator's responsibility to ensure that, before any user is allowed access to the database, the user is trained. The training should be appropriate to the level of access the person needs. If generic training materials are used, such as this book, Blackbaud training, or online resources, the DBA also needs to ensure that the user understands how The Raiser's Edge is used at your organization.

Training usually should be thought of in three parts:

1. *Training new users.* Although people have different learning styles, almost always the best way to train new users on software is one-on-one or in small group settings. Few fundraisers and others who will use The Raiser's Edge are going to learn what they need to know by being given long policy and procedure documentation. Ideally, the DBA will have or learn the soft skills necessary to provide that training to the organization's users. Hiring managers should work with the DBA to schedule short, one-hour time blocks with new hires over the first few weeks to teach them how The Raiser's Edge works in general and how it is specifically used at your organization. If you are fortunate to hire someone who already knows The Raiser's Edge, the organization-specific training is still of utmost importance. This face-to-face training can be *supplemented* by the more general resources available such as this book, user guides for The Raiser's

Edge, training classes, and online resources, and by your organization's specific policy and procedure documentation (but see the next section for details on creating this properly).

2. *Ongoing training for existing users.* Users will not learn or remember everything they need to know about The Raiser's Edge from one training. The DBA should schedule ongoing trainings as refreshers and opportunities for staff to deepen their level of knowledge. A great way to do this is to offer trainings over lunch, only providing the lunch to those who attend (or just asking staff to bring their own). Another way to do this is to send *short* weekly tips via e-mail.

3. *Training when software updates occur.* Many organizations seem to get updates for The Raiser's Edge, install them, and consider the update complete. It is the database administrator's job to train the staff on the new features of the update. The DBA should also work with all users whose processes should be changed to take advantage of the update.

DOCUMENTATION Many people will read the last section on training and think, "We need to get going on documenting our policies and procedures, and then we can give the information to our new staff to read."

Your organization should have policy and procedure documentation on The Raiser's Edge. However, I recommend a different approach to what most think of as policy and procedure documentation for The Raiser's Edge. The primary differentiation: *Good policy and procedure documentation for The Raiser's Edge at an organization is not written for new users to learn the program. The best policy and procedure documentation an organization can create for The Raiser's Edge is for the database administrators and power users.*

Let me explain. A few "cheat sheets" are a good idea for some users and tasks. And conceptually, yes, it makes great sense to have a document for "welcome to our organization, here is how The Raiser's Edge works, and here is how we use it." But:

- Most new users have no interest in reading a long manual with detailed, step-by-step data entry instructions about The Raiser's Edge, and so they will not.
- It takes a great deal of time to create such documentation, and it needs to be continually updated.
- Most of that kind of documentation has already been written, so why rewrite it?
- The more valuable documentation that is needed has not been written yet.

The kind of documentation that *is* needed and *should* be written—and I strongly advocate—is documentation that explains *exactly how and why your copy of The Raiser's Edge is set up and used as it is.* How is this different?

- It is written by and for the database administrator and power users to consult themselves and leave to their successors.
- It assumes the reader knows The Raiser's Edge. It does not teach them what The Raiser's Edge can do, how it does it, and what to click on. It does not say, "To add a new constituent, go to the Records page. Click on New Individual...." Instead it says, "Here at the Greater Bay Area Make-A-Wish Foundation, we

usually enter the following types of constituents. . . . The fields of note for those records include. . . ."

- It is not organized by the order of the pages in The Raiser's Edge, it is organized based on the business needs and processes your organization uses to make fundraising happen.
- There is as much emphasis on "why" and alternative options explored and rejected as there is on "how."
- It is always a set of working Word documents, never finished, never printed and put in a binder to say, "We're done."
- It covers so much more than just how to add a new constituent. I have seen dozens of such manuals that although well intentioned, just simply repeat the material in Blackbaud's *Constituent Data Entry Guide*.

I believe it is the database administrator's responsibility to oversee the creation of this documentation. If you wish to best serve your organization in the long term, I recommend that you make the creation of this documentation a job responsibility of the DBA, create measurable objectives for the annual job plan for the year, and rate performance against that plan in performance reviews. This will take time, a lot of time, but it can and should be done.

Documentation Structure   The documentation should be composed of three parts:

1. *Database setup*.
   - Each option in Configuration and User Options should be documented. The documentation should indicate the setting selected as best for your organization and why that setting is best.
   - The approach to Security should be explained. Not every right for every user needs to be documented, but key structures and decisions should be explained.
   - This is also the section to document database maintenance tasks.
2. *Data entry procedures*. This should be comprised of:
   - A tab-by-tab, field-by-field discussion of each field on each record on the Records page. This discussion should focus on your organization's specific use of each field. Each lookup field (a field where a list of choices is presented) should have each option documented about what it means and how it should be used in data output. For example, my consulting colleagues and I hear all the time, "We have no idea what that code means or why it's there."
   - Specific procedures should each be their own Word document and explained step-by-step. It is here that the greatest temptation exists to re-teach The Raiser's Edge. This should be avoided. Each procedure should be explained to a reader who already knows The Raiser's Edge. For example, procedures should be added for entering a new donor (not "entering a constituent"), entering gifts daily, processing recurring gifts, and reconciling with accounting.
3. *Data output procedures*. The few attempts at this I have seen try to re-create Blackbaud documentation about how the output modules of Query, Mail, Export, and Reports work. Instead, this type of documentation should include one Word document for each *output process* at your organization. These documents probably touch on two or more of these modules.

Examples of the procedures that are needed here include the steps necessary to generate the daily acknowledgement letters, direct mail files, newsletters, the annual report, and weekly fundraising performance reporting.

Each document should contain:

- The steps undertaken to set up the output process and why. Although output can be saved in The Raiser's Edge, we should have documentation as to why it was set up the way it was and how to re-create it if it is accidentally deleted.
- Once this is written, the beginning of the document should offer the quick steps needed to run the output now that it has been set up.

If your DBA is struggling to determine what to document, the issues raised in this book provide an ideal starting point. I have tried to identify the most key issues your organization should have defined approaches for, so start here if you do not know where to start. Use the concepts in Chapter 1 as inspiration to explain your campaign, fund, and appeal structure. Use the topics of Chapter 2 to explain your organization's approach to spouses and partners, add/sals, and contact types. And so forth.

Other Documentation Tips   Appendix C contains a sample of the kind of policy and procedure documentation I recommend. Here are some tips to help guide the DBA and to help you as you manage the DBA in writing this for your organization.

- *Identify authors and dates*. After the title of each document the name of the person who wrote it should be noted with the date the document was written. When the document is updated, the update author's name and date should be added.
- *Refer to positions, not names*. When referring to people in the text, however, the policy and procedure documentation should refer to positions by title and not by people's names: "The database administrator should . . . ," not "Dawn does. . . ." The exception to this recommendation is that when specific requirements or decisions have been made that guide the process, the name of the person who provided the direction should be noted along with the date. Consider copying and pasting e-mails with this direction right into the documentation, including the e-mail's header (From, Date, etc.).
- *Explain why*. It is important that the documentation explain why options were selected, not just what the selections were. Recording why is much more important, because usually the option selected will be reflected in the software. I have found that recording options considered and rejected can be helpful, as well. This explains clearly that the options were considered and not found as good so someone does not try that approach again.
- *Store electronically*. Work with IT to find a location on the network where a folder can be created to store these documents. Subfolders can be created as well. The documentation should exist as Word documents that are constantly updated as processes are changed and repeated. Rarely should it be printed. Certainly there is no need to make manuals of it to sit on shelves.
- *Keep focused on the intended purpose and audience*. If the writers seem to be losing focus about their audience, who they are writing to and who will be using their documentation, have them pretend they are writing for me, Bill Connors.

This loss of focus on the intended purpose and audience is usually indicated by too much detail about how to do standard steps in The Raiser's Edge. Have them assume they are going to win the lottery, leave your organization some money to hire interim help, and you are going to hire me to do that. They do not need to tell me what The Raiser's Edge can do or how to do it in general. I would need to know how *your* organization did things and why. Occasional reminders of nuances in The Raiser's Edge are fine, but the documentation should avoid statements like, "To start a new query, go to the Query page." It should say instead, "Start a new dynamic constituent query" or "Open the query named 'Direct Mail Includes' in the 'Direct Mail' query category."

- *Use screenshots judiciously.* I understand that "a picture is worth a thousand words." Microsoft Word has terrific tools for adding screenshots to documentation. Circles and arrows can be drawn to bring attention to certain parts of the screen. However, this functionality should be used judiciously. Careful use includes not only the circles and arrows but use of screenshots as well. The primary objective for the documentation should be content, not creating a good-looking manual. Adding and formatting the screenshots takes precious time. More importantly, however, screenshots are hard to update. The documentation is supposed to be updated frequently. When the software and your organization's needs change, it takes longer to recapture the screenshot than just update text. It is also important to be explaining why options and approaches are taken, not just how the options were set. Text makes this easy. Watch this as you review the documentation that is being created.

- *Distinguish between policies and procedures.* We often refer to "policies and procedures" so quickly in one breath that we forget these are actually two different things. Procedures are the steps for implementing the policies. The database administrator and power users will determine how to do things in The Raiser's Edge, but most of the policy decisions are up to the fundraisers. Managers and fundraisers set the policy, the database staff members implement them. For example:

  - Policy: "It is our policy to acknowledge all gifts within 24 hours of their receipt."
    Procedure: The parameters that have been set up in Mail—and why—to run your acknowledgement letters, and what someone needs to do each day to ensure that all gifts are acknowledged within 24 hours.

  - Policy: "Our annual report recognizes all donors of gifts, including pledges regardless of payment status, made in the past fiscal year..."
    Procedure: The parameters that have been set up in Reports, Analytical Reports, Donor Category Report to generate the annual report listing each year, plus any manual manipulation that is necessary to finalize the list for publication.

- *Make time.* Creating good documentation, even without making it look pretty, does take time. Lots of time. The way to get it done is to not think of it as "I've got to write our policy and procedure documentation." Instead, focus on documenting specific tasks. For example, the newsletter mailing list is due in two weeks. So as the DBA works on that list he or she should work on documentation for it at the same time. Note I said "*as* the DBA works on...." It is much easier, and the documentation will be better and more complete, if it is written as the process is worked on. Do not wait until the process is done and document it afterward. For the newsletter mailing:

- Work with the person in charge to document all the criteria discussed in Chapter 4.
- Work on the include query, and document the process and rationale for that.
- Work on the exclude query, and document the process and rationale for that.
- Work on the Quick Letter parameters in Mail, and document them.
- Include in the documentation the processes and contact information for storing the list, reviewing the list, getting the list to the mail house, and marking the records as having received the mailing.

If this documentation has not been created yet, it is probably not reasonable to write all the documentation for each process as each process is done in the next three months. It is possible, however, for the DBA and manager to sit down and spread out the responsibility for key processes over the next year. As the DBA's manager, think about what the most important processes are. Identify those you would be worried about, were you to lose your DBA and need someone else to pick up on them. Your leadership is helpful here.

You must give the DBA time to do this, especially if this is a process new to the DBA. It will take four to eight hours to make good documentation about one major process like generating the quarterly newsletter mailing list. That investment, however, will reap benefits for years.

- *Keep updating the documentation.* No one should ever say, "Whew, my documentation is done" and then stop looking at it because they feel they know it. It is never "done" because our use of the database is constantly changing. Both you and the DBA need to continually revisit the documentation. Use it. Encourage them to use it. While at the Greater Bay Area Make-A-Wish Foundation, I would always open the newsletter documentation and follow it rather than relying on my memory. This allowed me to:
  - *Get the mailing done much quicker.* I followed the directions I had written, not spending time searching for old queries or creating new ones.
  - *Get the mailing done more accurately.* The documentation reminded me of key points I was not going to remember quarter to quarter. It told me what fields in the queries to be sure to update for each quarter's edition.
  - *Review and confirm the process was correct or update it where needed.* Sometimes things needed to be changed because after the passage of time I had a different perspective. We also might have changed some codes or other procedures that needed to be reflected differently.

  Documentation is created for other's benefit, but it is for the DBA's benefit as well. You and your DBA should refer to the documentation when there are questions. That should be the repository of all known information about these processes.

- *Document database setup.* Some important topics to document are not processes like newsletters that are going to come up naturally in the annual schedule. Configuration settings and User Options, for example, are rarely modified. To get these documented—and perhaps for the first time, wisely evaluated and considered—have the DBA set aside one or two hours a week that is held inviolate for this purpose until its current state is documented. It needs to be updated every time the database setup is modified.

Data Oversight

With the previous areas correctly handled, there does not need to be a great deal of data oversight tasks to keep the database healthy. This section is divided into three types of work to help ensure the integrity of the data:

1. Providing support to run the regular reports that should be distributed at scheduled intervals. These were discussed in Chapter 7.
2. Runing maintenance queries to check to ensure that users are using the system correctly and not introducing mistakes. Examples include adding duplicates or leaving fields blank that should be filled out.
3. Setting up and modifying the settings in Configuration when needed.

It has been my preferred approach to train and empower users and allow them to use the system as much as possible. I prefer this more than a highly centralized data entry team. Each organization needs to make the decision that is right for them. I feel that most people, if trained, can do the required tasks.

I prefer to give users rights (reasonably, of course) and then check their work behind them. For most data entry tasks, The Raiser's Edge tracks at a sufficient level of detail who made the change and when. When mistakes are made, we can talk to the user as well as fix the mistake. This is not a matter of "getting after" the user but looking for training opportunities and making gentle reminders about what to do.

The maintenance queries give us the ability to allow this access and yet monitor the work. They are necessary even if we centralize some portions of data entry to help find mistakes even those users make.

Hiring

Finding a good database administrator or any other staff highly knowledgeable in The Raiser's Edge for support roles is hard. Much of that has to do with reasons we address in the next section on retaining database staff. So what do you do when you need to find someone to be your database administrator for The Raiser's Edge? This section should help answer that.

Job Position and Posting

In the introduction to the "Database Administrator Roles and Responsibilities" section, I listed the variety of roles that exist in an organization related to The Raiser's Edge:

- The database administrator, the role responsible for the setup, maintenance, and proper use of The Raiser's Edge.
- The power user who generates the most complicated mailings, reports, lists, and exports.
- The manager of constituent and gift data entry.
- Constituent and gift data entry staff.

A word of caution when crafting the job position for the database administrator if you want to find the best possible candidates: Be careful about including too much responsibility for the last role, day-to-day constituent and gift entry. DBA candidates should understand there will be times when they need to assist with regular entry: crises, anticipated busy times like large mailings and December, and when the regular data entry staff is out of the office. However, the kind of person who is going to best accomplish the DBA responsibilities does not have a personality that will respond well to responsibility to do significant amounts of data entry on a daily basis.

Some people are fine spending every day entering constituents and gifts and running acknowledgement letters, day in and day out. Thank goodness for those people and the patience and attention to detail they bring. A good DBA, however, is going to have more creativity, want more intellectual engagement, to figure things out, to set things up, to learn, and continue to grow.

If the first three responsibilities listed in the previous bullets are not sufficient to make a full-time job, consider other development or development support roles that might be more engaging for a good Raiser's Edge DBA than data entry. They could help with the newsletter, annual fund, office management, and other administration tasks. Try to reserve the daily constituent and gift data entry responsibilities for positions in more alignment with the routine nature of the work. We found a successful solution to this approach at the Greater Bay Area Make-A-Wish Foundation by combining the Raiser's Edge data entry role with the accounting system entry. The person who does this is terrific and happy. The combined roles make for easy relationships between the departments, and this approach allowed us to hire an excellent DBA for The Raiser's Edge who would not have been happy doing that data entry every day.

For examples of job descriptions and postings, see the resources listed in the following sections on "Where to Post" and "Retention." Most of these resources will have current and previous job postings and other examples of job descriptions for the DBA and related roles.

One final recommendation: in your job postings, please refer to the software correctly. The name of the software is "The Raiser's Edge." It is not "Razor's Edge" or even "Raiser's Edge." It is not "Blackbaud." It is "The Raiser's Edge." You will look much more knowledgeable to your applicants and leave a more favorable impression. You might also want to look for this focus on detail and familiarity with the software in the applicants' cover letters and resumes.

Where to Post

The specialty of fundraising database administration as a profession has not yet become large enough to have resulted in one key location or source where you can post your job openings. Not even the broader field of development and advancement services has become mature enough to have a local chapter of a national organization in each major city. It can be hard to get the word out, but the best places include:

- *Online resources.* You want someone who is savvy enough to have found the posting online to be on your database team. In the San Francisco Bay Area, craigslist.org is the best place to post jobs relating to The Raiser's Edge. Try to find your local equivalent by asking your peers.

- *AFP and CASE.* Try local chapters of fundraising-oriented organizations such as the Association of Fundraising Professionals (AFP) and the Council for Advancement and Support of Education (CASE). Typically, the people who specialize in the use of The Raiser's Edge within nonprofits may not be actual members, but the organizations are a conduit to others in the development shop who will help to get word out about openings.
- *Local consultants and trainers on The Raiser's Edge and other Blackbaud software.* Consultants and trainers on Blackbaud and other nonprofit technology can also be a resource because they are probably familiar with users and DBAs in your community.
- *Blackbaud's web site.* Blackbaud's web site has a public Job Postings forum, found in the Support section of the web site (specifically, in the Blackbaud Community Forums). Because Blackbaud's business spans the globe, the resource is international in scope, so be clear about your willingness to relocate someone when you post an opening.
- *Blackbaud User Society.* The primary web site for users of Blackbaud software that is independent of the company is the Blackbaud User Society at blackbus .org. They have a Job Postings forum, as well.
- *Other Resources.* You can also try the organizations listed in the following "Retention" section, but understand that their reach is wide in scope and geography.

To cast as broad a net as possible, you can use the general nonprofit job web sites such as opportunityknocks.org and idealist.org, The Chronicle of Philanthropy, and recruiters. But as I discuss in the "Retention" section, the fact that fundraising database work has not yet come into its own as a profession will limit the value of these resources.

Interviewing

When interviewing candidates for Raiser's Edge positions, be careful of the claim that the candidates "know" The Raiser's Edge. This caution is true for any fundraising position. I have heard people say they "know" The Raiser's Edge because they worked for an organization in which it was used and they were taught to log in.

In addition to your standard interview methodology and questions, I suggest your phone interviews include specific questions about The Raiser's Edge. Your on-site interviews should include hands-on exercises.

For telephone interviews, the topics in this book should give you plenty of material to find issues about which to ask questions. Even if you do not completely understand the issue or the answer, that is okay:

- The candidates being interviewed do not know that. The way they answer the question will give you a good sense of whether they seem to know what they are talking about. Do they speak confidently? Do they explain? Do they give examples?
- The ideal database administrator has both great hard and soft skills. Can this person explain the concepts behind an issue to you in terms you understand? This is exactly what you will need them to do if they join your team.

The following are some sample questions to consider when framing your own for an interview:

- What are the pros and cons of making spouses and partners constituents? How have you handled that situation in the past? From what you know about our organization, how would you be inclined to handle it here?
- What are some of the challenges with soft credits? How do you approach resolving them?
- If I were to ask you to do a mailing for me from The Raiser's Edge, what specific questions would you ask me to obtain the information you need to produce the mailing?

If you struggle with this, use your outgoing database administrator, other strong users on staff, and local consultants and trainers on The Raiser's Edge to get a few questions and key points to listen for in the answers. You do not need many.

Another tool I have used to mixed success is to set up an exercise to be completed in Excel. I prepared a basic list of data and a description about what I would like the data to look like instead. I e-mailed these items to the candidate, gave them one-half hour, and asked them to return the file to me. We then discussed what they did and how. This exercise should give you some sense of the candidates' general technical abilities. However, I have found with small organizations with lower paying positions, the candidates in the pool struggled with this exercise. It was more effective with a larger organization.

During on-site interviews, I recommend having the candidate perform actual work for you in The Raiser's Edge. Your organization has access to a sample database for The Raiser's Edge. Have the candidates work in the sample database and never use your live data. Ask them to do tasks such as the following:

- Add yourself as a constituent. It is okay to make up sensitive data such as birth date and private contact details when completing those fields in the sample database.
- Give me a list of all donors of $100 or more in the past three years who live in South Carolina *plus* anyone who is a current board member. (Because Blackbaud is in South Carolina, there is more data for these types of exercises in the U.S. sample database if you use South Carolina.)
- Give me mailing labels for the group in the previous exercise.

The activities are purposely vague so the candidates can interact with you the way they would need to if you hired them. Although you might not know how they are supposed to do the tasks in The Raiser's Edge, you should be able to tell by watching how quickly, confidently, and knowledgeably they seem to navigate the process. Also, assess how they interact with you in asking questions, bridging the development needs and Raiser's Edge technical requirements. They should be able to show you results that make sense to you. Not asking questions about the type of data you want and explaining clearly the decisions they are making are red flags.

Watch for how quickly the candidate learns and maneuvers the system, the kinds of questions asked and notes taken, thoroughness, attention to detail, ability to remember and follow direction, and the rapport that develops in the process.

The second exercise in the bullets is written to reflect the topics covered in Chapter 4. Labels need name and address information but require candidates to understand certain key concepts, including Mail and address processing, add/sal processing, and contact processing—key functionality that anyone in this role should know well.

These exercises should be completed quickly if the candidates know what they are doing. The give-and-take they have with you asking for appropriate clarification should take longer. Remember, the exercises are purposely written to be vague so the candidates have to interact with you to test *that* they interact with you and *how* they do it. For example, on the gift amount, they should be asking about cumulative or single gift; campaign, fund, and appeal criteria; gift type criteria; and the other issues discussed in Chapter 3. For the labels, they should ask about what add/sal, contacts, and address to use.

If you are not able to find candidates who know The Raiser's Edge, you still want to look for the same kind of communication skills discussed here. Also, introduce them to the sample database, see how they take to it, and what kinds of questions they ask you. This will be some indication of their ability to catch on quickly to it for you.

Retention

Turnover among staff members that work with The Raiser's Edge seems to be particularly high, perhaps because development and nonprofit turnover is usually high. There is little expertise I can share to address general development turnover, but what I can offer are the following suggestions on retention to fundraisers who are managers of the development department and directly of the database staff.

One reason I believe that finding good, experienced Raiser's Edge staff is hard is that those who have done the work do not stay in it. They are often not treated as though:

- They are part of the development team, have entered a profession, and have a potential career track.
- They are respected for their work by their colleagues and managers.

As I work with a variety of organizations in my consulting business, I get the sense that, in many organizations, the database staff members are treated like they are "just support staff." Few intelligent, capable, excited people are motivated to continue in the path of database work when this is their experience.

How you treat your database staff goes a long way in contributing to their decision to stay with your organization. It would also help our profession when those who find themselves in this work are treated well, enjoy it, decide to make it their career, and become really good at it. Here are some suggestions that I hope will help with that:

- *Pay competitive salaries, comparable to what fundraisers are paid at your organization.* Database administration is not simply a data entry or support role. Doing the job well requires a fine balance of technical skills and an understanding of the needs of nonprofits and fundraising. It also requires both hard technical skills and soft skills, including the ability to communicate, train, and write. Paying competitive salaries helps attract and retain the best database staff.

- *Treat the database staff, especially the database administrator, as an integral part of the development team.* The database administrator should be included in development meetings, not just the full-staff meetings, but small meetings where strategy and plans are developed. Decisions regarding mailings, events, and fundraising plans should not simply be conveyed later when work needs to be done. The DBA's work begins in the meeting, participating in the discussion about how to achieve the end goal and adding expertise. Treat the database staff as an integral, valued part of the professional development team.

- *Provide training opportunities.* Good DBAs always want to learn more. I know that training is not cheap, but it is a lot less expensive than having to hire and train a brand new DBA every year. Blackbaud offers a number of excellent classes, but your DBA should be interested in other types of training, as well. Use AFP, CASE, and other fundraising associations to expose the DBA to additional fundraising education. Classes on Microsoft Excel, Microsoft Word merges, Microsoft Access, and Crystal Reports are valuable to the role. You should confirm with your human resources staff, but you could consider offering training opportunities to staff contingent on their staying with you for a certain period of time, such as six months or one year.

- *Encourage conference participation and attendance.* As an attendee of most of Blackbaud's conferences over the years, I can assure you that the content is of high quality. These events offer excellent training opportunities. But even more than that, they create a sense of community, a sense that "what I'm doing is important, others do it, too; look what I'm a part of!" Sending staff to conferences can also communicate that you value them and their work. Over the past decade, Blackbaud's conferences have been offered regularly in a variety of locations, including Charleston, South Carolina (the company's headquarters); London, England; and in rotating cities in Canada.

- *Support participation in the industry.* Educational institutions for years have been in the forefront of taking development support work seriously. That sector, which refers to fundraising as "advancement," has a respected subsector it calls "advancement services." Those who work in advancement services are responsible for the database, for constituent and gift entry, and for reporting. At some institutions, advancement services might also include roles such as prospect research and tracking, department budgeting, and IT. Regardless of the sector of the nonprofit world your organization is in, however, you can take advantage of the resources that have developed out of advancement services and other places to provide education, networking, conferences, and support for your DBA. Of particular note I suggest:

  - *The Blackbaud User Society (blackbus.org).* This web site, independent of Blackbaud, though on good terms, is the best community for users and DBAs to interact with each other to share questions and ideas.
  - *Blackbaud's web site (Blackbaud.com).* Blackbaud's own web site has Forums so users can interact with each other.
  - *Blackbaud User Groups.* Your DBA should look for and attend these free events. If you have space, you should encourage your DBA to volunteer to host a user group at your facility.

- *The Council for Advancement and Support of Education (CASE, at case.org).* The Advancement Services pages of the CASE web site lists books, articles, trainings, and conferences that should be of interest to any serious Raiser's Edge DBA. Your organization does not have to be an educational institution or a member of CASE to benefit from most of these resources.
- *Association for Advancement Services Professionals (advserv.org).* This is a relatively new group formed largely of participants from CASE advancement services activities. This group is working to broaden the interaction of advancement and development services professionals beyond the education sector.
- *Fundsvcs.org.* This web site provides information about subscribing to FundSvcs, probably the best listserv (e-mail discussion group) available about gift processing and advancement and development services. The web site also provides an archive of previous discussions and downloads.
- *Other nonprofit technology organizations and web sites.* Many exist, especially if the DBA also has interest in Internet and e-mail fundraising. Reaching out to the specific resources previously listed and reviewing the web site of nonprofit technology consultant Robert Weiner (rlweiner.com/resources) are among the best ways to find them.
- *Books.* While there are no other books about The Raiser's Edge (beyond software user guides), there are a number of resources about nonprofit technology and fundraising of relevance to the Raiser's Edge database administrator. See the Bibliography of this book for some recommendations. Of particular note I suggest *Advancement Services: A Foundation for Fundraising.*

There are numerous resources to help you help your DBA so that she or he feels like a valued, professional member of your development team. You cannot keep DBAs forever, but you can inspire them to stay a lot longer than they otherwise might.

Version 8 of The Raiser's Edge

One of the benefits of the Blackbaud maintenance program is that upgrades to the software are included. Another benefit of being a Blackbaud customer is that the company has always been a cautious leader in nonprofit technology. For example, Blackbaud was one of the first companies in the 1990s to develop a Windows-based fundraising software package. However, the company has also moved forward with a certain amount of caution. Its management understands that nonprofits are usually not on the leading edge of technology.

Until the mid-1990s The Raiser's Edge was in DOS, the old black-screen format of software. The first version of The Raiser's Edge in Windows came out in 1995 (version 6). Understanding that Windows and technology had come a long way since the early 1990s when the first Windows version was written, Blackbaud released the next generation of The Raiser's Edge in 2000 (version 7). This is the one we use today.

Although the Internet has changed rapidly in the past decade, Windows and database technology have made more evolutionary changes in this time frame. The Raiser's Edge version 7 has had more than a dozen upgrades since its initial release, but it is the same core product it was then. It still works well today and will for several years to come. But the time is once again approaching when we will need to move to the next generation of The Raiser's Edge, version 8.

What does this mean to you as a fundraiser? Certainly, there should be no cause for immediate concern about work and expense. The Raiser's Edge is the most widely used fundraising software. It is a stable, mature, feature-rich product. It has been updated in most places necessary to allow it to work in today's Internet age. The fundamentals of fundraising have changed little since its release.

I bring up the new version for two reasons:

1. You and your DBA will begin to hear about it, if you have not already. Most of the concepts discussed in this book will apply to The Raiser's Edge version 8. Its eventual arrival is not a reason to postpone any of the activities this book recommends.

2. If history is our guide, Blackbaud will provide your organization with sufficient time to move from version 7 to version 8 because there will be some work and education involved. Blackbaud provided years for DOS customers of The Raiser's Edge to move to the Windows version and for version 6 clients to move to version 7. What we know at this time is that version 8 is an entirely new program. It is a complete rewrite of The Raiser's Edge based on the latest technology. It addresses challenges that users have expressed with version 7, some of which I have mentioned here. It is still The Raiser's Edge, and certainly all of your data will convert. However, your team will need to learn the new system and modify existing procedures to take advantage of the new and better tools available in version 8. The point?

   - Look forward to the release of version 8.
   - Make your current version 7 database and procedures operate as well as possible now so the necessary foundation is in place for a smooth upgrade.
   - Work with your database administrator to understand version 8's requirements and benefits when Blackbaud begins that discussion.
   - Listen to Blackbaud's recommendations about preparing for and doing the upgrade.
   - Take your time to plan and implement accordingly.

Summary

If you are a fundraiser and you have read this chapter, thank you. Your database administrator thanks you, your colleagues thank you, your constituents thank you—even your database thanks you.

The fundraising manager's understanding and support of the database administrator goes a long way toward the success of the DBA. If you understand what the DBA needs to do and help them do it, the DBA will do a better job for you and stay longer. This benefits you, your colleagues, and your constituents. Together, the database staff and the fundraising staff make a team. Thank you again for taking the time to learn more about and support your teammates.

Conclusion

As you have seen, The Raiser's Edge is a powerful tool. Contact management, mailings, events, membership, major gifts, stewardship, reporting—it seemingly does it all. Furthermore, there are many parts of the software we did not touch on because they do not affect fundraisers' day-to-day work.

No organization needs to use all of The Raiser's Edge. As with any software package, the key is to identify and use the tools and functions that support your needs and leave it at that.

Additionally, you are part of a team. It is not important that fundraisers know all the details about The Raiser's Edge because there should be a database administrator who has responsibility for that. The database administrator, however, should not be making the key fundraising decisions. Together you work as a team.

The fundraiser's responsibility is to:

- Understand the terminology and concepts of The Raiser's Edge to be able to work with the database staff to guide data entry and output needs.
- Use The Raiser's Edge where appropriate, such as:
  - Open records to see individual and organization data
  - Create and edit actions and notes
  - Use dashboards and summaries to track performance
  - Use the Home page for quick access to run reports and lists
- As assigned, manage the database administrator and staff to ensure the most accurate use and maintenance of the database.

If you would like to learn more about The Raiser's Edge, there are a number of resources available to you: Blackbaud documentation, trainings, and conferences. But I believe that if you focus on the concepts in this book, as a fundraiser you will know what you need to know to be a contributor to the data management part of the fundraising process.

Unlike a novel, the intent of this book is not that you just read it, enjoy it, and file it away on your bookcase. Its intent is to increase knowledge and understanding, but also to prompt activities and change and be an ongoing reference manual.

- After reading Chapter 1 about organizing fundraising and understanding campaigns, funds, and appeals, and after reading the book to see these records in their larger context, revisit the points made in that chapter to determine if your campaign, fund, and appeal structure are set up for the best effect for you and your organization.

- From Chapter 2 on constituent records:
  - Work with your database staff to ensure the key data entry fields are set up and being used properly for your fundraising needs, such as additional addressee and salutation types, contact types, and solicit codes.
  - Use the Notes and Actions sections as your instructions to begin entering your own notes and actions.
  - Look at how your user account for The Raiser's Edge is set up, such as the information on each of the tabs of lists, so that you can see the details of most help to you. Set up and begin using your Home page if you do not already.
- From Chapter 3 on gifts and gift processing:
  - Each time you ask for gift information from the database, refer to the list at the beginning of the chapter for the details you should provide to get the right information back.
  - Begin using the constituent Gift Summary to access and understand giving history and totals.
  - If you manage gift processing, work with your gift processor(s) to compare your organization's gift entry activities with the best practices discussed in the chapter to identify opportunities for efficiencies and better approaches.
- Whenever you request a mailing, reference the four Steps and the mailing process Chapter 4 discusses to ensure you provide complete direction for the production of the mailing.
- If you work with events or membership, ensure that your procedures follow those recommended in Chapter 5 or consider changing them to match.
- If you work with major gifts, follow the recommendations in Chapter 6 to establish your major gifts methodology, document it, and integrate it with The Raiser's Edge.
- Work with your fellow fundraisers and the database staff to start using the recommended dashboards and reports at the intervals recommended in Chapter 7.
- If you manage the database administrator:
  - Provide Chapter 8 and Appendixes B and C (if not this entire book) to your current database administrator and begin a series of meetings to ensure your DBA is properly managing your database for you: technical tasks, security, training, documentation, data integrity, and so forth.
  - When you need to hire a new DBA, use Chapter 8 to help craft and post the job position and interview the candidates.

I hope you have learned a lot by reading this book. But this book was structured with numerous sections and lists to make it easy for you to use as an ongoing reference tool. I hope you will share it with your colleagues. I also hope you will keep it close by so you can come back to specific chapters and sections to answer the question each time, "Now what should I know and do as a fundraiser to successfully accomplish this task in The Raiser's Edge?"

■ ■ ■

I joined my first nonprofit organization as an employee while I was still in college because that organization had such a major effect on my life in high school. The work you do is important. The work you do matters. The work you do makes the world a better place.

Thank you for doing it. Thank you for working so hard to do it so well. May you be incredibly successful for the mission of your organization. May it be exceedingly rewarding for you. And as I always say when departing my clients, I hope you have fun with it, too!

Reminder: Additional Resources and Follow-up to the Book on the Web

Given the technology subject matter of this book and the book's purpose to be a resource for fundraisers and their organizations, more information and resources can be found on Bill Connors' web site at www.billconnors.com/book at no charge. Included are:

- Bill's answers to frequently asked questions from readers of the book.
- More examples and documentation for the concepts discussed in the book.
- Other resources for The Raiser's Edge Bill has developed from his consulting and training practice, for both fundraisers and database administrators.

Converting to and Implementing
The Raiser's Edge

This appendix highlights the process of converting to and implementing The Raiser's Edge fundraising software from Blackbaud. The exact process and time frame for each organization is unique, but this outline provides a basic overview of the process.

It is common for management and staff to dramatically underestimate the work and time involved in implementing The Raiser's Edge. The work and time required is not due to The Raiser's Edge itself. The process and time commitment are similar regardless of the database to which an organization is converting.

As with any project, there are two time elements involved:

1. The total number of hours that staff and consultants must invest into the project.
2. The time frame or time period in which this work must be completed.

The biggest determinant of the total number of hours that staff and consultants must invest in the project is the organization's size and sophistication: the more data tracked and the more ways in which it needs to be tracked and managed, the more hours must be spent converting the data, setting up the database, replicating current business processes in the new database, and establishing new procedures with The Raiser's Edge. Most organizations do not realize their current complexity and have an oversimplified view of their data and processes.

The factors having the greatest impact on the time frame or time period in which the work must be completed include:

- The number of hours per day, week, and month staff can devote to the project. Staff cannot be expected to make rapid progress on such a project while maintaining their existing full-time responsibilities. Responsibilities need to be moved to other staff or temps to free up project staff time.
- The number of staff that can be assigned to the project.
- Resources that can be obtained to outsource the work to other programmers and consultants.

- External resources' time constraints and schedules, such as the availability of a Blackbaud programmer.

The following process is listed in chronological order.

Purchase Process

- Determine what modules of The Raiser's Edge to buy.
- Determine the number of user licenses to purchase.
- Determine related products (e.g., accounting, Internet) and services (e.g., data enrichment services) to buy initially.
- Determine appropriate maintenance plan.
- Determine other services needed of Blackbaud, such as consulting, training, conversion programming, customization programming, and custom reporting writing.
- Determine what services are necessary from independent resources, such as consulting, conversion, programming, and training.

Project Participant Training

In order to effectively participate in implementing The Raiser's Edge, project team members must be trained on the software *before* the conversion and business process development discussed in a later section. Ideally, team members are trained on data entry and storage capabilities of The Raiser's Edge (about two days of training) and data output functions such as reporting and mailing (two to three days of training).

Project Planning

- Make a list of what tasks need to be accomplished in order to "go live"—what has to be done to begin using the software and immediately thereafter? ("Go live" means to begin using the software for real work, but it should never be understood as the "project is over"—go-live is merely a transition point in the project.)
- Make a list of additional projects to address after the initial go-live.
- Determine who will be the project participants (staff and consultants).
- Determine the amount of time each participant can *reasonably* be expected to contribute.
- Determine the approximate amount of time that each task will take. Be conservative and estimate longer times rather than shorter.
- Assign project participants to tasks.
- Create an initial timeline.
- Based on the months the projected timeline falls into, modify the timeline to account for holidays, vacations, and particularly slow and busy times.

- Build in significant time for delays and tasks taking longer than expected.
- Identify a go-live date, a go-live definition, and milestones along the way.
- Inform all development staff of the requirements and dates.
- Create communication and change management plans.
- Create plans to involve senior management for support and needed decision making.

Conversion and Business Process Development

The core of the implementation project is composed of two parts:

1. Convert the data in the existing database(s) to The Raiser's Edge.
2. Develop new policies and procedures for use of The Raiser's Edge after go-live. I recommend that database uses needed in the first six months after go-live be documented prior to go-live. This helps ensure both an accurate setup of the database as well as the most successful results with The Raiser's Edge (with the least amount of stress) after go-live.

Note that, during this time, the source database continues to be used for daily work, kept fully up-to-date with new data entry, and used for all data output. The source database does not stop being used until the final set of data is provided for the final conversion.

Typically, the conversion is performed by a programmer outside the department's staff. Thus, two major processes occur at the same time:

1. Convert the data from the existing system to The Raiser's Edge.
2. Determine how The Raiser's Edge will be set up, data will be entered, and data will be retrieved.

As the conversion process usually takes the longest in terms of defining the time frame, it is given first priority. The business process development is worked on while the programmer is working on the conversion.

A third concurrent track is usually necessary to those above: cleaning up the source data that is best cleaned up prior to conversion rather than after the conversion. Usually, The Raiser's Edge has better tools for data cleanup than the source system. Often, however, data needs to be cleaned up in the source system so it can be converted correctly, because your organization has IT staff with the knowledge and tools in your existing database to do it faster or cheaper, or because there is more time available prior to go-live than afterward.

"Mapping" in the following table refers to the process of deciding where each field in the source system goes in The Raiser's Edge. Last Name goes to Last Name, of course. However, there are usually dozens or hundreds of fields that do not have this one-to-one correspondence. These fields must be understood and mapped accordingly.

<table>
<tr><th>Conversion</th><th rowspan="3">Preconversion Data Cleanup</th><th>Business Process Development</th></tr>
<tr><td>■ Data extracted from source system
■ Mapping
• Create map
• Create Cleanup Lists
○ Preconversion
○ Postconversion before go-live
○ Postconversion as time allows</td><td></td></tr>
<tr><td>■ Trial conversion 1 programmed by programmer

■ Trial conversion 1 validation
• Tested by project team
• Feedback from project team
• Additions to cleanup lists

■ Trial conversion 2
• Conversion program modified by programmer
• Tested by project team
• Feedback from project team
• Additions to cleanup lists</td><td>■ Data entry policies and procedures
• Constituent entry
○ New constituents
○ Constituent dies
○ Constituent moves
○ Constituent marries
○ Constituent divorces
○ Relationships
○ Etc.
• Gift entry
○ Cash
○ Pledges
○ Stock
○ Other gift situations
○ Batch
• Other records? For example:
○ Events
○ Membership
○ Volunteers
■ Data output procedures
• Mailings
○ Acknowledgement letters
○ Pledge reminders
○ Newsletters
○ Solicitations
○ Invitations
• Reporting
○ Daily
○ Executive
○ Board
• Integration with accounting
• Other? For example:
○ Membership cards
○ Membership renewal notices</td></tr>
</table>

Conversion	Business Process Development

■ Final conversion
 	
   • Conversion program modified
     by programmer
	■ Database setup
	   • User Options
	   • Security users
	   • Security groups
	   • Configuration
	     ○ Tables
	     ○ Attributes
	     ○ Business rules
	     ○ Membership
	   • Training plan and
	     curriculum development
	   • Help desk strategy
	     developed

■ Preconversion data cleanup must be completed ■ Final source data sent to programmer ■ Final conversion received back from programmer ■ Final conversion tested to ensure it is perfect ■ Database setup entered ■ Output functions required for go-live set up	

Custom Reports and Customizations

Large organizations often have a fourth concurrent track: the creation of custom reports (using Crystal Reports) and/or customizations. Customizations are custom-programmed software or small programs that integrate with The Raiser's Edge or change the behavior of The Raiser's Edge to meet the unique needs of specific organizations. Custom reports and customizations usually require the assistance of an external programmer. Proceed in a manner similar to the Conversion track discussed earlier. Customizations require:

- Related business process development and documentation
- Specification writing
- Programming
- Repeated testing and fixing
- Final testing

Final Push for Go-Live

- Postconversion priority cleanup completed.
- Initial group of end users trained.
- Go live!

After Go-Live

- Do postconversion cleanup not required for go-live.
- Perform ongoing maintenance tasks.
- Provide ongoing help desk assistance and training to current users.
- Add additional users.
- Add additional output functions not required for go-live.
- Implement additional projects deferred to post go-live.

Database Administrator Task List

There are a number of tasks the database administrator for The Raiser's Edge should ensure are completed on a regular basis to keep (or help get) your database healthy. Although there are tasks your organization should add to the following list that are specific to your needs and data, those listed below should be completed by most organizations.

This is a more technically-oriented list specifically for the database administrator, not for fundraisers. It is included in this book for fundraisers to share with their database administrators. More context for this document is provided in Chapter 8 of the book.

Technical Oversight

It is extremely important to oversee the correct handling of the "back end" of the data so that it does not become corrupted or lost. Otherwise, the perfect handling of the front end of the data might all be for naught.

Typically, these tasks are completed by IT staff or consultants, but the database administrator should ensure that these processes are being done regularly and successfully.

1. Backups should be performed regularly and thoroughly through the Blackbaud Management Console (BMC) on the server. By "thoroughly" I mean:
   - Schedule backups to run nightly.
   - Check the backup status in the BMC regularly, at least monthly. For a variety of reasons, the BMC backups may stop running on schedule.
   - Ensure that manual backups are run from the BMC before large imports, global changes, or global deletes.
   - Ensure that manual and scheduled backups do not build up on the server and create the risk of filling the hard drive. Servers should have enough disk space to save at least one month of compressed backups. Additional backup copies are nice to have but not necessary.
   - Copy the "backup" the BMC makes to tape or another portable media device using standard backup software.
   - Store portable media off-site. Fireproof safes on-site should not be considered acceptable alternatives. Consider the security of data stored off-site to ensure that it does not fall into the wrong hands or is used improperly.

- Rotate backup media. Do not copy a new backup on top of the most recent backup.
- Test backups at least monthly to ensure that the entire backup process is working. In the event that you have a server crash, you need to restore to a backup, and you want to make sure your backups are valid. Start by restoring from the backup media to ensure the entire backup process is working, including the copy to the external media stored off-site. Be extremely careful that you do not overwrite your current data in the process. More detailed and the most up-to-date procedures for testing backups can be found in the Blackbaud Knowledgebase (kb.blackbaud.com, solution BB96254).
- Develop and document a disaster recovery plan detailing the process for restoring the backed-up data from the portable media. Consider alternatives in the event your server or workstation is lost due to a power surge or natural disaster.

  Please make sure that your IT staff members know that Blackbaud does not test or support third-party software to make database backups. Using the Blackbaud Management Console is the only supported method for backing up. Backups made using Microsoft SQL Server tools and "live" backup agents for your network backup software are not supported by Blackbaud. They can be used in addition to backups made through the BMC but not instead of the BMC. For more information, review Knowledgebase solution BB291.

2. Ensure that the System Maintenance tasks on the BMC are scheduled to run weekly, generally early on Sunday mornings. Check at least monthly to ensure that these tasks are successfully running.
3. Ensure that your IT staff and anyone with technical abilities understand that, under no circumstances whatsoever, should data in the backend of the database be modified except using approved Blackbaud tools such as the API for The Raiser's Edge. It is risky but acceptable to read data from the Microsoft SQL Server data for The Raiser's Edge, but it is absolutely unacceptable to attempt to change data this way. Doing so invalidates your Blackbaud maintenance agreement, and fixing your data may incur significant expense.
4. Ensure that the server has plenty of free hard drive space. Be certain that your database is not growing, backup files are not increasing, and other files or applications are not being added at such a rate that there is any risk of your hard drive running out of room.
5. Watch the combined size of your database files if you use the SQL Server Express version of The Raiser's Edge. SQL Server Express has a size limit of 4 GB. Once your database reaches 3.7 GB, you begin to have problems and need to plan on upgrading to "full-blown" Microsoft SQL Server to run a larger database.
6. Ensure that IT staff and users do not upgrade software on machines with The Raiser's Edge that might interfere with the operation of The Raiser's Edge. Always check the Blackbaud web site for third-party compatibility before upgrading any of the following software:
   - Microsoft Windows Server
   - Microsoft Windows on workstations
   - Microsoft SQL Server
   - Microsoft Office applications (Word, Excel, and Outlook)
   - Microsoft Internet Explorer
   - Crystal Reports

Security updates are typically safe to install. However, upgrades to these programs should not be installed on any computer with The Raiser's Edge on it until Blackbaud announces compatibility.

7. Keep other software up-to-date. This is especially important for Microsoft Windows Server and Microsoft SQL Server, which Blackbaud occasionally requires to be updated more frequently than workstation software.

8. Implement upgrades to The Raiser's Edge when they become available (sign up on the Blackbaud web site for e-mail notifications). It is wise to wait one to two months if there is no urgency to gain access to the new features in the upgrade. However, there are bug fixes in upgrades, and Blackbaud customer support is able to assist you better if you are on the latest version. If a long time has passed since the last upgrade, you might wish to monitor the Blackbaud web site for patches and install them. Although you can install a patch to avoid issues it corrects, it is necessary only when the patch resolves an issue that affects your organization. Review the patch readme for the list of issues resolved; if you are experiencing an issue that is not in the patch readme, check the outstanding issues list to see if it is an issue that Blackbaud is currently working to resolve. Before downloading a patch, consider whether it addresses issues that impact your organization, and verify that you have the time and resources needed to test and install it.

Tip: Updating the Data

After upgrading the software on the server, log into the database from the client software on the server to get the data itself upgraded. Someone must log into the database for this final update process to occur.

If your data is hosted by Blackbaud, Blackbaud is responsible for doing most of these tasks, not your IT staff.

User Oversight

The database administrator is responsible for all the users who access The Raiser's Edge. The Raiser's Edge is not Word, Outlook, or the web—users must be trained, supported, and managed if your organization is going to be successful with The Raiser's Edge.

1. When you add a new staff person who will use The Raiser's Edge:
   a. Add the user as a constituent. Pay attention to the following areas:
      i. Mark the constituent as a solicitor so you can link the user's constituent record to the user account in Security and everyone can add the user as a solicitor in actions.
      ii. Use the **Business** button on the Bio 1 tab to link the constituent to your organization's constituent record, and complete the other fields.
      iii. Give the constituent a "Staff"-type constituent code. The **Date From** should be the day they started.

b. Globally add the user as a solicitor to her assigned constituents, if appropriate.

c. Add the user to Security. Give the user the appropriate default User Options. Consider having a security group with limited rights for use with new users until they have completed training and demonstrated competence on the system.

d. Use the option for Copy User Settings on the Plug-Ins page to copy the User Options, Home page, and Dashboard pages if the new user should have settings similar to those of an existing or previous user who has not been deleted.

   - If the settings are from a previous person whose user account you were keeping in order to do this copy, delete or update that user using the instructions in the following section.

e. Add the new staff person as a user to the Blackbaud web site. This will allow access to the user guides for The Raiser's Edge through the **Help** menu and other resources on the web site such as Knowledgebase and Case Central.

f. Train the user. The user needs training on both how The Raiser's Edge works, in general, and your organization's specific use of The Raiser's Edge. Time should be allocated in the new staff person's first week and month for proper training. A quick hour together is not sufficient training. Create a schedule together, along with the new user's manager, that reflects the speed and depth at which the new staff person needs to be using The Raiser's Edge.

g. Provide the user access to your cheat sheets and policy and procedure documentation, and note what sections are particularly relevant to her position. However, do not use them as a substitute for training.

h. Help the user set up her Dashboard and modify User Options.

2. When a staff person who has been using The Raiser's Edge at your organization leaves, do *not* begin by deleting her user account in Security. Instead:

a. Run an Action Detail Report to identify all incomplete actions for the user. Do this *before* deleting the user as, otherwise, the user's name is not available to be selected from the report criteria. Reassign, mark as complete, or delete the actions as appropriate. Check each of the following fields for the user's activity:

   i. Action solicitor
   ii. Action user
   iii. Action added by

b. Identify all open solicitor assignments for the user/constituent and reassign them.

c. Deactivate the user as a solicitor. When you do so, The Raiser's Edge will prompt you to add to date as the **Date To** field for the person's open solicitor assignments.

d. Update business and constituent code information in the user's constituent record to reflect that she is now a former employee. Also update other constituent fields as appropriate for the person.

e. Rename the user to First Name Last Name Position (as much as will fit) and *save*. This makes the name more meaningful for other users when they see it long after this user has left the organization.

f. Do *not* delete the user account if this user has User Options, a Home page, or a Dashboard page that would be difficult to re-create and is worth saving for the next user in the departing user's position. Save the user account until the new user begins so you can use the option in Plug-Ins to copy the old user's settings, but change the password on the account so it cannot be used inappropriately.

If you do not have this situation, you now have two options to consider for the user account:

i. *Delete the user from Security.* The user's name and work will remain in the database after the user name has been deleted. Leaving the user name in the database presents a small security risk of access through that account. Deleting users removes none of the work the person has done, such as queries and reports, and does not remove the person's name from Properties, such as **Added by** and **Last Changed by** in constituent and gift records. The only downside to deleting a user is that it is no longer possible to write a query with criteria of "Added by" and select that user's name. In my experience, that has not been a problem.

ii. *Move the user to a security group with no rights.* Due to the inability to query on deleted users' names, some database administrators prefer to leave the user name in the system. If you take this approach, it is recommended that you change the user's password so the account cannot be accessed (remember the password long enough to change it, but afterward it is no longer needed), and have a security group called "Inactive" with no rights and assign the user to that group only (remove the user from whatever group(s) the account was in previously). Some administrators add an "x" to the beginning of the user name to sort the user name to the bottom of the list of users.

For more information on deleting users, see Knowledgebase solution BB55385.

g. Remove the person as an authorized user of the Blackbaud web site for your organization.

h. Review all queries, reports, mailings, and exports the user created and used only under her name to reassign them as necessary. This may involve resaving the parameters using **Save As** if the user set up security on the parameters to allow only herself access to them or just changing the **Execute** and **Modify** options to allow other users access.

3. When Blackbaud provides upgrades for The Raiser's Edge, the database administrator should read the release documentation in advance of the upgrade being installed. The database administrator should then work with the users to train them on the new features and to modify existing policies and procedures to take advantage of the new features. Do not install upgrades without asking—and answering—"How does this upgrade affect what we do?"

4. Depending on the size and structure of your organization, you should have a committee of users that meets regularly to decide and learn about changes in data setup, policies, and procedures.

5. Mini-trainings should be held regularly, preferably at least monthly, for all staff for ongoing training about The Raiser's Edge. Consider one-hour get-togethers on a regular basis so new and old staff can stay up on the software. It is too much to learn and remember all at once. Perhaps do brown bag lunches or even provide lunch if you really want to get staff there. If the trainings

are held in the morning or afternoon, offer snacks as an incentive—and no, you cannot have any of the food if you do not come and stay for the session.

6. For most of your users, create cheat sheets when necessary, not documentation. Documentation should be developed for those who use the system extensively and need an internal policy and procedure reference on hand. Casual users are not going to read or reference long documentation. See Chapter 8 of this book.

7. Consider attending and/or sending users to the Blackbaud conferences, which are generally good for both education and motivation. Take a close look at the schedule, and determine how many people are needed to cover the sessions of interest. If different people go to each session and take good notes, everyone can share with the others the information learned (probably after returning). You should question, from an organization learning perspective, the value of multiple staff in the same session. Having to share information learned with others helps reinforce the note-taking during the session and the learning afterward.

   The exception to that is if you need to motivate, encourage, and reward someone who would be excited about the opportunity to attend and become a part of something that feels bigger than just using software. Sometimes the soft take-aways from these kinds of events are more important than the hard knowledge learned.

8. Some users may benefit from the Blackbaud courses offered in cities on a fairly regular basis. You should also consider the Blackbaud Learn training purchase program for classes and online training options. Independent options are also available.

9. The best way to get staff to use The Raiser's Edge is to have management require reports from the system. Have management insist that data be reported from The Raiser's Edge and not in spreadsheets and Word documents. Sometimes, that is the only way.

10. Have fun goodies and trinkets to hand out at internal user groups and trainings. Consider fun, computer- and money-oriented sticky notes, squish balls, pens, pencils, and notepads. Even certificates and toys for elementary school children can be used for fun effect. I always hand out chocolate for good questions and comments in my trainings. Check computer supply, party supply, toy and hobby stores and web sites for ideas.

Data Oversight

The most important tasks you can do to ensure the integrity of your data are not ongoing. Instead, they are foundational: training your users, ensuring all the options in Configuration are set up well, and setting up Security tightly. Establishing policies and procedures also helps ensure quality data. Once these are done well, it is difficult for users to make systematic mistakes that require much maintenance, but it is good to run the following tasks monthly to keep your data in tip-top shape. Add to these lists the issues you find when working with your users to keep your database clean.

Daily

Update policy and procedure documentation when decisions are made about the use of The Raiser's Edge. This is the database administrator's responsibility and is much more manageable if done as it occurs rather than saved for one overwhelming, large project.

Weekly

1. Run a query to ensure that all individuals have a primary addressee and primary salutation.
2. Run a query to ensure that all contacts have a primary addressee and primary salutation.
3. Run a query to ensure that no gifts are left marked as "Not Acknowledged."
4. Run a query to ensure that all tribute acknowledgement (notification) letters have been sent.
5. Run a query to ensure that all gifts from last week marked "Do Not Acknowledge" are properly marked this way.
6. Communicate to accounting all gift changes made this week beyond the addition of new gifts:
   a. Stocks sold
   b. Pledges written off
   c. Gifts adjusted
   d. Posted gifts deleted
7. Run a query of all constituents added and changed by your users in the last week and review their work for accuracy.
8. Do a search for "The," "A," and "An" where backslashes were not used properly, fix the records, and remind the staff person who added them about the correct procedure.
9. Review the blog for The Raiser's Edge (http://forums.blackbaud.com/blogs/raisersedge/default.aspx) and forums for The Raiser's Edge (http://forums.blackbaud.com/forums/3.aspx).

Monthly

1. Read the monthly e-mail newsletter from Blackbaud for The Raiser's Edge called *The User's Edge*, understand its contents, and implement its recommendations and notices as appropriate. If interested users of The Raiser's Edge are not receiving this newsletter, update their profiles on the Blackbaud web site or contact Blackbaud customer support.
2. Run the Past Due Report for pledges and recurring gifts, and ensure that your fundraisers are following up to collect these gifts.
3. Run the Duplicate Constituent report in Administration to identify any newly added duplicates.
   - Change the Duplicate Criteria, using different fields and different lengths, to be as thorough in checking as possible. After running the report, remember to set the criteria back to the day-to-day settings.

- If you find duplicates, use Properties to identify who added them and work with those users to help them avoid adding more.
4. Reconcile with accounting. Focus on:
   a. Fund balance totals
   b. Pledge balances/accounts receivable
5. Deactivate values that should no longer be used:
   a. Campaigns, funds, and appeals that should no longer be assigned to gifts.
   b. Table values that should no longer be used.
   c. Attributes that should no longer be used.
   d. Events that are no longer actively used.
6. Depending on your organization's definition of "Inactive" for constituents, perhaps perform global changes adding and/or removing a checkmark for this checkbox.
7. Drop lapsed members if you use the Membership module. Be sure you have a good backup before running this process.
8. Update the text of acknowledgement letters to keep them timely and to avoid sending the same letter repeatedly to regular donors.
9. Run a query of actions older than four weeks that are still marked as not completed. Work with the actions' solicitors to get the actions updated or deleted.
10. Review the following areas for saved parameters that have not been used for a long time and do not appear to be useful again in the future. Work with your users to have unneeded ones deleted.
    a. Batch
    b. Query—also check to ensure that remaining queries are being put into the appropriate categories and that users are only adding valuable categories.
    c. Export
    d. Mail
    e. Reports
    f. Import

Annually

END OF FISCAL YEAR

1. As you approach the end of a fiscal year, add campaigns and funds with fiscal designators for the next fiscal year if that is your policy. (Note: in The Raiser's Edge, there is no end-of-year or financial "closings" that need to occur before or after the end of a fiscal year.)
2. As you approach the end of a fiscal year, run the LYBUNT and SYBUNT reports to identify additional prospects to solicit to help you meet or further surpass your fundraising goals.
3. After the beginning of a fiscal year, consider deactivating any campaigns, funds, and appeals that should no longer be assigned to gifts. You may need to wait until all pledge payments with those values have been entered.

END OF CALENDAR YEAR

- December 1: Remind all sources of credit card donations to provide the credit card gift details within sufficient time for cards to be charged on December 31 or earlier to meet Internal Revenue Service requirements for tax-deductibility for the current calendar and tax year.

- December 15: Send a reminder to all staff about requirements and availability of staff to process gifts to meet the December 31 tax deadline, especially for credit card gifts.

- December 20: Ensure that staff coverage is in place for December 31 and that staff have access to all sources of credit card gift information (e.g., white mail, lockbox, phone-in, and walk-in).

- January 1 through 15: Make sure that gift entry staff follow the proper procedures for the gift date and GL post date for gifts. For example, although gift date is typically the date the gift is received, checks received in early January but postmarked by December 31 are usually given a gift date of December 31. Confirm with your accounting staff what date should be used for the **GL Post Date** field.

- Mid-January: Run annual statements for monthly donors, employees who gave through payroll deduction, and other donors who need a summary of their giving for the year.

Summary

With The Raiser's Edge, the greatest amount of work for the database administrator is setting it up properly, not maintaining it. If you get the system set up, data cleaned up, and data entry and output policy and procedures in place, maintenance of the system is fairly easy and takes little time.

Policy and Procedure Documentation Example

Generating Direct Mail File

This appendix supports two chapters in the book. First, this appendix is an example of the kind of information that fundraisers who are doing mailings should provide to the database staff to create those mailings as discussed in Chapter 4, supplemented with the kind of details the database administrator adds when using the fundraiser's document.

This appendix is also an example of the kind of policy and procedure documentation recommended in Chapter 8. It illustrates that an organization's documentation needs to record what is unique to that organization and should not be focused on teaching readers how to use The Raiser's Edge. Organization-specific policy and procedure documentation should be written such that a knowledgeable user can quickly repeat an established process, such as generating quarterly newsletter lists. The documentation should not be written to teach a novice user how Query and Mail work.

The following example reflects that approach in that it:

- Does not explain how to navigate in The Raiser's Edge but simply tells the user the names of the queries and mail export parameter sets to use.
- Notes the parameters used.
- Perhaps most importantly, it explains why those parameters are used—the fundraising rationale and management direction.
- Discusses related procedures outside The Raiser's Edge for which staff are not going to remember the details over time or that a new user would not automatically know (in this case, working with the organization's direct mail vendor).

This content is taken from the actual documentation I created at the Greater Bay Area Make-A-Wish Foundation. It is used to create the files needed by the direct mail consultant for one of the types of direct mail this chapter does called "special appeals." This is an example of a "real, live" document in process from an actual organization using The Raiser's Edge. It is not a perfected model but a realistic one. It demonstrates what can be reasonably created and updated over time as the person responsible for generating the mailing files runs and documents the process. In the interest of space and usefulness, some details have been deleted.

Process for Generating Special Appeal Direct Mail Files

Notes created by Bill Connors June to August 2009 for Challenge/Elephant Match MAW09AB.

Used again for Year-end Appeal MAW09AD (same as AB and AC except this *is* the appeal to send the 1x/year folks).

Criteria for Include Query

- Query named "Direct Mail Include Query for Special Appeal"
- Constituent query, including both individuals and organizations
- Those who have ever given a direct mail gift as indicated by the criteria of Gifts, Appeals, Appeal Category = Direct Mail. (As of 7/6/09, Appeal Category is a required field, the only options are "Direct Mail" and "Not Direct Mail," and Jackie and Bill have marked all direct mail appeals already in the system as Direct Mail.)

Criteria for Exclude Query

Note that some of the necessary exclusions are handled more easily in the Mail parameters in the next section and not in this query.

- Query named "Direct Mail Exclude Query for Special Appeal"
- Those with a *current* (current defined by blank Date To or Date To greater than today—needs to be updated) constituent code of
  - Board Member
  - Advisory Council
  - Staff
  - VIP (note that this is the *only* field by which we are excluding major donors and prospects; anyone who has given us any amount of money whatsoever that includes a direct mail gift and does not have this code will be solicited with this direct mail piece, no matter how much they have given)
- OR Preferred Address Country is one of any value except United States—check to make sure that no new countries have been added
- OR Well Wisher as defined by any single gift of $500 or more to a Well Wisher or Mini Proposal appeal (there are six; find with search on *mini and on *well) (due to confusion about how Well Wishers was defined—attribute or giving—this was the decision; we are *ignoring* the RE attribute for this purpose)—check to see if any new Well Wisher or Mini Proposal appeals have been added
- OR Approach Restriction applicable attribute (moved to query because some of the values are inactive and are not available for selection in Mail until I finish cleaning up this attribute)—1x/year to be excluded? YES for all but May and year-end, so remove from exclusion for May and year-end mailing and add back to mailings after that; there are VIP and non-VIP versions
- (Jackie says current volunteers should not be excluded)

Merge Query Results

- Query named "Direct Mail Merge Results for Special Appeal—STATIC!!"
- Running this query takes approximately 15 minutes.
  - 8/31/09 created a list of 36,428
  - (Sept was the mini proposal and that data is in a diff document)
  - 10/29/09 created a list of 37,103

Parameters for Export Files

There is no *single* tool in Mail that allows us to do all these things at once:

- Export 3 versions of a name (Addressee, Salutation, Sort Name)
- Use Head of Household processing
- Export address fields as separate fields rather than one address block

Export does not allow us to exclude individuals with no good address based on address processing or organizations without a valid contact.

Therefore Mail is used to produce an output query that is plugged into the constituent and gift exports.

Parameters for Mail, Quick Letters

- Parameters named "Direct Mail Data for Special Appeal"
- General:
  - Query: need merge subtract query of the two queries above
  - Will use Head of Household processing
  - Exclude Inactive, Deceased and Has no valid addresses
  - Create output query selected to be used to generate files
- Fields:
  - Constituent ID (file is created only to generate query)
  - Address Line 1 (to ensure address criteria gets processed)
- Filters: Exclude those with a Solicit Code of: update based on the time of year and relevance of 1x/year mailings—and do not forget to add back for next mailing after removing this
  - Direct Mail 1x/Year Only (this is not the one those folks should receive)
  - Do Not Mail Anything (had the RMT attributes of No Mail *and* No Newsletter)
  - No Direct Mail (RMT Attribute No Mail)
  - Renewals Only for Direct Mail (RMT Attribute Renewals Only; this is not a renewal mailing)
  - Do Not Solicit
- Attributes: Exclude those with a relevant Approach Restrictions attribute (not from RMT but still applicable to a direct mailing) now handled in Exclude query
- Individual Address tab:
  - Use Seasonal address as of [date based on mailing]
  - Otherwise preferred address
  - Remove from mailing if no valid address is found (NCOA will not be performed in advance)

- Organization Address tab:
  - Contacts: use Primary first, RMT second
  - Only send one per organization, NOT one per contact
  - If the contact also personally qualifies, they will get one to their personal address and one to their contact address
  - Remove from mailing if a contact is not available
- File exported to R:\Export Files Temp Folder
  - 7/25/09: 34,670 constituents
  - 8/7/09: 34,692 constituents
  - 8/31/09: 34,727 constituents
  - 10/29/09: 35,501 constituents

Parameters for Export for Constituent Data

- Saved parameters are named "Direct Mail Constituent Export for Special Appeal."
- Character-separated file using the ∧ as the separator per Margo's request at mail house.
- The input query here is the output query of the *Quick Letters,* not the merge query!
- The fields selected are:
  - Constituent ID
  - Key Indicator
  - Sort Key (by constituent name; so org name for orgs, not contact name)
  - Addressee
    - Individuals: Use Primary Addressee
    - Orgs: Leave blank
  - Salutation
    - Individuals: Use Primary Salutation
    - Orgs: Leave blank
  - Position
  - Organization Name
  - Address Lines 1–5 separately (Update Seasonal address date based on actual date of mailing)
  - City
  - State
  - ZIP
  - Country (including for now at Margo's request although international addresses are being excluded)
  - Contact Addressee
    - Use Main Constituent Only Addressee if present otherwise use the Primary Addressee
  - Contact Salutation
    - Use Main Constituent Only Salutation if present otherwise use the Primary Salutation
- Be sure to include the project code in the file name per mail house request. 10/29/07: 7 minutes to run the export

For more understanding about this process, see e-mail below sent to mail house 8/7/09 by Bill Connors: . . .

Parameters for Export for Gift Data

- Saved parameters are named "Direct Mail Gift Export for Special Appeal."
- Character-separated file using the ∧ as the separator per mail house request.
- The input query here is the output query of the *Quick Letters*, not the merge query!
- There is Gift Criteria built into the export to include only Cash, Pay-Cash, and Recurring Gift-Pay Cash. (Click on the name of the export in the Output display to select the Criteria button.)
- Be sure to include the project code in the file name per mail house request.

Uploading Data

Uploading Data to Mail House

Instructions provided by mail house staff:

- In your web browser, go to www … com and click on "Client Login."

Notify by E-mail of Upload …

After uploading the data, send an e-mail to …

Marking Appeals and Packages on Constituent Records

The mail house will send back to us the Cons ID with the Appeal and Package each constituent received for importing to the Appeals tab of each constituent.

Specifically (per mail house 8/09): "Also, to clarify, what we (she) will send you at conclusion of the job is a cross-reference of id number with the full RMT keycode. If you need to separate out Appeal and Package components from that keycode you need to take care of that on your end."

There is an Access database in the Direct Mail folder in the R: drive that illustrates how I easily created the import file and analyzed the codes received. I just used the standard import saved parameters to import them.

- Note that if the file is saved as an Excel file, Access will add decimal points to the export of the Cons ID. So, be sure to save it as a CSV file and when linking, be sure to specify the data type as Text and do not use the default of Long Integer.

In order to set up the appeal and packages in RE and add them to the constituents, find out the following information as well:

- Mailing name and purpose for the Appeal Description and notes
  - See previous mailings in Appeal for consistent names and descriptions
- Date mailing will be dropped
- Number solicited
- $ Goal and if desired, expenses for reporting and analysis purposes
- Meaning of the various package segments

Bibliography

This bibliography contains both works cited as well as additional resources for those who work with The Raiser's Edge and fundraising databases.

Bennett, Sue. *The Accidental Techie: Supporting, Managing, and Maximizing Your Nonprofit's Technology*. Saint Paul, MN: Fieldstone Alliance, 2005.

Blackbaud. *Campaigns, Funds & Appeals Data Entry Guide*. Charleston, SC: Blackbaud, 2008.

Council for Advancement and Support of Education. *CASE Reporting Standards & Management Guidelines*. Washington, DC: CASE, 2009.

Emlen, Julia S. *Intentional Stewardship: Bringing Your Donors to Their Highest Level of Philanthropy*. Washington, DC: CASE, 2007.

Hart, Ted, et al., eds. *Major Donors: Finding Big Gifts in Your Database and Online*. Hoboken, NJ: John Wiley & Sons, 2006.

Hedrick, Janet L. *Nonprofit Essentials: Effective Donor Relations*. Hoboken, NJ: John Wiley & Sons, 2008.

Maugham, W. Somerset. *The Razor's Edge*. New York: Vintage International, 2003.

McKinnon, Harvey. *Hidden Gold: How Monthly Giving Will Build Donor Loyalty, Boost Your Organization's Income, and Increase Financial Stability*. Chicago: Bonus Books, 1999.

Ross, Holly, Katrin Verclas, Allison Levine, eds. *Managing Technology to Meet Your Mission: A Strategic Guide for Nonprofit Leaders*. San Francisco: Jossey-Bass, 2009.

Stanionis, Madeline. *Raising Thousands (if Not Tens of Thousands) of Dollars with Email*. Medfield, MA: Emerson & Church, 2006.

Strand, Bobbie J. *A Kaleidoscope of Prospect Development: The Shapes and Shades of Major Donor Prospecting*. Washington, DC: CASE, 2008.

Sturtevant, William T. *The Artful Journey*. Chicago: Institutions Press, 2004. www.instituteforgiving.org.

——— *The Continuing Journey: Stewardship and Useful Case Studies in Philanthropy*. Chicago: Bonus Books, 2001.

Taylor, John H., ed. *Advancement Services: A Foundation for Fundraising*, 2nd edition. Washington, DC: CASE, 2007.

Woodward, Jeanette. *Nonprofit Essentials: Managing Technology*. Hoboken, NJ: John Wiley & Sons, 2006.

Blackbaud has a number of concise white papers on its web site that are helpful as well. Of particular note are white papers on implementing a recurring giving program (Bill Connors), major gifts (Kathryn Johnson and Bo Crader), and RFM analysis. The white papers can be found at www.blackbaud.com/company/resources/ whitepapers/whitepapers.aspx or under the Nonprofit Resources option on the Company link from the Blackbaud web site home page.

The Blackbaud web site also provides all the user guides for The Raiser's Edge. Of particular note to readers of this book is *The Raiser's Edge 7 for Beginners,* a more technical guide than this book but an excellent introduction to The Raiser's Edge and its use.

Index